A Gallery To Play To
The Story of the Mersey Poets

– Stride –

Phil Bowen is the author of *Variety's Hammer*, work from which was selected for inclusion in *The Forward Book of Poetry 1998*; and the editor of two Stride anthologies, *Jewels & Binoculars: fifty poets celebrate Bob Dylan* and *Things We Said Today: poems about The Beatles*. He has also recently written two plays: *Chimney Kids* (for children) and *A Handful of Rain*, about an imagined meeting between Bob Dylan and Dylan Thomas.

A GALLERY TO PLAY TO

The Story of the Mersey Poets

Phil Bowen

A GALLERY TO PLAY TO
First edition 1999
© Phil Bowen 1999
All rights reserved
ISBN 1 900152 63 0

Cover photo © Steve Tanner
Cover design by Neil Annat

Published by
Stride Publications
11 Sylvan Road, Exeter
Devon EX4 6EW
England

Acknowledgements:

Carol Ann Duffy's 'Liverpool Echo' (© Carol Ann Duffy, 1985)
is reproduced on page 127 by kind permission of Anvil Press,
and is taken from the collection *Standing Female Nude*.
© Carol Ann Duffy, 1985

Work by Roger McGough is reprinted by permission of
The Peters Fraser and Dunlop Group Ltd on his behalf.

Adrian Henri's books are published by Rapp & Whiting, Cape and Bloodaxe.

Work by Brian Patten reprinted by permission of the author
c/o Rogers, Coleridge & White Ltd, 20 Powis Mews, London W11 1JN.

Contents

Introduction *7*

'Our apparatniks will continue making
the usual squalid mess called History:
all we can pray for is that artists,
chefs and saints may still appear to blithe it.'

                     – 'Moon Landing', W.H. Auden

Introduction

'...small town demotic Mantovanis...'

In the summer of 1967, Tony Richardson of Penguin Books took a chance. Then Penguin Books' Poetry Editor, he devoted number ten of the highly prestigious Penguin Modern Poets series to three unknown and relatively unpublished young writers from Liverpool. The book, featuring Adrian Henri, Roger McGough and Brian Patten, would have its own generic title, *The Mersey Sound*, and be something of a leap in the dark. It would also be a big break for the three writers. The print run, as large as twenty thousand, would guarantee status, and steady sales were expected over the next ten years. Within three months it had sold out. The rest, as they say...

Chronologically, the Mersey Poets' niche amongst the various cabals – 'savage with gang-warfare' – that make up twentieth-century British Poetry, slots between The Group and the (post-Movement influenced) poets from Belfast (including the emerging Seamus Heaney, centred around Philip Hobsbaum's teaching at Queen's University). More than any others perhaps they symbolise the 'pop poetry movement of the sixties', to some, the leading poets of that fizzy, electrical decade. They were 'irreverent' and 'sardonic', perfectly in synch with the times they echoed. Innovative in both style and form, (said Penguin) *The Mersey Sound* – whose sales now head towards the million mark – became a watershed, widening both readership and boundaries of the genre. It brought 'poetry down from the dusty shelf and on to the street'.

Needless to say, the dusty shelf hit back. Writing in *Author 1970* about the growing reading circuit, Roy Fuller compared 'mountebank poets to ham tragedians looking for an easy laugh or tear', a view endorsed by John Wain who saw the 'instant' poetry readings as 'genial incontinence' at the expense of concentration and intensity. 'The troubadours of courtly love from Merseyside' were described by David Harsent in *The Guardian* as a fetchingly bittersweet cabaret turn', and were taken apart further by Douglas Dunn. In a lengthy article in *Encounter*, he claimed that '[they] represent an unliterary principle of making poems, subordinating craft to effect, [and are] small town demotic Mantovanis endorsing sentiments and expectations they have no need to create.' The criticism was by no means all from academia. Fellow troubadour Mike Horovitz also weighed in. Although acknowledging the Liverpool trio's considerable impact, Horovitz extrapulated that it was appropriate to their kind of 'almost precision tool poetry happening as it was on the crest of the wave created by the Beatles, and supported greatly by generous and effective publishers and agents. 'McGough and Henri were pop-stars' he claimed in the introduction to his anthology *The Children of Albion*, though more generous to Patten, citing his 'plangent erotic saxophonetrance' voice as the true evocation of the actual Liverpool scene.

Problems for anyone writing about the Mersey Poets involve doing so without the sound of special pleading and without further promulgating the myth. Unlike the misleadingly named Movement poets of the fifties, Henri, McGough and Patten knew one another well, held similar political and social views, were mutually influenced, and shared common beliefs regarding direction and audience. Yet all three are highly distinctive and very separate voices. This poses a further difficulty; they were never 'the band' so many felt them to be.

Critics have frequently made light of the trio's easily worn aesthetic, their quickly achieved sentiments and emotional excessiveness. Their continued success however – the honours, accolades, awards, the attendance at readings and genuine public affection – more than suggest that, with collectively over sixty books for adults and children between them, one feels they must have been getting something right during the last thirty years.

The challenge of this book is to present a spirited and readable account of their literary and social identity, rather than defensive protestations against 'dumbing down', or some belated critical exegesis. Nor is this a text whose general indebtedness draws entirely from the sixties, although a principal aim is to emphasise the cultural decentralization then taking place. As early as 1954, J.D. Scott in his formative article about the Movement had detected an impending mood soon to loom large as 'that tide pulling us through the Fifties towards the Sixties.'

Unlike The Movement and their literary heirs The Group, the Liverpool poets' educational diversity meant that the focus was the Art College rather than the university. The emphasis lay on what a poem did rather than what it was. This, along with a shared aversion for the concept of poetry as a specialised interest nurtured by professors in academic hothouses, made them something of a troublesome trio in the literary climate of the late sixties. In the French freewheeling style of Baudelaire and Rimbaud, influences uniform to all three writers, a current of feeling central to their aims revealed the poet as agent and 'provocateur' whose imaginative flights and transcendental longings were a spicy pointer to the zeitgeist pervading the hot summer of 1967.

This raises a final point: the poet and audience. Without actually writing for an audience, perhaps what at first separated the Liverpool poets from their contemporaries was the concern they showed for it. If an audience has made the effort to come to a reading, then the poet should accordingly present that reading as best as possible.

Hopefully, this study may go some way towards showing that the Mersey Poets were as central to the sixties and seventies (a period when achievements in British poetry were generally overshadowed by those in music and theatre), as 'the Auden generation', 'the Beats' and the Movement were to theirs. The development of the reading circuit from the 1960s onwards has served to raise public awareness of poetry and contributed greatly to poets being able to make a living by going on that circuit. As the poet Adrian Mitchell has endorsed, 'the Liverpool poets listened, learnt and led'. Moreover, they have always been full-timers in an age of part-timers. Practitioners rather than the type of leeching academics who bleed poetry dry, mastering prevailing fashion, writing formulaic impenetrable poems capable of winning competitions and running writing courses; but without any substantial readership and even less heart or passion. The Mersey Poets have critics in the let's-keep-poetry-solemn-domain but as Charles Causley has said, 'no one who matters'. A long time admirer of the three writers and the prevailing spirit of Liverpudlians – whose humour made his war years that more bearable – Causley feels that their work is not only representative of the place but also reaches out to enthusiasts everywhere. Often appalled at the envy, spite and negative attitudes so prevalent in the world of literature, Causley stands apart from trends and movements, asserting: 'I'm an enthusiast, I was told I had ability at an early age, but I'm always prepared to take my hat off to good stuff'.

We live in an age of dissembling, comfort language and equivocation. An age of euphemism, where management-speak and psycho-babble pours out of the mouths of executives and quacks. An age where language is polluted, misused, debased, seeks to impress by obscurity, and rings 'as false as an ill-kept vow' in times when even rhetoric has been replaced by the soundbite .

In Flecker's *Hassan*, the caliph asks: 'if there shall ever arise a nation whose people have forgotten poetry, or whose poets have forgotten the people – what of them?' The reply is 'they will be a dark patch upon the world.' The relative popularity of poetry today suggests that it has returned from what Philip Larkin called the 'loop-line that took it away from the general reader', and we have not yet arrived at such a dark patch. This is due in no small part to the efforts of Adrian Henri, Roger McGough and Brian Patten, whose imperative was never to bring down the establishment, but to put their own tribe on the map rather than proselytising without legitimate empirical knowledge.

Admittedly the success of The Beatles and the media interest in Liverpool deeply influenced Tony Richardson's decision at Penguin, and possibly lay behind Edward Lucie-Smith's thinking concerning his earlier book *The Liverpool Scene*. But poets who regard the Mersey Poets as merely a side-show often ignore their distinctiveness and the widely differing achievements of all three writers: the economy, edge and unblinkered concerns of McGough, the heartfelt preserving benevolence of Henri, and the straight-talking, sheer metaphysical charge of Patten.

Hopefully this account will reach a place where the people have not been forgotten, where poetry can be serious not earnest, make a simple statement (so much harder than a complicated one), and remind us in Brian Patten words 'of what we have forgotten we already know'.

The Fifties and the Beginning of the Liverpool Scene

'...we're all artists. It's a shilling!...'

To understand the Sixties is to understand the period that provoked them. As described in Ian MacDonald's account of The Beatles' music, *Revolution in the Head*, 'any domestic film of the fifties conveys the genteel, class-segregated staidness of British society at that time. The braying upper-class voices on newsreels, the tired nostalgia for the war, all of which conspired to breed unrest among the young'. John Lennon in particular, loathed the decade's stiff and pompous soullessness, which may have been relatively comfortable for the generation that endured the war, but for the newly-termed 'teenagers' it was a stifling time against which they reacted initially with Rock'n'Roll.

Fuelled by three closely connected events, there emerged in Britain between the years 1956-58, a new and much-disputed 'angry generation'. On May 8th, John Osborne's *Look Back in Anger* opened at The Royal Court, closely followed by the publication of Colin Wilson's *The Outsider*. A leader in *The Times* linked both with Kingsley Amis whose *Lucky Jim* had created a new anti-hero described as a 'thoroughly cross young man'. Largely concerned with intellectual restrictions, the Angry Young Men came around the time of the Suez Crisis and went after Harold Macmillan's election triumph in 1959.

Less apparently significant was the opening of a club called The Cavern in Mathew Street, central Liverpool in 1957, only days after Anthony Eden resigned as Prime Minister in the wake of Suez, to be succeeded by the pragmatic Macmillan. Equally propitious was the 'Beat Generation' in America, whose heresy during the Eisenhower era, in a country of mounting racial tension, was a resonant foretaste of things to come. In September, a state of emergency had arisen in Little Rock Arkansas when two hundred of the National Guard's finest were ordered to prevent nine black children entering a school. Two days later, Eisenhower had a stroke.

It was not only Little Rock that laid Eisenhower low. Coincident with ensuring that one small-town school could accommodate black and white children side by side, Eisenhower also had to cope with a small Russian sputnik flying over his head.

Even in the context of Europe, Russia was thought of as the backwoodsman of the continent, so the launching of Sputnik One on October 4th 1957 caused a universal sensation. The world gaped in wonder. America had been outsmarted at last.

Clearly modelled on the sputnik, but entirely American in origin and nicknamed by the San Francisco journalist Herb Caen, was the 'beatnik'. Jack Kerouac, an unknown novelist who according to legend had written *On the Road* during a three-week nonstop session in 1951 on a tele-type roll, became its talisman. Kerouac's writing career since the appearance of *The Town and the City* in 1950 had amounted to little more than a collection of rejection slips. He had finally got his novel on the bookstalls by mid-1957, where it remained on the best seller lists for over a month. It struck a chord not only with his own generation but later with the youth of the 1960s and 1970s who wanted to be 'the only people' of whom Kerouac approved, 'who would burn, burn, burn, like fabulous yellow roman candles exploding like spiders across the stars'.

In 1956, fellow Beat, Allen Ginsberg's sexually explicit *Howl and other Poems* was published by Lawrence Ferlinghetti's City Lights bookshop in San Francisco. Only paperbacks were sold and the shop was open from ten till midnight, attracting poets and writers of every persuasion. It was raided in 1957, and the police charged Ferlinghetti with bringing out an obscene book.

By the time an acquittal was won, the shop was a Mecca, Ginsberg and other authors such as William Burroughs becoming household names. As early as 1952 John Clellon Holmes had written about 'The Beat Generation' in *The New York Times*. Now it was happening. The mystic state of 'beatitude' was being achieved – a state of being stripped of social insulation and endowed with epiphanic clarity as a result. The mass media however were not bothered with the finer points. Beatniks meant news. They meant beards, jeans, alcohol, long hair and bare feet. They meant drugs and squalor. And they meant group sex.

For Britain in 1957 it was the year of Harold Macmillan's 'never had it so good', speech which took place in Bedford during a hot July.

World fashion too found rallying points in the new acceptance of trousers for women and sexy bikinis on the beach. Sunglasses were worn even at midnight and enlightened young women flaunted the shapeless 'sack dress', inspired by new natural styles in early acknowledgement of street chic.

In the theatre, a major new playwright Harold Pinter, emerged with *The Birthday Party*, whilst unexpectedly wide coverage was given to Samuel Beckett's *Endgame* recognising experimental influences from Europe.

Above all, there was Rock'n'Roll. More specifically, there was Elvis Presley.

In February 1956, H.M.V. had released Presley's 'Heartbreak Hotel'. Within days it became number one in the Top Twenty, remaining there for eighteen weeks. 'Blue Suede Shoes' and 'Hound Dog' soon followed. British parents became worried. Presley himself was simply giving a Blues intonation and phrasing to songs in the white Country and Western tradition. Sentimental cowboy songs sung like a black man, with an overt sexuality and 'suggestive movements' despite the lyrics being purged for more conservative white ears. Clearly something had happened to those long cherished Victorian values based on respect for one's elders and betters, the Empire, the clergy, the Law and the Queen. All of a sudden in 1957, 'the kids today just got no respect'. Music became a battleground between the young who loved the wild new noise, and parents who hated it.

Skiffle groups sprang up all over Britain. The craze centred on London's Soho jazz cellars and in the recently fashionable expresso coffee bars. Arising from an infatuation with all things Italian – sharp suits, sultry actresses, and contemporary design – they were the places in which to be seen. Crammed with foliage, wicker chairs and candle-filled Chianti bottles, they had exotic sounding names such as The Latin Quarter, The Partisan, El Cabala and The Cafe des Artistes. Frothy coffee was dispensed from huge gurgling silver machines; Teddy Boys, beatniks, bohemians and layabouts alike uniting around that most iconic of all Rock'n'Roll's symbols, the jukebox.

In the leafy Liverpool suburb of Woolton, sixteen -year old John Lennon's aunt and guardian Mimi Smith was worried about the effect the skiffle craze was having on him. He too was losing respect.

Based on three chords, the main appeal of skiffle was its accessibility. Consisting of a primitive rhythm section of double bass, kitchen washboard and banjo, it meant almost anybody could play. Although smitten by Rock'n'Roll after first hearing Elvis, if the swivel-hipped American provided the spark for John Lennon, it was a skinny trad jazz player, the Chris Barber Band's ex-banjoist Lonnie Donegan, whose hits included 'Rock Island Line', who fanned the flame.

Surprisingly it was Lennon's authoritarian Aunt Mimi who bought his first 'guaranteed not to split' guitar from Frank Hessy's music shop in Whitechapel, central Liverpool. Around the corner runs Mathew Street – little more than two rows of seven-storey warehouses in the late fifties – where lorry-loads of fruit and vegetables were delivered daily. At number 10, electrical goods were stored, piled high in cardboard boxes, but the basement was vacant. It was here, early in 1957, that Alan Sytner opened his apocalyptic jazz club based on Le Caveau in Paris's Left Bank.

Liverpool in the fifties meant business, factories and ships. Along the docks, the overhead railway passed above funnels and warehouses, the Pier Head's giant clock giving the river a fresh shimmer as spectacular sunsets threw a regular crimson wash across the skyline. Trams would arrive outside the city's three waterside palaces: the Cunard Company Building, the Mersey Docks and Harbour Board and the Liver Building. With its twin belfries, crowned by the two heraldic, eighteen-foot Liver Birds, Liverpool's most famous building stands proudly next to its neighbours in dramatic harmony with local mythology, sea and sky.

'Over the water' echoing to the mournful piping of ships' horns, lies Birkenhead. Here at Cammel Laird's, *The Mauretania*, and *The Ark Royal* were built. Tugs' sirens could be heard as river ferries and ocean liners entered what was still the biggest shipping pool in Europe. A melting pot of races, it spawned a vital working-class characterized by resilience and an extreme sense of humour. It was also famous for its sarcasm; the distinctive quickly spoken glottal accent giving rise to a dynasty of music-hall comedians from Billy Bennett, Robb Wilton and Arthur Askey, to later maestros such as Ted Ray and Ken Dodd.

Beginning at Lime Street, driving past The Adelphi Hotel and Epstein's famous naked statue of 'Dickie' Lewis, one passes small hotels in Mount Pleasant, a proliferation of Baptist chapels, Irish meeting halls and grassed-over bomb sites, pub signs on every corner. A sharp right into Hope Street suddenly brings into view one of the most eclectic and truly monumental buildings of our time. Designed by Giles Gilbert Scott, the sandstone Anglican Cathedral looms over the graveyard of St James' Cemetery and the monument to William Huskisson, dominating the entire landscape; and more immediately Liverpool 8 and the oldest Chinatown in Europe.

In the late fifties, this entire district was a Scouse bohemia. Bordering the Art College and the Institute High School for Boys, Hope Street bisects a faded area of cast-iron letters on street-ends enshrining the great shipping dynasties of Canning, Rodney, Roscoe and Huskisson. A haunt of painters, sculptors, poets and writers, it housed West Indian immigrant families, students, layabouts and artists living in studio flats within crumbling town houses built originally for wealthy slave merchants. Socially, it centred around two pubs; the Philharmonic Hotel – sumptuously fashioned by Cunard shipwrights in crystal and mahogany, where even the Gents' toilets was carved in rose-coloured marble – and for the more discerning bohemian, Ye Cracke in Rice Street.

The summer of 1957 saw John Lennon, having formed a group at school called The Quarrymen, enrol at the Liverpool College Of Art, where he met and befriended Stuart Sutcliffe, its most gifted student. The unlikely pair's respective tutor, Arthur Ballard had recently returned from Paris, meeting

Giacometti and Poliakoff. He had absorbed avant-garde French painting, and introduced it to his students. In the same year sculptor Arthur Dooley, having left his job as janitor at St Martin's School of Art, returned to Liverpool to spend two years working in Speke for the Dunlop Rubber Company. Here his highly innovative welded scrap metal and molten bronze casts were germinated.

1957 saw the beginning of a coterie of coffee bars, basements and bohemian dives, gay bars and West Indian drinking clubs. It was the age of the prime movers of the 'Liverpool scene': names such as Yankel Feather, Alan Blease, Brian Gilbertson, Alan Isaacs, Neil English, Eddie Mooney and 'the man who gave the Beatles away', Alan Williams.

Whilst homogeneously Scouse in outlook, Liverpool beatnik culture in the late fifties was mainly about looking and sounding the part. Everyone was called 'man', names such as Monk and Bird dropped, words like Zen and 'warmonger' common coinage. Aficionados all dressed in black, wore duffle-coats or donkey jackets, long scarfs, CND badges, polonecks and sandals. Girls had either no make-up or copied Juliette Greco's black-eyed and skull-white face. Hair was long and straight or elfin-like as Audrey Hepburn's in Roman Holiday. Figures were hidden in oversized sweaters borrowed from boyfriends who wore Fidel Castro beards, had uncombed hair over their ears or sported crew-cuts aping Gerry Mulligan. Favoured literature of the day included James Joyce, Henry Miller and Colin Wilson. Other required reading was Jean-Paul Sartre, Kerouac and William Burroughs. Their poets were Gregory Corso, Ginsberg and Lawrence Ferlinghetti.

Dublin born playwright and screen-writer Johnny Byrne was an early player:'I fell in with a group like me, absolutely crazy about the beats. In a very short time we were into jazz, poetry – straight out of the beatniks – and all around us were the incredible beginnings of the Liverpool scene.' He and art student Mal Dean, who was in the same illustration class as John Lennon, would meet at Alan Williams' coffee bar The Jacaranda, where The Beatles first played. They would hitch-hike to St. Ives for the summer, then go to the Beaulieu Jazz Festival; 'there was an amazing meeting between Pete Brown and Mike Horovitz,' Byrne remembers. 'Almost like Stanley and Livingstone. We all recognised kindred spirits and had long all-night jazzy, druggy conversations, rapping, just as in the books. Even though we were all falling to pieces we thought this was the way it should be.'

This was the way it had always been since 1954 in a garden hut in Plantation Road, Oxford. Michael Horovitz, having left his native London, had gone up to Oxford fully intending to do a B. Lit (first on Blake, then on Beckett) but various things happened including meeting a Canadian expatriate Ray Cortenz who introduced him to this earliest of beat communes. He shared it with barefoot Bermudan Teddy Gordon, and poet-philosophers, artists and jazz musicians would all pass through. 'Life there began at twilight as party-goers would fall in, and there'd be jiving to bop and post-bop records – and smoking dope was a wild new thing, and the utter difference of how everything looked and felt on those early joints'. Horovitz underwent a process of reaffirmation. Deciding that criticism was the enemy, he became an 'anti-intellectual intellectual'. The real work was to make poetry and realise visions in the same way Blake realised Jerusalem. He decided to collect the work of all the writers and artists he knew and publish them in a magazine called *New Departures*.

Displaying early acumen for hustling, publicity and organisation, Horovitz managed to print three thousand copies, all of which sold. 'We had a bit of backing and a certain amount of goodwill. I think we helped to sow seeds then that a lot of underground presses inherited and developed'.

Soon after the first issue of *New Departures* came out, emerging from a tent one morning at the Beaulieu Jazz Festival, Horovitz was greeted by a small, plaid jacketed, bearded figure: 'Horovitz, ecch! Horovitz ecch!'

For someone as synonymous with the 'English Beat Generation' it was no surprise that, after initial respectable early years spent near Hendon in Surrey, Pete Brown was expelled from the Hasmonean Grammar School for anti-religious behaviour. Thus began a period as an itinerant poet, musician, journalist and labourer, culminating in the apochryphal meeting with Horovitz at Beaulieu. A hitch-hike journey to Edinburgh soon followed, their scribbled exchanges en route becoming the endless English jazz epic of the road, *Blues for the Hitch-Hiking Dead*. The hot summer of 1959 saw the beginning of some lasting, if at times fraught relationships. Johnny Byrne recalls a girl that he and Mal Dean had taken up with in Cornwall. She told them about a poet who lived in a hedge outside Aylesbury and gave precise directions how to find him; 'so we went to Aylesbury, followed the instructions, found the hedge, spotted signs of habitation, went to the local pub and discovered Spike Hawkins.

John Frederick Hawkins knew about the literary scene in America at a relatively early age:

> I picked it up from my English teacher who opened up a lot of alleyways. Through these the way led to a beautiful house, and within the house I found books and bookshops such as Better Books, and tiny volumes which were marked City Lights, (and I found) this poem called 'Howl' by Allen Ginsberg and I thought, 'My god...'

Hawkins did all he could to stoke the rumour about the hedge. All too aware of the corollary between village idiot, local writer and eccentric genius, he worked hard at his image for the people of Buckinghamshire. 'And one day this scruffy figure emerged, beard, with a very neatly wrapped Italian suit in brown paper, which I presumed to be some sign or omen – perhaps he'd been released from jail... it was Byrne.'

At Beaulieu, Hawkins, Byrne, Horovitz and Brown decided to split the country, rather like the Popes splitting Europe between Avignon and Rome. Hawkins and Byrne would have everything north of Stafford, Horovitz and Brown, everything south. Byrne had already fallen in love with the energy of Liverpool; he persuaded Hawkins to come up, and together they shared a flat (with newly-arrived Irish painter Sam Walsh in the basement) at 3 Hillary Mansions in a windswept Victorian parade, rich in faded elegance.

Designed by John Foster in 1836, high above the gorge of St James's Cemetry surrounding the Anglican cathedral, and yards from the Art College and Ye Cracke pub, Gambier Terrace has long been seen as something of a prerequisite for infamy or renown in Liverpudlian artistic circles. Its projecting end bays, Ionic columns and Doric pilasters gave it immense style and a raffish charm. It was here that John Lennon and Stuart Sutcliffe had an upstairs flat. It was here that the first murky photograph Britain ever saw of Lennon appeared on the 24th July 1960.

Two hacks from The Sunday People, hearing about the area's growing bohemian reputation descended on the terrace, found the flat, noted the squalor and duly published an article revealing the Dharma bums of number 3 in an exposé headlined 'THE BEATNIK HORROR!' It was a cruel and bitter winter Johnny Byrne recalls. 'The water used to come through the flagstones when it rained, and heating was practically non-existent.' One day he found some paintings lying around in the backyard, rotting. 'So I went out and got all of them and burnt the lot to keep us warm. They turned out to be Lennon's!' Byrne was also present at the Art College dance where Hawkins read his poetry, and was later approached by Eddie Mooney who ran Streate's Coffee Bar. Mooney wanted to start some readings there and perhaps get a scene together. Hawkins' reputation at that time was purely word of mouth, but he was able to find some jazz musicians glad of a place to play:

> It was a wonderful joining together of talent: people from Liverpool, the States, a lot of first-timers. There was this connection, a complete network of people, virtually penniless, travelling to and fro as they spread the word, bringing out new literature, new poems, prose, books...

Pete Brown recalls:

> We were all busy being bums in London. Mal Dean and Johnny Byrne were in Liverpool and they said, 'Come up and steam about.' Hawkins had been living in a hedge or a haystack. Anyway something clicked in

17

his head and he left a note pinned to his sleeping girlfriend saying, 'Brown. Gone to Liverpool. Please follow.'

In London there were certain 'residencies' – the Cafe des Artistes, the left-wing Partisan Cafe in Soho where folk singers and musicians converged. Michael Horovitz remembers more and more jazz becoming involved. Then it was poetry and jazz. 'And gradually we moved out of London to Cambridge, to the north-east, and a bit later to Liverpool where Byrne and Hawkins were resident'.

By any early sixties provincial standards Eddie Mooney was innovative. It was largely his flair, sense of camp and vision that gave Streate's Coffee Bar a similar reputation in the mythology and folk-lore of poetry that The Cavern gained with Rock'n'Roll. A candle-lit, whitewashed basement with a distinct Left Bank flavour, where you could hear the sounds of Ornette Coleman and Charlie Parker, it was dominated by a painting of a Victorian gentleman who posthumously gave the venue its name. The first poetry events consisted mainly of Hawkins, Byrne and Brown reading their work, and poems in the revered *Evergreen Review* stolen by Hawkins from Better Books in London.

Hartlepool born Maurice Cockrill, having moved to nearby Wrexham, had aspirations of becoming a painter, and after meeting a girl called Judy Dunn at a party started visiting Liverpool regularly. 'Judy was amazing, she had long hair and was sitting barefoot on the stairs playing the guitar. She was well into what was happening in Liverpool, introduced me to Arthur Ballard in Ye Cracke and took me down to Streate's.' Although not moving to Liverpool for some time, Cockrill has vivid recollections of those early times: 'Spike Hawkins was like some character out of a surrealist poem in the days when nobody took their coats off at parties. Streate's was gloomy really, full of smoke – a lot of duffle coats'.

Waspish Yankel Feather, now an established artist, ran a rival place almost opposite. He remembers an arty crowd frequenting Streate's, but as it was competition, never went in. His place, The Basement, consisting of a ship's beam, an old iron grate, chains over bare bricks, a wildly vivid African motif and a genuine Elizabethan chair, catered for a much more eclectic mix. 'There would be local beauty queens bringing footballers, and on one night the chief of police turned up with his wife.' He up-staged Streate's by acquiring a licence through his connection with Liverpool solicitor Rex Makin, and charged a shilling entrance at the door. Stuart Sutcliffe and John Lennon turned up one day. When Sutcliffe asked how much it was to get in, Feather replied a shilling. Lennon retorted, 'But we're artists!' 'We're all artists',

Feather camply informed him, 'It's a shilling!'

Yankel employed the painter Henry Graham – later connected to the poetry scene – as resident musician:

Henry Graham was a quiet, rather disapproving, high-presbyterian young man who played the guitar very well, it had a sort of a Spanish twang to it – it was nothing like The Beatles! – and he'd sit there moaning and singing these songs, and it gave the place wonderful atmosphere, very decadent, and I was paying him a fortune, about three pound a week! So I wanted a shilling.

In the afternoons, The Basement attracted a quieter, slightly older, more studious clientele: students, teachers, out-of-towners – all flirting with a kind of vicarious bohemia. One such newly qualified graduate teacher was an introspective, bespectacled young man in his early twenties from Litherland, whom Yankel Feather remembers as 'having a bereft sort of look about him'.

Seaforth, born Roger Joseph McGough, had come home from Hull University in 1958 full of impassioned ideals, with a burning desire to write or paint. He had stayed on an extra year after graduating and obtained a teaching certificate specialising in the psychology of learning. Now he was learning about a new way of life, quite disassociated from his home background, fiancée, and job at St Kevin's Secondary School for Boys in Kirkby.

Returning from work on the bus, sitting at the back, McGough would notice a group of teachers who would regularly catch the bus and go down to the front. One of them – easily the biggest – had a two-seater all to himself :

He'd turn round to talk to his mates, but he'd talk to the whole bus. I used to think he was an interesting guy. He knew a lot. He had a dark beard and glasses – was very distinctive – at a time when there weren't many individuals around or eccentrics. And he seemed one. I thought yes, a man to watch.

Roger McGough 1937-1958

'...keep your head down...'

Less than a mile north of Bootle, Liverpool's most lugubrious outreach, the arid suburban plain of Seaforth spreads monotonously along Bridge Road, heading northwards to Waterloo, before reaching the more desirable expanses of Litherland and Crosby. Bordered by the drab waters of the Liverpool-Leeds canal, it was in this distinctly unpromising location, that on 9th November 1937, Roger McGough was born in a three-up three-down at 11 Ruthven Road, close to, but the wrong side of 'posher parts over the hill'.

The sounds of tugs' foghorns on the Mersey were early memories. They also stimulated images and ideas that were to remain important throughout his life. Snuggled up in bed, these sounds were warm and reassuring to the young McGough, but also mysterious and exciting; both a coming home and a going away. Wartime Liverpool meant nights spent in shelters, foraging for bomb fins in the yard, uncles coming home from the war. It meant hiding in a small room under the stairs in a cot with his sister Brenda, born in 1939. Later it meant collecting bottle tops for the war effort – the debris, the paraphernalia, the insignia of war when 'all men wore uniforms' or were either away on service or home on leave. His father, Roger Francis McGough was one of seven brothers, and young Roger's many uncles would turn up at all hours, often with exciting presents, would talk, smoke Woodbines and stay up late into the night. Cupboards and drawers were filled with bayonets, cap badges, and 303 rifles; the noise of the sirens, the drone of the bombers and the desperate flashing of search-lights trying to find them.

His mother Mary McGough, formerly McGarry, also came from a large Roman Catholic family. One of twelve, her lively teenage sisters would later teach Roger and Brenda how to jive, samba and waltz. McGough Senior had made a private arrangement for his family to evacuate to Chirk in North Wales, to avoid the bombing but after three months Mary, worried about her husband moved the family back adopting the maxim, 'if we are going to die we'll all die together'. The bottom end of Ruthven Road had been blown to bits. Brenda McGough vividly remembers standing in a shelter doorway with her father, holding his hand, looking at the bombsite of Bridge Road entirely ablaze. She also recalls watching prisoners-of-war knocking down unsafe buildings that would later become the playgrounds in which she and equally adventurous friends would roam.

It was an uncle who had been an heroic prisoner-of-war in the Far East that her brother – who always seemed to have 'his nose in a book' – remembers. In his later poem 'Snipers', their uncle would scan the ceiling nervously with shaking hands:

'For snipers,' everyone later agreed. 'A difficult habit to break.'

Another uncle, not a favourite, would encourage his wife – who had the onset of dementia – to tell stories about hearing Hitler talking to her on the radio. Hitler would become Mussolini, the imagined lover of the furniture-kissing 'Sad Aunt Madge'. There was also the prodigal, exotic Uncle Bill in 'Casablanca' who became a jockey in Morocco, but his 'letters / like silver cups, were few and far between,' until he eventually ended up back in Liverpool: 'Fog rolling in from the Mersey. As time goes by.'

It had always been Roger McGough Senior's ambition to own a house 'over the canal'. Both a non-drinker and keen sportsman he had played amateur football for Liverpool. Promoted to foreman on the docks – a hiring and firing position then – he had instilled into his children that the McGoughs were the exemplary family in the neighbourhood. 'That little bit better, that little bit more intelligent'.

His already observant son remembers his maternal grandfather William McGarry, who despite being shell-shocked and gassed in the First World War held down a good job at Bryant & May match factory. The noise of the May blitz brought the carnage all back causing him to talk to himself, 'walking round the block with a yardbrush / Over his shoulder.' In his day he had been the most straight-backed and best-looking man in Seaforth, 'just like Charlie Chaplin.' his grandmother would say. A talented, kind old man, who could play both the piano and accordion and tap-dance, McGough sees him sadly and ironically in 'Tramp Tramp Tramp', a poem written nearly forty years after his death. Then, as later, these images create an evanescent backdrop where the shadow of death is never far away. Being there for the final scene:

In the parlour, among suppurating candles
And severed flowers, I see him smiling
Like I'd never seen him smile before.
Coat-hanger at his back. Marching off to war.

McGough's father used to think 'certain McGoughs and a few close friends' were the only normal ones, and all the neighbours were either bonkers or 'barzydown'. That special working-class pride, always trying to be that bit better than your neighbours, keeping your front-step cleaner than anyone else in the road, the sort of family that the Liverpool playwright Willy Russell empathises with: 'the type of family that wants to better themselves. Not the

hooligans, but those who wanted to get on, read proper books, join the library.'
Great emphasis was placed on education in the McGough household, Roger's
extrovert mother able to persuade Brother Thompson, head of St Mary's Prep
School, to allow her son to sit the entrance examination late. He passed it, left
his primary school, the Star of the Sea and quickly achieved the scholarship
to St. Mary's Grammar School, an institution that includes John Birt, Laurie
Taylor and Kevin McNamara amongst its alumni.

Always near the top of the class, an avid reader, he had clearly shown the
promise that merited parental sacrifices. Because Prep school meant fees, his
mother worked part-time in offices and at the family-owned Lincolnshire
Laundry in Stoneycroft in the way that the pre-Baby Boomer generation did,
ensuring their children the education they themselves never had:

Having me meant sacrifices. Going without.
And then to cap it all, the Scholarship
School uniforms, violin lessons,
Elocution, extra tuition.

Being at St Mary's meant more altar boy duties, 7 a.m. Mass, Gregorian
chants and Lourdes water. 'There were prayers of course, hymns and litanies,
often in Latin, which became my private mantras'. There were also elocution
lessons arranged by Mary McGough in a vain attempt to cure her son's habit
of talking too quickly. Referring wryly to the origin of the clipped delivery to
become one of the most distinctive trademarks in contemporary poetry,
McGough recalls 'When I was twelve I spoke too fast and ran
allthewordstogether'. He didn't 'writeanywordstogether' though. Poetry at
school was dull, the language of the poems he was made to study, stale and old-
fashioned. He loved the first poems he heard, 'handed down by mothers,
poems that you could smell and taste, nursery rhymes and fairy tales, strong
in rhythm and image'. After the age of eleven the poetry disappeared. 'I don't
know where it went but it came back with a painful bang. Great chunks of
Palgrave's Golden Treasury were heaved at us by teachers. They were paid to,
and the syllabus demanded it. The poems seemed heavy and dusty and outside
my emotional range. At the time I don't think any of us could name one living
poet'.

The elocution lessons paid off in a much more beneficial way. For the first
time in his life McGough realised he enjoyed recitation: pieces like
'Jabberwocky' and John Masefield's 'Cargoes'. He was beginning to get a feel
for reading aloud, but – in an early indication of a dichotomy in his make-up
– did not like people looking at him. The extrovert side came from his mother,
a woman of little education, who admired teachers, and was less uncomfortable
with them than her husband.

McGough Senior loved playing the piano and could pick up any tune. He was a skilled wood craftsman making beautifully carved and varnished toys for both his children. Despite a busy life he found time to work as a reserve fireman and later a special policeman. He would watch his son playing cricket for the school 'through the railings' and not join the other dads at the end of the innings for tea: 'he needn't have done, but he did.' The boxing gloves bought on his son's thirteenth birthday made a telling metaphor years later in 'Squaring Up': 'You said sorry / And you were. I didn't. And I wasn't.'

McGough has regularly squared up to familial themes ever since. As a teenager he would take out books for his father who was wary of libraries – they were for educated people and full of traps. His sister remembers: 'Mum wanted us both to get on academically, while Dad wanted us to excel at sport. Mum got her way with Roger. Dad got his way with me.'

Another benefit from her brother's elocution lessons – still in the days when being intelligent and have a working-class accent were felt to be incompatible – was that McGough became involved in choral work and entered music and verse competitions. Winning his first award in the world of poetry, an Elementary Grade One, at the age of twelve in 1949, McGough remembers other people who had better voices or seemed to have; were 'that bit posher, but would freeze up on stage and couldn't do it. And I always could'.

He was 'keen' to do a lot of things during his formative years, but not always particularly good at them, although he did play cricket for the first eleven. He kept his head down, and despite his love of reading, was never bookish and was always out with his mates. He sometimes did his homework on the bus in marked similarity to Paul McCartney whose promising school career nose-dived much later at the Liverpool Institute. McGough gradually slipped from the top six in class to the bottom twenties. He stopped wearing his cap, but always kept any greater rebellion in check by the family ethic: 'don't make a show, don't draw attention to yourself'. A vital part of him always deemed this to be so, but he liked to go onstage (something his boisterous sister would never do). Later he would wear dandified clothes, later still, green glasses, an earring, a pigtail – but got embarrassed when people pointed these things out.

He failed English Literature at O Level and did French, History and Geography in the sixth-form, in contrast to Brenda, who was more interested in boys and sport, feeling that she was the one who always got found out whereas Roger, his mother's favourite, never would. He regretted not continuing English, but felt in retrospect, perhaps it was a blessing in disguise. 'It meant I didn't get to dissect and unappreciate more poems at university.' McGough was always one of the gang, witty, but not the wittiest; he contributed to the gang, was popular and wanted to be popular. He was good at reciting poetry onstage but felt that it was not important, because his peers had little respect for it. Better to have won a race.

At seventeen, McGough went to Hull University to study Geography and French. The choice was limited. Kevin McNamara, a former altar boy from Star of the Sea – later a senior Labour politician – recommended it, so a group from St Mary's went. They were the first of their generation to do so.

Through McNamara's influence McGough got into Needler Hall, where his attitudes soon started changing. 'I felt a strong need to express myself, to communicate. I was the outsider, the seer, the shaman, I was the duck who thought he'd invented water. I tried music first, then painting and then I began to listen to the rhythms inside my head and the poetry began.' Coming home on holiday, he would meet friends who had gone to other universities, talk about writing, and make ventures out of Seaforth into the centre of Liverpool; places like Yankel Feather's Basement Club. McGough was studying Sartre and existentialism – it was the beginnings of the beatniks – French cigarettes, duffle coats and polo necks, the start of his long-term attachment to image, fashion and style.

Hull at this time was a mixture of schisms and differing groups taking themselves very seriously indeed. McGough recalls fellow Scouser Neville Smith – later to write *Gumshoe* – bravely joining the Drama Society, but not being taken seriously because 'his accent wasn't right and he was too small'. There was the sophisticated London-based crowd discussing modern jazz; it was the end of one era and the beginning of another. McGough was 'eighteen, getting on fifteen' and in some ways made to feel even younger by students just above him (including Roy Hattersley), who had done National Service. Not many years ahead educationally, they gave the impression of being much more than that in their maturity and overall experience, giving McGough mixed feelings of both awe and contempt.

The duality in McGough prevailed again: chairman of the Catholic Society, social secretary, cricket club secretary, but also tea-chest bass in Tinhorn Timmins and the Rattlesnakes with fellow students Frank Tyrell and Pete Connor who recall 'that he didn't have much musical ability, but practised hard on his charisma'. He also started to practise hard on his writing.

The almost universal critical acclaim that greeted *The Less Deceived* published in November 1955 by the unknown Marvell Press, found its author Philip Larkin the spokesman for the newly emerging meritocratic class. It marked a decisive turning point in his career and Larkin became the most important poet to establish himself in England since the war. He spoke for those who had turned their back on Modernism, Eurosceptics before their time in their suspicion of all things 'abroad'. In March of that year Larkin had been appointed as Head Librarian at the University Library in Hull. He was the warden of Roger McGough's Hall of Residence, making McGough realise it was possible to be a poet and alive at the same time. Until then he thought that poetry was just English Literature, and that meant the Past. Seeing Larkin, was a living embodiment – a poet, and someone whose work he enjoyed. Roger McGough made the decision to be a poet in Hull:

> Once I put pen to paper words flowed. I thought this is poetry, I must be a poet. I spent three days and nights solidly writing. It came out like St John of the Cross to some extent but it was also the nearest thing I've ever had to what could be called a mystic experience.

At first he copied the forms he was studying: Baudelaire, Apollinaire, Rimbaud and other French symbolists. Gradually, as he read more, he became aware of other forms, other ways of working, ways of experimenting and learning contrasting techniques He tried dealing with ideas, more cognisant methods, but above all, emotions and feeling. The idiosyncratic e.e. cummings was an early influence, as were Eliot, Wilfred Owen and Hopkins. It was around this time that he first heard a recording of Dylan Thomas reading *Under Milk Wood*:

> For me, in the early days, it was a pure emotional outburst that I tried to shape and control. But of course, I wasn't speaking with my own voice; I was using the ghosts of other voices – Dylan Thomas, and the French poets. It took me a while to discover my own voice; but when I did, I found that it was very close to the actual voice I speak with.

He was put off submitting to the university magazine because the poetry published was too prolix and full of Latin quotations, as if the poets were moving the furniture of their education into their work. He showed some poems to a student doing an M.A. in English, saying they were from 'a friend', thinking that he would recognise genius immediately. 'He didn't. And they weren't.' The reply, not without acuity, was 'tell your friend he might try writing monologues'. Later he showed some early work to Philip Larkin who was supportive, and continued to be so, congratulating him in a letter dated March 27th 1980, on the 'library condition' of McGough's books, which showed 'signs of a good deal more wear' than his own. In 1958 Larkin felt McGough 'was walking an impressionistic tightrope – sometimes it works, sometimes you fall off'. In that same year McGough attended his first poetry reading given by an established poet.

Born in 1926, having learnt to write poetry through those twin monuments to modernism, Eliot and Pound, Christopher Logue had moved to Paris in the early fifties, becoming influenced by Brecht and Pablo Neruda. Returning to London from Cyprus in 1957, Logue wrote plays for The Royal Court, poems for *The New Statesman*, and became something of a shaping spirit for dissent. Later that year, through the film director Lindsay Anderson he gave his first large-scale poetry reading at The National Film Theatre. This was such a success that he was asked to read at various universities. One of those selected was Hull.

The effect Logue had on McGough – who had only heard lecturers read poetry – cannot be underestimated:

> He definitely made quite an impact, and it was the image too - the existentialist look – hair brushed forward – this was the way you did it.

This was the way, McGough imagined, the Americans did it, taking issues such as war or urban life, incorporate travel, worldliness, passion, and rhythm. 'Logue read well. Very well. The accessibility too, that struck me. That instant accessibility.'

Adrian Henri 1932-1956

'...the contender...'

The island of Mauritius is a remote dot in the Indian Ocean. Famous as the home of the dodo and two renowned stamps, the 1847 Penny Red and the Twopenny Blue, it had long impressed travellers and writers. One was Charles Baudelaire, who saw the seductive beaches in 'Parfum Exotique' as a place where

> nature gives
> Peculiar trees and tasty fruits.
> Men whose bodies are slim and strong
> And women whose eye is astonishing in its frankness.

It was here that Louis Ernest Henri Celine was born in 1854. The son of a Master Mariner, a natural traveller and adventurer, he had sailed the world three times before reaching the age of thirty. His restlessness continued, and in 1887 he set sail once more on yet another marathon voyage, arriving this time at the city of Liverpool.

Here he found a place basking in the glory of being the most significant port and third richest city in the British Empire, its name echoing from the sea fronts of Singapore to the tobacco plantations of Nyasaland. Collectively, it generated more tax revenue than Birmingham, Bristol, Leeds and Sheffield and was where Cunard and the White Star lines had based their headquarters. Ten miles of docks and shipyards provided employment for 100,000 people. It was where huge ships from all corners of the earth brought cargoes of pilchards, tobacco, cotton, metals and gems. Its bustling streets were paraded equally by a mixture of bankers, barrow-boys and beggars and it reminded Louis Ernest Henri (having now dropped Celine) of Marseilles. He decided to drop anchor and stay for a while, perhaps even set up home.

A year later, whilst visiting the small nearby Cheshire town of Birkenhead, he met a local pattern maker's daughter whose eye to him was 'astonishing in its frankness'. They immediately fell in love. Louis Henri and the much younger Edith Shaw were married shortly afterwards in 1889.

Their first home was in Whetstone Lane, Bebington, before they moved to the much larger 7 Lowood Road to accommodate their quickly growing family. It was here that Edith Henri 'ruled the roost', and where music and laughter were always in the air. It was also where their fifth son Arthur Maurice was born on July 6th 1898.

Small, but good-looking, Arthur never quite shared the musical talent of his other brothers, particularly the dashing Emile, closest to him in age, if not in temperament. What ambitions he did have were rudely shattered by World War One. Barely old enough to serve, he was still called up, and to compound his misery got shot in the leg.

Life then resumed uneventfully for Arthur Henri. Work was scarce; the only real action, the regular dance bands he and his brothers, Emile, Noel and Paul would form such as 'Les Freres Henri'. They would often play at local tea dances where Arthur developed into a fine ballroom performer. It was the Depression, the age of forced 'labour-camps' – he would tirelessly help others but found it difficult to help himself. In his late thirties, marriage seemed to have eluded him when, at a local dance, he was introduced by brother Emile – now performing in Professor Dossors Alfredo Orchestra – to a young girl with bright eyes, exquisitely fine cheekbones and the most curious gaze.

Emma Johnson was born on the 26th June 1911 in Birkenhead. An only child, bright, emotional, with high aspirations, she was quick at most things and very imaginative. Captivated by Arthur's sleekback hairstyle, dark matinee idol looks, skilful steps across the dance floor, and lured by the camaraderie of his exotic, unconventional family, she felt an irresistible attraction. They were married in 1931, living at first at 7 Lowood Road before moving to nearby Tranmere, and 17 Sydney Buildings, home of Emma's father Albert and stepmother Frances. Opposite Mersey Park, it lay directly above Cammel Lairds Shipyard, home of the *Ark Royal*. It was here that their first son Adrian Maurice Henri was born on 10th April 1932.

Birkenhead in the thirties was still a very separate entity from Liverpool. A more even mix of countryside and industry, the town would give the Henris' son early images that would influence him both as an artist and writer throughout his career. The flags and funnels of the ships, the ferryboats, smells from the tannery, his maternal grandfather's 'darkblue suit gleaming black boots shiny watch chain / striped shirt no collar but always a collarstud', (from *Autobiography*). There was the old man's allotment, the cobblestone path, and the shadowy figure of his great-uncle Bill, smelling of beer and horses, 'rolling up the hill / in Sydney Road' then falling fast asleep in his chair. And at night, he would remember ominously:

lying in bed
in the dark crying
listening to my mother and father argue
dead eyes looking out from flyblown photographs
empty mirrors reflecting the silence

The seaside town of Rhyl sits rather jauntily on the North Wales coastline between Prestatyn and Colwyn Bay looking out into Kinmel Bay. 'Things started to go downhill', according to performer and theatre producer Juan Vitti, 'when they demolished the Pavilion Theatre and replaced it with a Nissen hut'. Laurel and Hardy and Buffalo Bill had appeared at the prestigious Queens Theatre, replaced later by an arcade. 'When the Pavilion went, a great piece of history was taken away from this town', says Vitti remembering 'the children's paradise' of three fairgrounds, and miles of beautiful sands: 'when summers were never hotter and kids would burst tar bubbles without shoes or socks on their feet.'

It was this 'sunny Rhyl' in its heyday that the Henri family moved to in 1938. Arthur Henri had got his first real break in life. He had been appointed as a redcoat at Sunnyvale Camp. Within a year the bad luck that had dogged him struck again, this time in the shape of World War Two.

Starkly contrasting with Roger McGough's wartime experiences in Seaforth – huddling under the stairs with his sister, listening to the war – Adrian Henri's experiences were typically visual. Although only one bomb was dropped on Rhyl in anger – 'which landed in a field and killed a cow' – as he would write much later (casting himself as the wartime child in 'Rhinestone Rhino'), he had no need for toy soldiers or toy tanks, they were there in reality. The military had taken over the stables next door to their home in Vale Road. Sherman tanks would rumble past each day, and starry-eyed the young Henri would go to the railway-station to watch soldiers coming back from Dunkirk. Many would be shivering, wrapped in blankets; some giving the children centimes riddled with holes. In May 1941 Adrian Henri and his mother went to stay for a week in Birkenhead. That day the Blitz broke out. Henri still remembers looking out across at Liverpool from Mersey Park – the whole of the horizon on fire.

Sunnyvale Camp had also been taken over by the military, which meant that the job that Arthur Henri had finally found was gone. His new post was the lowest level of war department clerk, a position in which he was to remain for the rest of his working life. Those early arguments that Henri overheard as a boy in Sydney Building began to increase, the 'empty mirrors reflecting the silence' that ensued becoming even more desolate. Emma, increasingly frustrated, sublimated her ambitions in her only son. In what seemed a template for that generation, similarly to Roger McGough's mother Mary, Emma wanted Adrian to better himself through learning. An omnivorous reader herself – 'anything from sloppy romances to *Ulysses*,' she was a great library-goer, encouraging her rather overweight and short-sighted son to be the same. When other boys were in the snooker halls or playing football, he was in heaven with 'these wonderful creatures (young female librarians) behind the desk'.

St Anne's Voluntary Primary School in Vale Road was even by pre-1944 standards, old-fashioned and inept, the upshot being that no pupil had passed the scholarship in years. Bright, artistic, 'a contender' for the 11-plus, his highly distinctive 'calligraphic' hand writing already emerging, Henri became aware that he was not achieving what he should be. His friend at that time, Dennis Cramer, felt a kindred spirit. 'We were two little fat kids with glasses sitting at the back. I liked Adrian a lot, but even then', Cramer remembers, 'he had a strange sort of abstract, other-worldliness about him, a sense of being permanently preoccupied with something far, far away.'

Plump, shortsighted and rather foreign-looking, Henri was bullied at school and became something of a classic victim figure. By using his wits and drawing skills however, he overcame these problems. He discovered Frank Wootton's *How To Draw Planes,* quickly learning how to do Spitfires and Hurricanes, which pleased the other boys at playtime. This way they would leave him alone. It also 'drew' him towards Art. Academically it was of little use because, par for the course at St Anne's, he failed the 11-plus and went to Emmanuel Secondary Modern School, in Rhyl, where from

Being the bright boy in the junior school I became this hopeless figure... because all the boys had to be vocationally trained and do either woodwork or metalwork and I was hopeless at that, and so obviously so, that they said - oh well - if you can't be technical you must be commercial, so they got me and some other boys who weren't very good at technical either in with the girls, and we did short-hand and typing, and if anything I was worse at that, and completely a square peg in a round hole.

To compound his problems the strain in his parents' marriage was becoming more apparent: 'never marry for love', he remembers his mother saying, 'it's not enough.' His childhood was a 'border zone where skirmishes, rocket-attacks, dogfights took place daily', he felt, 'a lonely observer, fired on by both sides at once! Then, at the age of twelve, getting used to the idea of

being a
sad
boy-to-be-poet
head full of words
understood by no one

he found himself with a sister.

Avril Henri was born in 1944. Her brother remembers running with her pram up and down Rhyl sands, 'hair in curls it's rolled up in every night'. Avril, now a senior civil-servant, sardonically recalls being left outside the post-office by her brother, 'who only remembered me when mentally checking his shopping list as he felt sure he had forgotten something'. For a short while life at home became more relaxed and was further enhanced by another event that occurred during the same year. The company of Manchester Repertory Theatre had been evacuated to Rhyl, one of their productions, *Emil and the Detectives* requiring a number of the local children. Actor and director Joe Holroyd who loved the place so much and was, in Juan Vitti's words, 'a professional from his toenails upwards' decided to stay on in Rhyl after the theatre's extended run, forming the celebrated Rhyl Children's Theatre Club which remains to this day. Henri, at the behest of his mother, joined, becoming one of the children still remembered in the town as 'one of the ones who got it all going'.

I never got the romantic leads, I played the Beadle in Jack and the Beanstalk, sang in the chorus, but I got a lot of elocution and basic stagecraft. It was very important to me; it was confidence building, and the nearest thing I had to a girlfriend at that time came out of the Theatre Club.

It gave him an early opportunity to display early artistic skills, one entry in the Rhyl Journal of 1947 under 'Scenery Design' commending 'fifteen year old Adrian Henri of 133, Vale Road... who will be in charge of the Scenery Design and Painting Department. He plans to be a commercial artist when he grows up and his Club experience will no doubt be of considerable help.' Henri was involved in the Children's Theatre for four years and it was an important part of his life. It was also where he caught chickenpox from one of the girls, passing it on to Avril causing a delay in the family's move to their new council house in 1948.

Rhyl in the forties was full of evacuees, children from London, Birmingham, Manchester and Liverpool, all playing a large part in giving the theatre such a broad cultural mix. Still very much the square peg at school, and having been so badly let down by the system, miraculously Adrian Henri was saved by it.

As part of R.A. Butler's Education Act in 1944 (described by Evelyn Waugh as 'one of the things politicians did when no-one was looking, towards the end of the war'), greater opportunity in the Welfare State was promised to encourage social mobility. A new examination, the 13-plus arose specifically to give certain pupils a second chance. Henri sat it, passed, and it changed his life.

The small market town of St Asaph, some ten miles south of Rhyl, is notable perhaps for one reason only, that it is a city by virtue of the fact that it has a cathedral. It also has a Grammar School, which numbered only one hundred and fifty pupils in the forties. It was the school where Adrian Henri went in 1945. It was the place in which he took off and blossomed. From the bullied 'Bunter' figure at junior school, the misfit at Secondary Modern, he became the 'school character' at St. Asaph. International photo-journalist, Rhuddlan born Philip Jones Griffiths recalls Henri as the person who made school bearable for him. 'I didn't realise there were other people like me until I met this strange character who did all these outrageous things, but was also interested in art and music. And that was Adrian.'

No longer needing to draw planes for the other boys, Henri became the school's star pupil at Art. In the sixth form he discovered Picasso, Magritte and Matisse, later the work of T.S. Eliot and Ezra Pound. These were his own discoveries, but at school, studying French at A level, he empathised with the nineteenth century French Romantic poets such as Rimbaud and Baudelaire. From the 'hopeless case' at school, the eighteen-year old Henri found himself in a position where his English teacher wanted him to study literature at university, his French teacher, languages; whereas he himself was totally fixed on Art.

The Henris' marriage was coming apart. From being an only child for twelve years, then one of two, Adrian Henri found himself the eldest of six. Next came his brother Tony, born in 1946. Referred to in *Autobiography* as 'hitchhiking round Europe / laying girls in my spare bedroom tired eyes at the dead / morning railway station', he became the sibling that Henri would remain closest to. Tony was followed by two more sisters, dark haired Christine and brown-eyed Michelle – 'dancing at parties kissing on the stairs'. Unfortunately the more children, the worse things got; armed neutrality set in whereby neither parent spoke. Arthur Henri had become active in Civil Service Trade Unionism, showing great skill in writing letters and reports, but his wife Emma was constantly reproachful of her husband's lack of ambition. Despite being proud of his son's achievements, Arthur Henri felt all this education was a waste of time as there seemed no prospect of a job at the end of it all. In the early fifties most art colleges offered Diploma courses which did not provide grants. Money was scarce so this was essential. Newcastle and Reading did degree courses, which were grant-aided, and as Henri's results were good enough, his application to King's College, Newcastle was accepted shortly after the birth of his second brother Andre in 1951.

As a young artist, Lawrence Gowing had been a pupil of the Euston Road School. Established in 1937, it centred on the work of four artists, Victor Pasmore, William Coldstream, Claude Rogers and Graham Bell. Its teaching emphasised 'humility', 'honesty' and 'realism', thus challenging the 'vociferation and pretentious flourish' of the Surrealists, whose leading figures included Andre Breton and Paul Eluard.The English base for surrealism was the London Gallery in Cork Street, run by E.L.T. Mesens, where the jazz singer George Melly would later work. Gowing was Henri's tutor at King's, but his teaching, based on strong visual narrative, had little effect on him. So much so, that at the beginning of his second year Gowing, realising that he was getting nowhere with Henri – 'whatever ability he had, it wasn't coming through in his work' – and instinctively feeling that he did have something, told him 'you just better do it'. He had faith in him as a personality who would eventually express himself somehow.

Rhyl's three fairgrounds in the forties and early fifties consisted of as picaresque a section of humanity as one could hope to find outside the East End of London. Run by such meretricious operators as Joe Sales, Joe Brownlee and Arthur Webber, characters reminscent of Syd Field's spiv sketch, they would drive big American cars and had a taste for child labour as it was so cheap. Juan Vitti worked with Bob Denzer who had a skeleton act. 'A very good one, so good he took it all over the world. He was married to an ex-Tiller girl, and when he wasn't working, which was most of the time he'd be in one of his brother Tom's stalls.' It was in this netherworld of minor villains, down-on-their-luck theatricals, Romanies and the horse-racing fraternity that Adrian Henri found himself ('expressing it somehow'), for several summers during his later school and university years. Working on the hoop-la at Lake Walk by the Marine Lake with its distinctive blue bridge, Henri learnt the art of talking to people and more importantly, persuading them to part with their money:

> So I'd be this arty person in the daytime, and then a minor member of this sub-culture at night or in the holidays. Even years later when I was quite well known, I'd walk round the fairground and people would say, who are you working for this season? Some of them were real heroes to me; legendary con-men and gamblers. The fact that they'd have a drink with you in the bar later was wonderful - as much approval as someone liking your picture – it was where I really started to learn about language, slang and dialect, and another tremendous confidence builder.

'You grew up quickly', Juan Vitti recalls, 'you got street-wise and learnt to take ridicule, if you were small, or fat, or had a foreign sounding name or other problems – you overcame them. We found out that we could do things other children couldn't do. And I'm sure Adrian found that out too'.

What Henri also found in Rhyl was a record shop called Albert's. Albert himself was a semi-pro musician and jazz buff. He would stock Dixieland music, the big bands, and also Swing and Be-bop. Here, at the age of sixteen, with music already in his background, Henri began his lifelong vocation as a frustrated jazz musician. At Albert's he would hang around listening to the music and look at the girls who would wander in, all so desirable in the latest fashions of the time but sadly, equally unattainable as none of them would ever look back.

Later at Newcastle he mixed with a crowd who would sit on the suburban train coming into town whistling the second chorus of Potato Head Blues. He learnt the washboard, played in the College Jazz Band (once with the trumpeter Ian Carr), and stretched to singing a bit of blues. Playwright Alan Plater, then in the Architecture Department, remembers 'this overweight bespectacled character standing on a table in the Union bar singing "Frankie And Johnny" in the style of George Melly'.

Melly himself would later become a lifelong friend, but at that time Henri knew him vicariously, through Jim 'Jasper' Livesey, clarinettist in the Mick Mulligan Band. Playwright David Mercer, then a painter, was in the year above. A higher case Oliver Reed, he was a dominant figure, imperious, drunk and rude to everyone in sight. A former Merchant seaman, in the days when ex-servicemen had their G.I. Bill of Rights, he was one of the many young men who had seen action, played hard, but were as serious about their studies as the National Service students that Roger McGough encountered at Hull. Half a generation later, Art Colleges would become breeding grounds for English Rock and Roll, but for Henri, studying Art at university offered him a broader cultural base, crucial to his later eclectic development.

He graduated in 1955 with a B.A. Hons in Fine Art, but without any immediate career opportunities. Turned down for National Service on grounds of shortsightedness, he found himself in something of a vacuum. To fill it he applied for a temporary post as a teacher. The Catholic College for Boys in Preston wanted an art master for a year. Henri was their man. He took to it surprisingly well, some friends remarking 'how straight' he suddenly became. This newly found respectability did not stop him from shocking one or two of his more adventurous sixth-formers, who were amazed to find their art teacher sitting in at the local Jazz Club one night, strumming his washboard and singing passable blues with the band. It was here in 1956 that Adrian Henri met Joyce Wilson.

Liverpool 1957-1961

'...Where's the best place to buy a pair of winklepickers?...'

In the fifties, with the exception of Soho, the place for any aspirational painter, poet, musician, bohemian or 'bon viveur' on a tight budget was Liverpool 8. Described by George Melly in *The Observer* as a 'multi-racial slum waiting in raddled beauty for the planners' bulldozers', and more positively in Adrian Henri's prose-poem 'Liverpool 8' as a place 'where you play out after tea... Back doors and walls / with names, kisses scrawled or painted... A new cathedral at the end of Hope Street...Wind / blowing inland from Pierhead bringing the smell of breweries / and engine oil from ferry boats...'

In his introduction to *The Liverpool Scene* (published in 1967), Edward Lucie-Smith took a more expansive view:

> The city continues to think of itself as something pretty special. 'The most obvious thing about Liverpool at the moment is that [it] has a lot of feathers in its cap...Liverpool knows its own standards and imposes them firmly.

Unlike Soho, Liverpool 8 in the fifties was bereft of clip-joints and nightclubs such as The Mandrake, or pubs like The Fitzroy and The Golden Lion, with their blatant disregard for licensing laws, sexuality and outwardly respectable behaviour. In Liverpool, closing time meant ten o'clock, so a place to make the most of one's allotted drinking time was essential. Such a place was Ye Cracke. Formerly the Ruthin Castle, it acquired its name around 1900. Squeezed between two larger buildings, one of which was the War Office, its owners were the renowned Liverpool publican family the Egertons. Here, the main attraction, the long-suffering landlady Doris would dispense beer to the whole of Liverpool bohemia crammed into one small bar. On a good night there would be the Art College crowd centred around Arthur Ballard, including Jeff Mohammed, Stuart Sutcliffe, the life-model June Furlong and John Lennon whom Yankel Feather noticed surprisingly for 'the quietness about that boy'. A pint of Bass's breath away would be Arthur Dooley and his eccentric cohort 'Mayfair Ben' in eavesdropping distance of the poet and painter Henry Graham, his wife Liz and her friend Josephine the current girlfriend of the 'professionally bohemian' coffee-bar owner Alan Blease. Beryl Bainbridge, then at the Playhouse would drop in with her husband, the painter Austin Davis often in the company of fellow artists Rod Murray, Sam Walsh and Don McKinlay. To complete the melting pot would be a coterie of local gays surrounding Brian Epstein, and when he was in Liverpool, the 'English Jack Kerouac' – Pete Brown.

If anyone 'looked the part' in this assembly it was Alan Blease. Ruth in School educated, handsome, with long dark hair and drooping moustache, open-toed sandals and a beret, Blease had spent some time in Paris, and with his almost military self-confidence was the epitome of fifties bohemian chic. He ran the Studio Club in Bold Street and was a consummate seducer of women. In the summer of 1956 his girlfriend Josephine, a blonde Juliet Greco lookalike and art school model, took a job at Rhyl Fairground as did Blease himself, with the artist Don McKinlay, as street photographers. When Josephine's stall was quiet she would read poems by Louis MacNeice, which, combined with her striking appearance, brought her to the attention of the large, bearded, heavily bespectacled young man working on the stall opposite.

Joyce Wilson knew her mind right from the start: Talking about the woman he had met at the Jazz Club in Preston Adrian Henri states:

she had very definite tastes and ideas without ever nurturing any great desire for a career of her own. She was always sceptical about arty types, but was very sociable. People reacted to her generally in a positive way; she was full of ideas and had good taste. She was largely content with being happily unemployed – but never in any negative way.

Before meeting Henri in Preston she had been going out with a musician. Her father, Inspector Wilson of the Lancashire Constabulary had found her a clerical job computing policemen's wages, which she grudgingly accepted as it provided her with money to spend. She needed it on her first date with Henri who turned up with 2/6d in his pocket! This inauspicious start notwithstanding, they got on well, the bearded and already highly aspirational artist an increasing focus against her doctrinaire father. Inspector Wilson took an immediate dislike to the totally unsuitable 'artist type' his daughter was associating with, which was never resolved. Things at home became so difficult that in the summer of 1956 Joyce upped and left, deciding to move in for a few months with a friend.

For the principal cause of the upset, that hot summer was a case of (Adrian Henri's) 'Back to the Fairground Blues', dealing with hoops and balloons. This continued for the next two seasons interspersed with teaching jobs in Chorlton, Cheadle Hulme and Netherton. It was during his final season that Henri having acquired a state-of-the-art brown-box Pye record player, bought a rare Chet Baker L.P. to accompany it. 'One day the record just happened to be propped up on the counter and this kid came up and started talking about Chet Baker. I couldn't believe it. In Rhyl that was quite something.' The 'kid' happened to be Mike Evans, later a vital component of what would become The Liverpool Scene.

Evans remembers that first meeting equally well. 'I was working on some kind of Bingo stall and Ade was working a couple of stalls up from me where you fired balls from catapults at these cardboard cats. So there was this interesting bohemian looking character and he had these two voluptuous women with him, one of whom was Joyce, and the other, I later discovered, was Eddy Macphearson the Art College model over on vacation work. For a while I was under the impression that this bohemian character was really that bohemian – he had two women in tow!'

If Evans's later precosity was startling to Henri, the blonde Juliette Greco look-alike reading Louis MacNeice in the stall opposite was infinitely more fascinating. He began a conversation, found out her name (Josephine), and met her boyfriend Alan Blease, who suggested he should come over to Liverpool...

and I came over and discovered this wonderful bohemia that was like all the things I'd ever read about – Paris in the twenties and London in the nineties – and I just thought this is wonderful, the place is full of artists, everybody goes to the pub, everybody knows one another and I want to go there. So I did.

Joyce Wilson was still in Preston but not for long, her father's anger becoming seismic when she left town with Henri, the Pye brown-box record player and all her belongings in the back of Alan Blease's sign-of-the-times red open-top sports-car.

For a short while she and Henri lived on the premises at Blease's Studio Club, playing all-night sessions of the fiendish (fall-out-with your-friends) 'truth game', endlessly discussing starry-eyed trips to Spain, at times living off the money collected from bottles they would return to The Swan in Wood Street, when times were tough. 'We used to sleep on a rolled-up mattress kept under the counter, so we couldn't go to bed until all the customers had gone home'. Things looked up when Henri became part of a dynastic job situation involving himself, Don McKinlay and Rod Murray, which began with employment at The Liverpool Playhouse as a scenic artist.

He and Joyce Wilson married at the registry office in Gregson's Well, Liverpool 8 in 1957, Mr and Mrs Wilson in grudging attendance. Soon they acquired their first place, a bedsit' at 24 Falkner Square. It was here they also 'acquired' 'Mayfair Ben'.

Christopher Morris-Jones had one immaculate Saville Row suit, one overcoat, two Jermyn Street striped shirts, and two coat hangers. Hence the epithet. Before moving to the basement of Falkner Square he lived on a mattress at the foot of sculptor Arthur Dooley's bed in his ramshackle studio in Slater Street near Allan Williams's Jacaranda Club and The Swan pub.

'He always looked immaculate', Henri recalls, 'had this "terribly far-back" accent and was completely penniless, but somehow convinced our landlord that he could turn this basement into a club. And he did and we called it the Half Moon. Joyce did the bar, this marvellous black guy Alfred was the cook, and it was great. They had my brown box as the music centre, and some nights Henry Graham would play the guitar, and you went down these steps and knocked on this door.'

Despite being unlicensed and open all hours the club managed to run for a year and a half during which time Henri, having been sacked by The Playhouse, job-swapped with McKinlay to Warwick Bolam Secondary School in Netherton where he remained until 1960. However, one night, a hilarious 'Keystone Cops' police raid saw the demise of The Half Moon and also the end of Mayfair Ben. This meant that the Henris were able to move into the basement, the old bar becoming a studio, allowing for a spare bed. Yankel Feather recalls Henri in those days:

He used to come and see me quite frequently and I'd go and see him, and one day he said to me, if you're ever hungry and the shops are closed don't be afraid to call on us because we've always got food. And one night I was starving – it was about one or two in the morning and I thought, I know what I'll do, I'll go round to Adrian's. I knocked on the door and he said, what do you want? And I said, well I'm a bit hungry and he said, I've got nothing in. So I said, can I go to the toilet – and I had to go through the kitchen – and on the draining board there was something covered up, and I just happened to move the cloth and there was all sorts of food prepared. So I shouted, Adrian I thought you'd got nothing to eat. And he said, oh that's for tomorrow. So I decided that as Adrian was getting fatter and fatter and fatter and I was getting thinner and thinner I'd better look elsewhere if I was ever hungry. So I never called on Adrian again.

Only two miles north of the burgeoning bohemia of Liverpool 8, but spiritually oceans away, Roger McGough was living in the all too nagging familiarity of Litherland. Tragically his father had died from a heart-attack at the age of fifty-three, not long after McGough's twenty-first birthday:

He'd had his first attack two years before, he was a strong man, but it was almost like an epidemic of people dying – all these guys he'd worked with at the docks started dropping off. All men of different builds too – some smoked, some didn't – and it seemed like once he'd had his first attack that was it. It was just a matter of time; unlike nowadays with various heart operations. So that was frightening. At a time when your own life is opening up, your home-life is falling apart as you move away from it. I'd fled the roost as it were – so there were all sorts of feelings of guilt.

Perhaps this early experience sheds some light on the way the theme of death haunts so much of McGough's writing. Understandable in a writer's work in their fifties, or even forties, but this early preoccupation has always given him cause for concern. He was teaching in Kirkby, trying out some of his own poems on his pupils, because the set-texts 'weren't suitable', making the occasional Saturday afternoon visit to Liverpool 8 and The Basement Club. Full of undefined aspirations, he had found a room above a boxing-club in Litherland that he used as a studio with his friend Paddy Lynch. Here he would paint for hours into the night. He had become engaged to a student called Josephine Twist during his last year at Hull, but was beginning to feel uneasy about it. 'I was changing and she wasn't .' He was racked with indecision; the urge to be a poet all consuming, he needed something to happen in his life before his passion was undercut.

Adrian Henri claims that the only person he knows less decisive than himself is Roger McGough. However, events were now making things happen. Having served his teaching dues in Kirkby at St Kevin's, McGough had been accepted by Mabel Fletcher College in Mount Pleasant as a lecturer. Close to the city centre, it gave him far greater freedom and mobility. His outward behaviour changed too – former student Rosalind Harbutt remembers him as full of fun, 'like a big kid at times, flicking chalk and always fooling around. He was like one of us really. If we ever had any parties on the go he'd always be there.' He finally made the decision to break up with Josephine Twist, feeling that perhaps his life was going to be different. Something was about to happen, but it was hard to say what. Like Adrian Henri before him, he was becoming increasingly drawn towards Liverpool 8.

> It was the place to go to really, it was where the students lived, the poets, the painters, and an exciting place to be. I felt at some stage I'm going to have to get a flat here.

Gradually he started going down to Streate's, became more adventurous, and started looking the part. He got to know Pete Brown, who around Christmas of 1960 introduced him to someone he had seen somewhere before. It was that guy. The huge bearded guy with the heavy glasses on the bus that he had been so fascinated by. Not knowing what to say he decided to play it cool, be impressive:

Where's the best place to buy a pair of winklepickers?

McGough and Henri hit it off: 'Adrian's was the first arty place I'd ever been to – polished bare floorboards, lots of paintings and real coffee.' McGough also met Sam Walsh who had moved from the flat he had shared with Hawkins and Byrne in Gambier Terrace becoming a close friend of Henri's.

Born in 1935, Walsh studied painting at the Dublin College of Art before coming to England in 1955, to lead 'a double life as a portrait painter for money and an abstract painter for love'. From this uneasy compromise, Walsh heavily influenced by Francis Bacon, moved into a kind of pop-art all of his own based around large air-brushed faces, including one of Bacon bought by The Walker Art Gallery in 1963. The previous year he and Henri had exhibited together at The Portal Gallery in London where they both met Bacon who gave them encouragement and champagne.

Although holding similar artistic preoccupations, Walsh was the senior partner, regarded in the early sixties as the most interesting local painter around. The distinguished critic Roderick Bisson bought a Walsh painting for the Sandon Rooms beneath the Bluecoat Chambers, although reportedly, he would dine deliberately with his back to it. George Melly was a frequent visitor in those days. Unlike Yankel Feather, he speaks highly of the Henri hospitality:

> The first time I met Adrian was when I'd picked up a girl known as Mary the flower-seller's daughter. We decided to spend the night together but didn't know where; so she said, I know where to go. So we went up to Falkner Square, and there in a basement was Adrian. He was very hospitable, Mary and I were permitted to stay, but what pleased me was that I saw his pictures. I particularly loved one of them – very much of its time – so I bought it for very little. He said it was the first picture he'd ever sold'.

Thus began a lasting friendship, Melly becoming a consistent, if at times frustrated and impatient champion of Henri's painting.

Henri, by now a part-time lecturer at Manchester College of Art, had been persuaded by Pete Brown to become involved in Liverpool's growing poetry scene:

> Poetry had just been a sort of hobby, I had a notebook, would write in it then put it back in the drawer. I went along to help organise it more than anything else and very reluctantly did I have anything to do with poetry. But what I discovered was, that all this poetry that I thought was so wonderful that I'd been writing in private – all this sub-Eliot, sub-Auden stuff – when I tried to read it out to a crowd of Scousers with a pint in their hands it was acutely and deeply embarrassing.

McGough remembers Streate's poetry and jazz nights as 'a beatniky, existentialist sort of thing; and in those days I was a beatniky existentialist sort of guy'. Other local poets were the hunched, manic Phil Tasker and the darkly mysterious arch-beat Tonk. Pete Brown, still a constant visitor and catalyst, would endlessly hitchhike between Roy Fisher's spare bed in Birmingham, Adrian Henri's place in Liverpool, invariably ending up at Ian Hamilton-Finlay's flat in Edinburgh.

It was through Brown that some exciting news spread about a fifteen-year old 'wunderkind' poet whom nobody knew. On 6th November 1961 McGough read at 'Streate's', later to be told, 'there's a guy here from *The Bootle Times* – a journalist'. 'And I expected this hard-bitten forty year old', McGough remembers 'and there instead was this hard-bitten fifteen year old'.

Brian Patten 1946-1961

'...if only I could crack it...'

I never knew my father. My mother married him but they were separated before I remember. I was brought up in this really tiny house with this crippled grandmother – and she and my grandfather never spoke. It was a very small, frightening, claustrophobic space. And there was an auntie who sat in a chair – lived sitting in a chair in the kitchen – and my mother was a woman called Stella. And I felt very much that if I opened my mouth or said anything it would rock the boat. And I didn't want to rock a boat.

Born on 7th February 1946 at 100 Wavertree Vale into a family with quite a name in the local criminal fraternity, Brian Patten was an only child, withdrawn, dark haired, with dark eyes that cautiously appraised the world right from the start. He never did know his father, and to this day is not interested.

Wavertree Vale ran into the unfashionable city end of Picton Road on the fringes of Liverpool 8. Flanked by two dark Victorian and uncompromisingly 'working-man's' pubs, the Ashgrove and the Belle Vue, it sat approximately two miles from the short-spired Picton Clock whose square face gazes benignly at the greener pastures of Mossley Hill and Childwall. Patten remembers cousins in and out of prison. Tommy (known as 'the brace and bit man') was the 'mouthiest', so much so one night that Sergeant Frank Jones vividly recalls throwing him against a prison-cell wall at Lawrence Road Police Station with such force that he thought he had killed him.

Unlike Henri and McGough, both of whom can name favourite early childhood authors, Patten grew up in a house with only one book. It had a green cover, smelt of mothballs because it had lain on top of a shelf for a long time, and was an 'innocuous book about a fox'. He was six when he found it, and it filled him with a disproportionate sense of mystery because it seemed so out of place.

At Lawrence Road Juniors he was just as out of place himself. Bottom of the class, the last to read and write, he was considered by his teachers to be in need of remedial teaching. There was no improvement later at Sefton Park Secondary Modern School. At fourteen he still couldn't spell (still can't), and despite acquiring some basic learning, the barriers of his indifference remained rooted as he himself did at the bottom of the C-Stream.

The 13-plus was a godsend for Adrian Henri but not for Patten. Not only did he fail it but walked out half-way through. It was a sunny day, so he slipped out to the park. Quarry Bank: 'the kids wore uniforms and the area looked posh, the kind of upmarket place my friends' parents aspired to.' He remembers the school because it was where John Lennon went – an indifferent scholar himself – but Patten was far worse, his loathing of academia in general, and exams in particular, a defensive but constant theme to permeate throughout his work. He also hated sport (still does) but would not be picked on or bullied, was always in fights and hung out on street corners in gangs: 'we would get cistern chains from outside-toilets and go looking for other gangs. It was a tough area. To survive, that's what you had to be.'

Patten developed an aggressive, 'gloves-off' personality, referring to himself later in 'Lament for the Angels Who've Left My Street' as the 'monster who scared my playmates'. It is a side of his personality that has been a problem: 'there was a violent part of my nature which for a long time I had a fight with, but now it's gone'. Patten remembers genuinely being half-hearted about the gang member he had become, and around the age of fourteen started drifting away. The solitary, intense observations on life, so characteristic of much of his poetry and later years were now beginning to accrue:

I was a pretty isolated child at first, and began writing poetry really to try and articulate the chaos I felt in me at fifteen. The people who I grew up with weren't very articulate, and the only way I felt I could try and explain anything in me was to write poetry.

Apart from coded references in *Little Johnny's Confession* and his children's novel, *Mr Moon's Last Case*, it took his most recent collection, *Armada*, published in 1996, for his childhood, with its 'crushed hopes', 'the derelict playgrounds of back-alleys and bomb-sites', to be voiced. In 'The Betrayal' personal guilt is expressed because he could never read the nature of

What those who shaped me could not articulate
Still howls for recognition as a century closes
And their homes are pulled down and replaced,
And their backgrounds are wiped from the face of the earth.

Other things caught his attention:

A caterpillar climbing a tree in a playground,
A butterfly resting on a doorknob.

Only Lizzy Graham, who lived in the Patten's crammed bickering household, is recalled fondly. His early experience with the loneliness of old age instilled a recurrent thread that would nag away continually in future collections. In his early poem 'Cheque for A Dream' Lizzy is remembered taking him to the Magnet cinema, a place highly central in his personal iconography:

And through it all your sad figure creeps
With Chaplin movements, and sometimes you turn around
And smiling wave at the empty auditorium. But only memories
Clap back and cheer you from the dusty streets

Here he met the world of 'celluloid imaginations' for the first time. A far cry from the uninspired and stagnant minds of the teachers he was still being stifled by at Sefton Park School. Despite this, in 1960, salvation occurred.

Incredibly, an essay, long since disappeared, but firmly rooted in popular poetry folklore, and as unpromising a title as could be imagined, of the traditional – 'What we did in our summer holidays' kind – changed everything. That he did the essay at all was a revelation, but the untapped reserves of imaginative power that headmaster Mr Woolley saw when shown it, was a bigger one. If at first Patten found writing essays 'a very good way of avoiding cross-country which was really running around the gasworks and across the park', he had for the first time in his life been told that he could do something well. It also speaks volumes for Mr Woolley, the one teacher whom Patten has to thank.

The poet's flippant response belies the fact that Patten had received an enlightening encouragment and he latched on to it like someone drowning. Drifting away, he lost interest in the gang he felt increasingly isolated from. He had nothing, but felt desperately that he wanted to articulate the mish-mash of feelings inside him.

Something was in the air. It was called the sixties – not quite the fizzy electrical storm yet – but Patten had a premonition of freedom. He would follow the street singers; war-damaged men whose sea shanties and Irish ballads filled him with a sense of melancholy and awe.

He began to wonder more about the innocuous book with the green cover that smelt of moth-balls. Did his grandfather have a secret passion for reading? Had he stolen it? What was it doing there? Nobody in the household read.

Unlike Henri and McGough's mothers' efforts to encourage their eldest sons to succeed, when asked did he get any push from his family Patten replied: 'only over!'

He started reading avidly. Jack London became an early favourite author, the desire for identity, given credence through the discovery of his imaginative powers further triggered by another formative experience approximately a year earlier than his famous essay.

Frieda's house looked no different from any other in Wavertree Vale. It was certainly no bigger. Once inside however, it seemed enormous, largely because of the amount of books it contained. Frieda, an Austrian Jewess, was regarded suspiciously by other neighbours in Wavertree Vale because of the strange way in which she dressed. Patten never did find out 'how she ever got washed up on our street'. Seven doors down, the last house to change from gaslight to electricity, he remembers scratchy opera records, the smell of bitter coffee making it a far more exciting place to be and easily the most mysterious house he had ever visited. He felt both a frightening and a comforting sensation, as if being there meant thematic streams starting to flow. The gas-mantles would splutter, bathing the room in a lambent sepia tint, a much gentler, warmer light than the electric bulbs to which he was so accustomed.

Later in his introduction to *The Puffin Book Of Children's Verse* Patten said he wanted the anthology to be a modern version of Frieda's room; 'a vast coffee-scented cavern in which there were forests to get lost in, and oceans in which mermaids might drown'. Recalling how Frieda would read from Rip Van Winkle, later lend him musky bitter-scented books, he would run wild with the wolves, be transported through snowstorms, up mountains and across vast deserts. Free from the restraints imposed on him by adults, Frieda's Room became a sanctuary, a fountainhead of source material that would rarely dry.

One story, the parable of the little mermaid, particularly struck him. Concluding with the mermaid leaving the man she loves and coming ashore – a sensation comparable to walking on broken glass – he started to realise that beautiful things could also be painful and cruel. And that fascinated him.

1961. Patten was fifteen. It was to be one of the most crucial and remarkable years of his life. It hardly began well. On leaving school, he failed to get a job with the local butcher, was redirected to a local newspaper editor; where, instead of becoming what Roger McGough calls an 'up and coming pork butcher' he became, in the tradition of Dylan Thomas, a cub-reporter. The newspaper was *The Bootle Times*. Like Thomas it was to be the only bona-fide job he would ever have.

His first assignment was a pop music column that included some short pieces on McGough and Henri, probably representing their earliest publicity. He also started reading Dylan Thomas. To Patten, Thomas was the most remarkable writer he had so far encountered, his poetry and short stories resonating with the treasures he had discovered in Frieda's room. He hardly understood it but it excited him. Someone had shown him T.S. Eliot's work around the same time but he felt it was dry, grandly deciding it was boring and had nothing to do with the world he wanted. This he found in an anthology of translations by Arthur Symons (ironically an influence on Eliot) concerning the French Symbolist Movement. Published in 1899, it gave prominence to Arthur Rimbaud and Baudelaire both of whom had greatly impressed McGough and Henri. Patten neither knew whether the translations were good or what the poems were about, but again he found them fascinating.

Reading avidly now and absorbing fresh material like a sponge (in the same way the young and newly-named Bob Dylan was on discovering the folk clubs of Greenwich Village), Patten plundered the main city library. He took on board Walt Whitman, the longer poems and 'secret texts' of William Blake and the surreal poems of Garcia Lorca. Freely admitting he understood them no more than Eliot – to him that was irrelevant – they were teaching him something for the first time in his life. Eliot was a brain. They sang from the soul. Their work was like a magic spell. It was giving him something that he wanted, it was strong but also intangible and elusive: 'I had to have it, it was hard but I knew that I'd know something more than I know, if only I could crack it'.

And this, he began to do on reading an advert in *The Liverpool Echo* which was to change his life. Enigmatically it read: MEET PETE THE BEAT AT STREATE'S.

1961-1968

'Read poem! Read poem!'

I found my way down to this basement club, and there was a lot of beatnicky type people in it. I was fascinated by them at fifteen, and there were impromptu poetry readings and things like that.

Brian Patten's own first reading took place on the second of November, four days before meeting McGough, who introduced him to Adrian Henri on November 9th. Michael Horovitz remembers taking a troupe of musicians to Liverpool to do a jazz-poetry event at the Crane Theatre in Hanover Street: 'At the party afterwards, Adrian Henri, who was the host, said, 'oh this poetry stuff is alright, I think I'm gonna start doing it.' Henri himself has no such recollection: 'I was never much of a fan of poetry-and-jazz – certainly not the Horovitz brand, it just didn't seem to gel.'

Horovitz refers to Patten as being 'this marvellous boy who sat in the front row trying to hide his school cap' (hard to believe), 'and who later came up and read rather different, passionate romantic poems.' Horovitz sees a direct link with Patten, Henri and McGough and the emergence of the Beatles around 1963:

They were pop poetry, whereas we were more bop poetry. Our analogy was with bop and to some extent we related to the beat poets, plus American and international protest and jazz poetry.

He was encouraging to Patten, on his own admission 'a ragbag of bits of information' at that time, when the aspiring young poet sent him some poems to look at. Brian Patten still admires Michael Horovitz, grateful for his early help, regarding him as one of the great enablers of contemporary poetry. Despite his youth, Patten had a strongly developed, single-minded sense of vocation, and was confident enough to suggest to the much older Henri to move away from his 'acutely and deeply embarrassing' formal poems and write directly in his own voice. This became Henri's personal release as a writer, discovering that:

not entirely unconsciously, but somehow or other it just seemed it was important that you didn't do it like the Americans did it, you did it like you would do it; so you didn't pretend you were coming from San Francisco or New Jersey, you actually came from Birkenhead or Bootle. So you did it in your own voice not theirs. And that was the great breakthrough.

McGough agrees. Impressed by Horovitz and Brown because they were 'doing it in smoke-filled rooms, and it seemed exciting', but somehow feeling it wasn't quite what he wanted to do:

> We wanted to put Liverpool on the map and give it a voice. Other poets in these clubs were writing about American landscapes. Although they'd never been there it seemed O.K. to write a poem in beatnik jargon about getting into a yellow cab and going down 43rd Street.

McGough had already made his own personal breakthrough, writing even then in the clipped idiosyncratic, 'user-friendly' way that became his instant trademark. His poems were firmly rooted in Lime Street, Skelhorn Street, Dale Street and the Kardomah Cafe at a time when it was felt one would never write poems specific to Liverpool as 'it wasn't poetic'.

Patten remembers the early days with the same excitement, acknowledging his debt to Pete Brown but feeling that:

> It wasn't so much what I was writing that amazed them, but the fact that it was this fifteen year old kid that was doing it! They brought a lot of excitement up to Liverpool, but the big difference between Horovitz, Brown and Hawkins and us, was that they came from a jazz base – which was still exclusively university or middle class – while we were working more from a folky humour, Rock and Roll base. And that related to people much more directly'.

Unlike Henri and McGough, Patten's personality has always been decisive (though not in matters of the heart!) – 'I'm more fuck it, let's do it'. After a brief unhappy spell living in Underley Street with his mother who attempted suicide due to the bullying nature of his step-father – David Bevan an alcoholic policeman – Patten, at the age of seventeen decided to move out. He rented an attic at 32 Canning Street, where in his own improbable way he speedily galvanised the whole of the scene.

The winter of 1962-3 was the worst of the century. For three months the whole country was in siege under the snow. Old people died, zoo animals were wiped out, the football season was on hold, beer would explode in bottles; and Sylvia Plath, the most original poet of her generation gassed herself in London aged thirty-one. Ironically, a year so cataclysmic both socially and culturally began with the usual British concerns about the weather. That was until January 12th when the Beatles appeared on ABC-TV's *Thank Your Lucky Stars*.

Beatlemania did not become official until their Palladium performance on 13th October, two months after their 274th and final gig at the now world-famous Cavern Club. However, it was being talked up. Following a surfeit of unappetising news ranging from the Profumo scandal and subsequent suicide of Stephen Ward, to Macmillan's illness and resignation, via the defection of the spy Kim Philby, and the Great Train Robbery, a diversion was required. A good-luck story needed hyping, something blameless – possibly even working class – above all, happy. The Beatles became that story. Although it was not until 1967 that the Mersey Poets gained wide recognition, the focus that the Beatles gave to Liverpool was undoubtedly crucial to their success.

During the early part of 1962, cub-reporter Brian Patten was encouraged to develop a pop column for *The Bootle Times* in which he included early articles on Henri and McGough. It also gave him ideas for a magazine:

> I started *Underdog* I suppose because being surrounded by the printing works, one had access to bits and pieces of paper that one used to nick. It just seemed easier for me to do it than a lot of other people.

Underdog ran from 1962 until issue eight in 1966, and was regarded by Johnny Byrne, himself involved with *Beat Train*, as 'a very important small magazine'. To Mike Horovitz it established Patten – with his 'purest of little mags' as the man 'most responsible for building the Liverpool scene'. Patten himself is more ambivalent. 'It began as a broadsheet, I used to flog it around the pubs, and it was the first time that all the Liverpool people were pulled together'. Gradually it developed from its original stencil-format, becoming more professional in appearance, publishing poets of international stature such as Anselm Hollo, Allen Ginsberg and Robert Creeley. Patten's move to the attic in Canning Street meant that he now found more like-minded people. One frosty morning in a bus shelter after an all-night party he wrote his first poem in his own voice on the back of a Woodbine packet. 'Party Piece' with its implications of loneliness in a crowd and botched communication became the first of many urban cameos written by Patten around this theme. The poem resignedly concludes:

> So they did,
> Right there among the woodbines and the Guinness stains.
> And later he caught a bus and she a train
> And all there was between them then
> Was rain.

He was 'living on chips, amphetamines, sexual adrenalin and hope'. Still on *The Bootle Times* he was covering seedy court cases and fetes by day, and running poetry gigs at night. He had found a new venue – the short-lived Green Moose ('going to the Green Moose man') – had his own group of friends, but more importantly discovered Sampson and Barlows in London Road.

Situated under the restaurant of the same name, the new venue was a hired room which doubled both as a washroom and folk club. On first appearance it looked inappropriate in comparison to Streate's. Despite its outward dreariness and unforgiving wrought iron grills over the bar it was a big success, providing the Liverpool poets with the first outlet that they ran themselves.

One day, sitting beneath the skylight of his attic, and feeling young and foolish, the beginning of a poem that would have far-reaching effects for Brian Patten 'just came out'.

> This morning
> being rather young and foolish
> I borrowed a machinegun my father
> had left hidden since the war, went out,
> and eliminated a number of small enemies.
> Since then I have not returned home.

'Little Johnny's Confession' and its forthcoming sequel gave Patten an alter ego and a quirkily assured voice placing him at the heart of what was now becoming an all-embracing artistic spirit in Liverpool.

The idea of the Merseyside Arts Festival, first held in August 1962 stemmed from an event in 1960 called the South Liverpool Festival of Art. This was an attempt to express the spirit of the city in a deliberately non-establishment way. The new festival in this pioneering mode looked towards young emerging artists such as Brian Patten that the establishment had ignored. Henri and McGough seemed natural choices as committee members. John Gorman however, did not.

A post-office engineer with something of a reputation as a wheeler and dealer, Gorman with his lugubrious features and thick Scouse accent was making a reputation for himself as something of a practical joker. With his dog-toothed check suit and bowler hat, he would stand at the entrance of the Mersey Tunnel stopping motorists with a clipboard full of absurdist instructions. A Scouse Johnathan Routh doing his own *Candid Camera*, he was a prankster ahead of his time, doing it for no good reason other than an innate distrust of the bogus articulacy of officialdom. His uninhibited zaniness could also be easily aligned to Zurich Dada should any precious artistic sensibiltities be offended. Gorman wrote poetry too, but quickly realised his main talent was comedy. The ideal venue presented itself – Hope Hall, near the new Roman Catholic Cathedral – courtesy of Leslie Blond, property owner and patron-cum-landlord of the arts who began the premises as a continental cinema having run a similar outlet in Wallasey.

John Gorman and Roger McGough were an unlikely pairing, but both immediately recognised each other's strengths. McGough, happy in his job at Mabel Fletcher College was enjoying a particularly fruitful period of his life. No longer the bereft individual Yankel Feather remembers, he was now clearly someone who would know exactly where to buy a pair of winklepickers. Gorman quickly picked up on McGough's urbane wit, direct, quirky poetry, but above all his ability to handle dialogue. McGough in his turn, by nature diffident and circumspect, responded to Gorman's outward-going personality and determination to succeed at all costs: 'John was a good organiser, he could type, and he always wanted to be working. At times possibly too much and things would get frenetic. To John, not working would be negative. He always had to be working.'

The unlikely hit-band Scaffold was starting to happen whilst McGough – though not quite the poet Laurie Lee called 'a poet for us all: laconic, ironic, at times Byronic' – was turning over ideas for what would become a sixties classic.

With its lightness of touch, colour and irreverence adroitly juxtaposing universal irony with the failure of urban domestic love, *Summer With Monika* seemed to catch the mood of the times perfectly. Eventually published in 1967, also an L.P. which guitarist Andy Roberts (who collaborated on the album) felt never got due recognition, it later became a stage play directed by Mel Smith. It was later re-issued featuring illustrations by Peter Blake, who enjoyed the project as much as working on the sleeve for *Sgt Pepper*. More recently it was re-mastered as a C.D. and latterly adapted by McGough as a radio play. The title was taken from a film poster outside Hope Hall, (which McGough never saw), but its origins were far from visionary. 'It began as different poems that were hanging round at the time for different girls and different experiences and just having got this person, this girl's name, it seemed to focus it all.'

One different experience and a very early break for McGough came courtesy of Michael Horovitz who invited him to read at the Cellars Club as part of the Edinburgh Fringe Festival in 1963. It was the first visit to a place that would become a mainstay in the careers of the Mersey Poets and many of their subsequent associates. Strangely, on this trip he went with neither Henri nor Patten, but the sculptor Arthur Dooley:

Arthur had an exhibition at a shop in Princes Street, and I went up with him – we collected junk and stuff, took up a whole floor, just made it together really. It was funny – we didn't have a hotel, we were just sleeping on floors, sticking papers down our jeans – but I was a teacher, it was pretend; it was very exciting, but I always wanted to be on the road like Brown seemed to be, or like Brian later. I was a teacher. I was always part-time. I always had to get back.

At least 'back' was the developing Liverpool scene. There was the Arts Festival and the 'events' at Hope Hall based on Allan Kaprow's New York 'Happenings'. There was *City* and *Death of a Bird in the City* that McGough would participate in with Adrian Henri, John Gorman and other local experimentalists. McGough contributed 'Mother the Wardrobe is full of Infantrymen', to the later piece with its universally ominous coda:

mother don't just lie there say something please
mother don't just lie there say something please

The Monday night poetry reading at Sampson and Barlows were a far cry from the earnest po-faced gatherings usually attributed to such events. At variance too with the Streate's readings, where audiences were confused by Horovitz, baffled by Hawkins or intimidated by Phil Tasker and Tonk, Cornwall-based school teacher Pat Thomas, then a student, remembers them as 'great fun – what poetry should be like, but hardly ever is'. Described by Adrian Henri in Liverpool University's *Sphinx* magazine (whose then editor Martin Kay helped promote the developing talents of Henri, McGough, particularly Patten), as 'predominantly teenage, non-intellectual, and non-student who like to laugh with McGough and cry with Patten about the sort of problems we all share'. Pioneering, with a penchant for obscurists, Kay influenced Patten a great deal at the time. 'I owe quite a lot to Martin, he was the first person to publish me and he got me interested in Rimbaud, Whitman and Lorca. He helped us all I suppose just by being enthusiastic in the days when not that many people outside our own crowd were.'

Run by all three writers, the Sampson & Barlow's readings continued into 1964, peaking with the visit of the world-famous and highly influential Black Mountain poet Robert Creeley. McGough felt it was an important venue as it gave them the opportunity to try out ideas and methods without fear of failure or embarrassment. 'The kids didn't look on it as Poetry with a capital 'P', they looked on it as modern entertainment, part of the pop movement. They may go away crying, or they may go away very sad, but it was a certain experience to them, all part of experience.' Henri also spoke of 'audience poems' – removing the barrier between performer and audience whenever possible. 'We'd get everyone to write a word or sentence, collect them at the interval then read out the results later.' In this way they echoed the 'events' he was organising at Hope Hall.

Wherever one looked in non-establishment Liverpool culture in the early sixties (apart from the music boom) the bulky frame of Adrian Henri was omnipresent. Judy Dunn introduced Maurice Cockrill to Henri in The Philharmonic Hotel, who remembers him in those days as 'Mister Art, into everything, larger than life, charismatic, but always sociable and I suppose a useful person to know.' Locally based, Sean Hignett had just published a book called *A Picture to Hang on the Wall* which Cockrill recalls caused quite a stir. 'It wasn't that well written, but what was interesting was that the characters were all based on people like Adrian, Sam Walsh and Arthur Ballard. A rumour got round about them making a film of it with Marlon Brando playing Henry Graham!'

Having exhibited nationally with Peter Blake, Hockney and Patrick Hughes, and more locally with Graham, Walsh and McKinlay, Henri was now commuting daily to Manchester College of Art. He was also about to begin his polymorphous homage to James Ensor, *The Entry of Christ into Liverpool*. A major prize-winner in Belfast, his painting career was off to a promising start, but already flawed in George Melly's view by an over-casual attitude to his work:

He's always been underestimated as a painter. Everyone knows him as a poet, and I've always thought he was certainly as good a painter as he was a poet and sometimes even better. But he has lent work without limit and in consequence some of it has been lost or damaged. This cavalier approach is exemplified by the fact that what is probably his masterpiece *The Entry Of Christ into Liverpool* was recently discovered off its stretcher and rolled away in a garage.

Melly did not much care for the 'Happenings' that Henri was organising at that time, feeling they 'weren't very exciting', a view not shared by the distinguished writer, historian and translator John Willett. Art critic for *The Guardian*, Willett had been asked by his friend Nicholas Horsfield to act as a part-time consultant regarding the visual arts on Merseyside. Allocated an office in the Bluecoat Chambers, in the process of researching his subsequent book *Art in a City*, he was recommended to visit

a mysterious, virtually abandoned house. No bell. No names on the door... then I tried the area steps and found a bell by the basement. That was Henri's, his wife [took me into] a room with books, sofa, cast-iron nineteenth century fireplace, some paintings [his and Sam Walsh's]. No Henri, but Mrs. H. told me there would be some form of Event in Hope Hall that night. Adrian was chasing around in connection with it.

Willett duly went to the crammed basement where the 'event' was taking place, witnessing 'a broad, mildly Turkish-looking figure with beard and glasses' introduce a mixed programme of sketches, poetry and folk songs, whose liveliness, Willett felt, was its best feature. The 'events', later documented in Henri's *Environments and Happenings* published by Thames and Hudson in 1974, began to gather momentum, attracting an increasingly diverse crowd – art college students, lecturers, club-goers, in fact anyone wanting to be part of a scene. As the Beatles popularity was sweeping the country in 1963, the 'events' peaked in their home town with *Nightblues* featuring Henri, McGough, Gorman, Patten and local R'n'B band, The Roadrunners. The success of the venue was also largely due to Leslie Blond's wife Dorothy who converted the basement into a bistro, the first of its kind in Liverpool. It was a special place to be. John Willett recalls *Nightblues* as including:

> some really good things, especially by Roger McGough, and was accompanied by an electric-guitar group, the Roadrunners: the first time I've heard poetry and jazz that really came off. There were two good poems by McG – the second, 'Summer with Monika', describing his stay-at-home, kitchen sink holiday in the summer of the Profumo scandal. Also a very effective turn with all three poets, Gorman, him and Brian Patten, reading verses to a tune of the group's, which then let its own vocalist [Mike Hart] loose. [Also] a really funny, originally conceived and written sketch by McG with a nuclear disarmer in a bomb proof suit being questioned: this acted by Gorman and himself. A girl dancer from Oldham. Henri acting as compere. Patten now and again disclosed by the curtain, typing away at a great epic poem that finally he never read. Large pictures by Don McKinlay. A finale with all the company running round and round the cinema, waving flags; I later found out that signified 'Roadrunners'. There really was something there. It was spontaneous, unpretentious, I thought, and above all indigenous. It seemed to meet the demands of a young and attractive audience, who later packed out the club downstairs'.

Nightblues is something of template for the three poets' performing styles. Henri, the front-man, but self-deprecating and still uncertain of himself as a poet. Patten, young – but as McGough had noted 'mature in the sense that he knew he was a poet' – but uneasy and uncomfortable regarding performance, and McGough, already the assured poet-performer, handling both aspects with consummate skill.

John Willett still remains a friend and advocate of Henri's. 'He's certainly not straightforward, but always fresh with an energy and a generosity, unlike so many poets, that is not only concerned with pushing his own work, but others that he respects. He has never believed in any arts hierarchy in which he's forced to fit into. Whether it's Bulldog Drummond or Gertrude Stein, it all comes alike to Adrian.'

Roger McGough, still in Litherland, was flirting with Bohemia more and more but without ever losing his Catholic faith. He still had his aspirations. Yet something kept nagging away. It became something that would nag away throughout his work – the 'failed reveller', the one 'never to run naked in the rain' in 'Here I Am', or the overcautious one in the later 'Crazy Bastard' keeping his head down, staying behind, having to keep 'an eye on the clothes'. The one who always had to get back, but always wanting to be this more exciting character – with a bright red sports car perhaps – but always wanting to be a poet: 'Even if it meant sacrificing your life for the work, all well and good – by being a poet I thought that's what you have to do.'

These contrasting and conflicting emotions provoked in McGough what was to become his signature poem; the seminal 'Let Me Die A Youngman's Death'. It also gave him the added confidence to chat up Thelma Monaghan at the Art College Dance.

Adrian Henri had a bigger problem. Standing in a corner of the disused library that served as studios for foundation course art students in Manchester, and carrying a copy of an obscure volume of philosophy, was Heather Holden. Long-haired – a sixties' beauty before her time – she not only painted beautifully, but also wrote poetry of a childlike Blakean simplicity, causing Henri to fall hopelessly in love. To compound matters, Art was involved making things even headier, his amour fou, or late 'adolescent' first love becoming part of a belated self-discovery of poetic associations, the ephemeral and of lust. Raised in Haslingden, Lancashire in the remote unforgiving landscape of the Rossendale Valley, Holden was equally taken by Henri's cultural awareness, humour and sophistication. She was flattered by the disproportionate interest he took in her work. After a long chat in the local pub, followed by a party in Wythenshawe things quickly started to hot up.

Even in the emerging hedonism of the early Sixties, having affairs with one's students was a sackable offence, so the relationship was by necessity strictly clandestine:

We used to meet in pubs in town and go – oh fancy meeting you here – we were laughing all the time I have to say… and I suppose I was quite a refreshing person for Adrian to meet because I didn't have any boring culturally-formed aspirations. I was very naive and had a very fresh response to everything. The Beatles were just getting cracking and we'd meet in the snow in Piccadilly Gardens, and there'd be the usual Christmas music, and then suddenly The Beatles would be blaring out, and our song was 'You've Really Gotta Hold On Me'. There was a Mother's Pride sign, and Adrian did drawings of Pere Ubu in the

Gardens... yes it was very, very exciting and romantic, and it was a right good laugh.

Prankster playwright Albert Jarry's famous grotesque has loomed large within the ambit of Henri's cultural references. Cropping up ubiquitously in much of his work, at times a comic alter ego, Ubu is a character he feels that can be readily placed 'just about anywhere'. George Melly felt it was simply 'a good excuse for Adrian to exploit his fatness, but it served him well'.

Henri and Heather Holden's relationship was rich in wistful personal fantasies in the force field they generated. The two developed a private mythology that included artificial lilies of the valley that seemed somehow appropriate to many of Henri's love poems originally published in *Underdog*. Eulogies such as 'Tonight At Noon' (the title poem of his first collection), and 'I Want To Paint' were all directly about Heather Holden.

In similar fashion to her contemporary, Brian Patten, Henri found himself influenced by a much younger person. He and Heather would play their own form of poetic consequences, Henri discovering he was able to write with the direct simplicity he had long craved. Here began his notorious fondness for referring to female underwear. Edward Lucie-Smith once remarked that 'Adrian always secretly hoped that every schoolgirl in Britain would tuck a booklet of his poetry into the elastic of her bloomers'. It became a distinctive if risible and easily caricatured feature of much of his work. 'A red bra with I love you written inside one of the cups / A painting of a shocking pink heart with your name scratched on it.' ('Love Poem'). Holden became his first mythologised muse and he would list other familiar semiotics: a dark blue suspender belt, faded pink folders, scribbled kisses, and her navy school knickers.

The relationship was doomed from the start, Henri's love never being returned in the same obsessive way. Having his adolescence in his thirties rather than his twenties meant waiting for the coin-box phone to ring, or the next blue envelope to arrive, coming to dread holidays spent without her:

> Without you they'd forget to
> change the weather
> Without you blind men would
> sell unlucky heather

If Heather Holden was all wide-eyed innocence, then Thelma Monaghan had been round the block. Striking, with an already sharpened eye for style and fashion setting her apart from most Liverpool girls of the time, she had graduated from the College of Art, married, divorced and had a child. To Roger McGough there was something attractively 'forbidden' about her:

She knew about things I didn't, was very independent so I suppose there was something of a femme fatale about her. It was flying in the face of everything I'd been brought up to believe. I was entranced, at the same time always thinking that in other ways perhaps we weren't suited.

Formerly Thelma Pickles, she dated John Lennon whilst at college, accompanying him to Quarrymen rehearsals at Aunt Mimi's. Talking to the writer Ray Coleman, Thelma remembers Paul McCartney, who had just started in the sixth form at the nearby Liverpool Institute. 'He used to come into the Art College canteen with George Harrison. Paul was quite young then, and George even more so. They were both overshadowed by John's personality.' Some years later, just before she met McGough, Thelma went out briefly with McCartney after he had split up with his girlfriend Dot Rhone.' He'd developed from the plump young schoolboy into someone very much his own person'. No fan of Rock and Roll and oblivious to the burgeoning local scene – not even aware that Love Me Do had been released – Thelma was amazed when a girl in a coffee bar on Church Street asked for Paul's autograph. 'Paul said, oh it's just this Beatles business. I wasn't clued in at all as to what was happening at this stage.' On several occasions she would go to The Cavern with him. 'They were certainly very big down there. People were screaming. I found the whole thing really strange. When we walked to the car afterwards, groups of girls would follow and they'd be extremely rude to me. I found it very odd that girls would behave like that. I must have been very naive.'

She hardly seemed that to McGough. Still living at home, his aspirations still undetermined, the contrast between Thelma and his former girlfriend Josephine Twist could not have been greater:

I met Thelma at the Art College, then saw her again at Hope Hall, and started taking her out. She had a flat in Princes Park, a three year old son, Nathan, and she made her own clothes, was up-to-the-minute in fashion, went to London when we didn't, painted these abstract pictures and knew Paul McCartney. He would come round to the flat, so I saw a bit of him, which was interesting rather than exciting. Thelma was sassy and very much a woman of the age.

Everything about Thelma represented an entirely different set of values to those McGough had been brought up on, and inevitably the relationship drew parental disapproval in similar fashion to the Wilsons and Adrian Henri. Eventually, after staying over at her flat on weekends McGough took the plunge and moved in. He would soon have another big decision to make shortly afterwards.

As 1964 approached, things were moving quickly. Due to The Beatles' success, Liverpool, having gone from no media attention at all was suddenly becoming saturated with it. Television crews were everywhere looking for the next 'new thing'. McGough, still at Mabel Fletcher, and on the Merseyside Arts Committee, had been introduced by Mike Weinblatt (a hairdresser/poet published in *Underdog*) to a colleague at Andre Bernard's Salon. Shy about revealing his surname, the good looking young man was briefly christened Mike Blank.

Offering his services as a photographer, he took pictures of the various revues being promoted around the city, particularly at the newly opened Everyman Theatre above Hope Hall. Gradually he found himself being given small parts in some of the events. 'Mike was invariably the straight man', says McGough, 'although later he became the 'handsome one'. He was quite good at reading and enjoyed being onstage'. He was also Paul McCartney's brother, and as his position in the group became more secure, and wanting to maintain a separate identity, he gave himself the rather too fashionably coy surname of McGear. In his later book *Thank U Very Much*, Mike McCartney remembers:

> Mike Weinblatt took me down to Hope Hall beneath the Everyman where 'arty things' were going on. Whether it be oblique blues artists like Muddy Waters, the MJQ and Bo Diddley, or surrealist painters like Magritte, Dali or Max Ernst, I had always succumbed to anything 'different'. So I was easy prey for the quick-thinking-speaking McGough whose machine-gun word imagery soon splattered my mind against the Hope Hall wall.

After a visit by an ABC-TV producer to *The Liverpool One Fat Lady All Electric Show*, the cast – Henri, McGough, Gorman, McGear and local performer Jennie Beattie, were auditioned for a new satirical programme called *Gazette*. Three were picked: McGear, on his looks and versatility; Gorman as the comedian; and McGough, the writer whose 'hobby' was poetry. Less than famous for decisiveness, McGough quit his job at the college, which Adrian Henri recalls 'surprised a lot of people at the time and we all felt it was very brave'. Thus began Scaffold and McGough's uneasy if successful, and ultimately beneficial relationship with show business.

Henri himself was still in a quandary over Heather Holden. Now working on the Foundation Course at the by now legendary Art College in Liverpool, the affair always meant more to him than her. The situation was ameliorated one night by a hilarious if hardly romantic stay-over on a bottom bunk, two foot-six wide ('Adrian was very plump in those days') at George Melly's house in London, and by her frequent visits to Liverpool. The Henris' relationship, since the days of Preston Jazz Club, the open-top sports car and The Half-Moon Club had always been unconventional; now it was at the tentative beginning of what was to become known as an 'open marriage'. Heather would sleep on their sofa, got on well with Joyce, still the social person of Henri's poem 'Who?' ('Who else / drinks as much bitter'), tacitly accepting the cultural awakening Holden was giving her husband. The two women would go out drinking in Ye Cracke. Holden fondly recalls 'always getting on fine with Joyce. She had this amazing cat called Darling, and there was no guilt about stealing her husband because I wasn't.' Heather also read at Sampson and Barlow's. Crowded with 'interesting people who all looked like poets', she found McGough somewhat distant but hit it off with Patten who published some of her poems in *Underdog*. 'Brian was fine, I'd sometimes go round to his attic in Canning Street near where Adrian lived and we'd just sit and talk for hours.'

Patten, who had delegated the sales aspect of *Underdog* to the photographer Eddie O'Neill, was even then a much less social figure than Henri or McGough. Solitariness, however, is something he has always come to terms with, even taken advantage of, whether it be the figure in the 'room without any curtains' underneath the skylight or Little Johnny writing his final letter in his designated hideaway.

Having left *The Bootle Times* late in 1963, he took the occasional odd job, spending a brief period in Paris chalking poems on pavements. He survived on 'a bit of this and a bit of that – if you see what I mean – ducking and diving, selling dope, selling this, selling that – all that kind of stuff – slightly on the edge of what was legal'.

Initially fascinated by the bohemian world, Patten soon became reproachful, developing a scepticism concerning the 'long-haired philosophers', that he found hard to jettison. He was also disinclined to fit into the growing conflation of words and music, the early cross-overs between poetry and performance. Looking back, McGough felt 'Brian wasn't very good as a reader at first, he found it difficult; it didn't bother me, and it never worried Adrian, but Brian was nervous and found it harder. Later he finally made great capital out of his voice. So it came with time.'

Drugs were another matter. They came quickly. Here Patten did feel at home: 'I took them an awful lot. Much more than Adrian and Roger. They dabbled, I took.' Although comparatively scarce then, hard drugs were available in the early sixties in Liverpool if you had the right connections. Patten had.

There was an underground drug culture that was very separate from the poetry scene that was going on, and I was wrapped up in that as well. There were people that Adrian and Roger steered clear of that I didn't, and I was dealing in that world. When I was eighteen and nineteen I was taking heroin. I was fixing, but I realised the dangers, I had a few bad times but had enough sense to stay away from it. I got involved but then I got out.

If Hamburg was the second home for the early Liverpool beat groups, then Edinburgh was the poetry scene's cultural equivalent. Roger McGough sees it as a focal point since his first trip with Arthur Dooley in 1961:

Going back years and years, every year, come back, sometimes do a show with Brian, sometimes with Adrian, sometimes the three of us; various permutations, and Andy Roberts – usually there as well.

Roberts, who became something of a George Martin figure for the three poets remembers that first meeting vivdly:

We all met at Edinburgh when I was involved as a musician with two shows that were playing at The Traverse Theatre Club. And in the same time-slot was this team from Liverpool – I'd never heard of them – called The Scaffold. And in the afternoons there were poetry readings which included people like Hugh MacDiarmid, Anselm Hollo and Alex Trocchi – and Roger McGough was part of that – and I used to go to the readings, got to know the Scaffold as well as Adrian and Brian and other poets from Liverpool. So this all appeared to be one big package of people from Liverpool really. Then when I got back, after the festival – which was just a one-off as far as I was concerned – I had been offered university places in Hull and Liverpool, and I thought... well... I'll go to Liverpool, I've just met these really interesting blokes there, so I fancy that.'

Of all the artists who have worked with the 'big three' over the years, none have matched Roberts for consistency and staying power. During his first year at university he played it straight, taking on board the fact that he was there to be a lawyer. However things gradually became subverted when McGough asked Roberts to collaborate with him, which led to active involvement in other musical events around the town and Roberts' transformation into musical director of the Scaffold in the mid-sixties.

Due to the success of the B.B.C's *That Was the Week That Was*, satire became fashionable in the mid-sixties and much of Scaffold's early work was informed accordingly. Largely an index of Gorman's energy, and organisational skills, McGough's dialogues and McGear's presence and adaptability, Scaffold moved from being established local heroes improvising around news headlines on *Gazette*, (broadcast only in the north), to a top-earning and widely-touring comical/Dadaesque ensemble – from Huddersfield to Milan. 'When we went to the Edinburgh Festival,' McGough remembers, 'we were seen as a refreshing new review group, as opposed to *Beyond The Fringe*, we were billed as a 'Liverpool group in a new revue'. The only other revues were universities – Oxford and Cambridge – our roots were working class, which was partly political, partly comic and partly poetic, and that was what we were.' Scaffold would appear in Edinburgh with artists as diverse as Lindsey Kemp and Larry Adler, and on the same bill as play readings of Beckett and new work by Paul Ableman. One review in *The Scotsman* felt they had 'succeeded in breaking the mould which *Beyond the Fringe* had imposed on its successors'. Because of their increasingly tight work-load, McGough found it hard to find time for writing. Even so, he managed to publish some poems (most notably 'My Busconductor', with the pay-off 'One day he'll clock on and never clock off / or clock off and never clock on.') in the new prestigious magazine *Ambit*.

Begun and still edited by Martin Bax, *Ambit*'s reputation for innovation and originality in both poetry and artwork was soon established and still remains. McGough was invited to visit Bax's home in Highgate, giving him an early insight into the 'literary London life' not dissimilar to the 'bohemia' of the Henris' first flat in Liverpool 8. An *Ambit* reading was arranged in Salford where McGough read with two local poets, Tony Connor and Jack Marriott. This reading remains something of a curiosity in McGough's career. Here he was in a decidedly unfashionable setting a long way from the gathering media attention and press interest surrounding Liverpool, which culminated in an article and photograph in *The Daily Express* of the leading local artistic luminaries on St George's Plateau. This coincided with a B.B.C. radio crew recording Brian Patten reading 'Little Johnny's Confession' for Jack de Manio's breakfast show.

The broadcast was heard by Philip Unwin, of George Allen & Unwin. He liked it so much that, despite not having a poetry list, he felt he had made a discovery. Somehow he managed to track Patten down to the attic in 32 Canning St, where the bemused poet – taking the call on the landing – found himself with a major first book deal at the age of nineteen. 1965 was one momentous event after another for McGough, Patten and Henri. Before the summer was through, Patten took another call. This time it was from Allen Ginsberg.

Ginsberg arrived in England as a result of being initially deported from Cuba due to his homosexuality, so he was sent to Prague. The Czechs made the same response and sent him to Moscow from where he was duly sent back to Prague where he was voted the King of May. Then he was deported to London, where he stayed with Barry Miles. Cheltenham born, a veteran Aldermaston marcher, Miles edited a small magazine called *Tree* featuring the first publication of Ginsberg and Ferlinghetti in this country. Miles had got close to the doyen of the counterculture, John 'Hoppy' Hopkins and later moved to his flat at 108 Westbourne Terrace in Notting Hill Gate. Alexander Trocchi, Michael de Freitas and other prime movers and activists in what was becoming known as the 'underground' also lived here centred around places such as Frank Critchlow's cafe, The Rio, in Westbourne Park Road.

Miles was publishing *Longhair* magazine and managing Better Books in the Charing Cross Road. He seemed the natural choice to accomodate the newly arrived Ginsberg, quickly becoming what Michael Horovitz called his 'St Paul and archivist, secretary, or English agent.' It was through Ginsberg that Miles met The Beatles, getting on particularly well with McCartney, the Beatle most in touch with the developing counterculture at that time.

'I met The Beatles through Ginsy. He didn't know them but he wanted to and was introduced to them by Bob Dylan. It wasn't a very successful meeting. It was his birthday on June 3, he wanted to have the Beatles at his birthday party, he thought that would be nice. Like anyone who was anyone at that time, he also wanted to visit Liverpool.'

Brian Patten met Ginsberg at Lime Street Station. It was cold so he lent him a multi-coloured jumper his grandmother had knitted him long before the coming of flowerpower. He never saw it again. He had no room in his attic either so he asked Adrian Henri if he could put Ginsberg up which Henri gladly agreed to:

George Melly had Allen and Gregory Corso to stay once and was appalled by them – they behaved very badly – so I was slightly nervous about this; not that it was a particurlarly bourgeois kind of institution I was living in. Anyway he duly arrived and he was charming. But what I'll always remember is the morning after we'd been to The Cavern, I woke up and heard this noise downstairs, so I went down - there was a sink on the half-landing – and it was Allen washing the dishes and singing one of those Buddhist chants to himself. It was really an amazing revelation – Allen Ginsberg washing my dishes'.

Henri took Ginsberg to the Art College where he met Arthur Ballard and was delighted by what was happening at the College. Ballard, a man of many contradictions, both warm-hearted and pugilistic, a Bohemian who lived in the Wirral; was totally charmed by Ginsberg and offered to drive Ginsberg and Henri (described by Roger McGough as a meeting of beards) to various places of interest. One such place was the cast-iron church in Everton. It was here in

Albion Street, that Henri wrote what was to be his first major poem. Dedicated to Allen Ginsberg, 'Mrs Albion You've Got A Lovely Daughter' surpassingly links William Blake, Herman's Hermits and Liverpool girls in a mental universe orchestrated by time and place, elucidating the 'popular modernism' to be so prevalent throughout his career:

> The daughters of Albion
> taking the dawn ferry to tomorrow
> worrying about what happened
> worrying about what hasn't happened
>
> Mrs Albion you've got a lovely daughter

A 'Ginsberg reading' during his brief stay in Liverpool was a must. Sampson & Barlow's was defunct at the time, so another venue had to be found. Parry's Bookshop in Hardman Street next to The Philharmonic Hotel, had a vacant room so this was deemed the place. Pete Brown who was in Liverpool at the time, agreed to introduce Ginsberg and read briefly, but as Adrian Henri remembers:

> Just as we were about to start, Michael Horovitz appeared and totally monopolised the proceedings when we were all waiting for Ginsberg. He just charged in with a large raffia bag full of *New Departures* to sell and insisted on reading at length. But despite that it was one of the best poetry readings I've ever been to, certainly the best I've ever heard Allen do. It was a late spring evening, sunlight coming through the window, and he sat cross-legged and just read and it was totally intimate and beautiful, and it just flowed out, not even preaching, just talking to you, but talking like some sort of prophet.

As there was no publicity there were fewer than forty people present, the evening concluding at Fat Johnny's (a West Indian drinking club off Falkner Square) whereby Ginsberg took revenge on Horovitz filling his raffia bag with a large rock. Henri felt Ginsberg had a fantastic effect on Liverpool. 'Nobody knew who he was – you'd take him to the pub and Allen would talk to you for five minutes then wander away and talk to lots of other people. The most unlikely people were terribly impressed by him.' Not Yankel Feather however, then running an antique shop at the top of Wood Street, who remembers 'this famous poet coming in with Adrian, and I thought these two don't look like they're going to spend much money with me, so I more or less told them to fuck off.' The Cavern was more welcoming. Henri remembers Ginsberg in the club's office in discussion with two drummers, playing Tibetan rhythms with his finger-cymbals. 'He made it with one of the guys. We never did find out who.'

Ginsberg then returned to London still determined to have The Beatles at his birthday bash on June 3. As Miles knew how to contact them, they came to the party in Chester Square. The ubiquitous Michael Horovitz was there. 'By the time The Beatles arrived with their wives, Allen had stripped naked, with his underpants on his head and a No Waiting sign round his dick. He thought this was appropriate – 'be in your birthday suit for your birthday party'.

Horovitz felt that although Lennon and McCartney quite liked Ginsberg, they all kept this 'piss-taking distance from it all'. Miles he felt was a useful shield who kept them apart from the 'heavy paranoia of poets such as Harry Fainlight who wanted to be promoted on the pop level'. Lennon, Miles recalls, was particurlarly upset at finding Ginsberg naked: 'You don't do that in front of the birds.'

Ginsberg gave a reading at Better Books which, like the Liverpool reading was unadvertised, but in this case totally packed. Half the audience were American including Andy Warhol, Gerard Malanga, Barbara Rubin and all the people from *Fuck You* magazine. Miles's wife Sue remembers an afternoon shortly afterwards when Ginsberg, realising that Gregory Corso was in Paris, Ferlinghetti, soon to be in London, and Pablo Neruda and Pablo Fernandez, also both over, declaimed: 'major international poets, nearly all in London, so this should be celebrated with a big poetry reading'. Hired by Barbara Rubin for £450, The Albert Hall was promptly booked for 11th June 1965.

The Albert Hall reading, on the day before the Queen awarded The Beatles their MBE's, is rightly seen as one of the great watersheds of contemporary poetry, with everyone present seeming to have a different perspective. Peter Whitehead made a film of the event called *Wholly Communion*, the disadvantage of which according to Christopher Logue, was that the audience was missing. To him they were more interesting than the performers. In his introduction to the commemorative book, the poet and novelist Alexis Lykiard describes it as: 'if not quite the hoped for Blakean jamboree and feast of illumination, [it] was in many ways an undoubted success. It was the first large-scale Happening. 7000 people thronged the Albert Hall.'

Ginsberg's appearance was like Bob Dylan's at the Isle of Wight four years later, and the mythology surrounding The Albert Hall reading compares with Woodstock in the world of Rock. Miles is less than praiseworthy: 'The reading itself was dreadful. Ginsberg was very upset by it. It was bad because he got drunk and gave a very poor reading.' Adrian Henri remembers 'Ginsberg raving and shouting, a different person completely and not half as impressive somehow as he had been in Liverpool'. It was here that the Mersey poets met Adrian Mitchell.

Six months younger than Henri, born in London, Mitchell had left Oxford without a degree, worked as a reporter on *The Evening Standard,* then as a journalist for *The Daily Mail.* He was the first person to write an article on the Beatles and remains a huge fan and friend of Paul's. As a poet he had been on the fringes of The Group, who included George Macbeth, Martin Bell and Peter Redgrove, then meeting at Edward Lucie-Smith's flat in Chelsea, where he introduced his poem 'Veteran With A Head Wound'. It was about a victim of Hiroshima and it had a great impact on Michael Horovitz.'It affected me more than the American Beats. I thought this was better poetry. At the Albert Hall, his two short poems about racism in Alabama and the Vietnam War, got the most concerted audience response. Pete Brown and Mitchell formed the nucleus of my basic poets' team in *Live New Departures.*' Mitchell himself saw the Albert Hall meeting as an on-going influence. In a broadcast he said:

> The whole movement surfaced for one night at which Ginsberg, Corso, and Ferlinghetti were joined by many British and European poets. It was a spectacular and strange evening. It was a huge party and like a party, some people loved it and celebrated it later in poems, while others hated it. But the excitement of that rally gave an added momentum to the small readings with audiences of 100 to 200 people which are usually the most valuable to both poet and audience.

Mitchell has remained a friend and supporter of the Mersey poets ever since having worked with them individually and collectively on numerous occasions. All three regard him amongst their most formative contemporary influences; so much so that he is frequently mistaken as a 'Liverpool Poet'. The beginnings of such cultural camaraderie are endorsed by Jeff Nuttall whose *Bomb Culture* became a seminal sixties text:

> There was a frisson for us all to savour as there had been at the first Aldermaston, and the Underground was suddenly there on the surface in open ground with a following of thousands.... after The Albert Hall I wrote to Klaus Lea crying: 'London is in flames. The spirit of William Blake walks on the water of the Thames. Come and drink the dew.' Miles however, provides something of a disclaimer. 'There were a lot of fuck-ups which no one really knew much about. Alex Trocchi was the compere; he insisted he had a major role being the elder statesman. Out of his brain on heroin in front of 7000 people.'

Nuttall remembers Harry Fainlight as the star by default:

> He got pilloried. He was going to read his poem 'Spider' and he started to talk about 'Spider' and it was clear he couldn't stop talking about it. He was out of his bonce on amphetamines.

Brian Patten still feels that Fainlight was 'one of the great mad poets' celebrating him years later in his poem 'Friends':

And now Harry, you too are caught in your own
Miraculous stream that flows uphill,

Fainlight's rambling introduction about acid visions of horror had him physically caught in his own stream and introduced real conflict into the evening. Horovitz remembers people shouting 'Get him off!' and Fainlight becoming agitated. 'Then Trocchi got up with his pipe and tried to behave nicely and said, "Come on just read your poem, it's a good poem..." – and Ginsberg was shouting, "Read poem! Read poem!" – and it all got very strident. But for Fainlight himself it was not only dramatic but traumatic and it haunted him for the rest of his tragic, short life.'

The 'renaissance' was not enthusastically felt by all. Edward Lucie-Smith, about to give up his chairmanship of The Group, writing in *Encounter* under the title 'A Wild Night' said :

There was a triumph one might have wished otherwise. Adrian Mitchell, already well known for his powers as a reader, declaimed a clever but more than slightly smug poem about Vietnam, and was rewarded with the biggest ovation of the evening. Yet there was an awareness that this was applause without catharsis, and the spectators were applauding the echo of their own sentiments, and willing themselves to be moved without truly being so.

This is firmly repudiated by Horovitz who felt that Mitchell's line, 'Tell me Lies about Vietnam' did offer 'a kind of catharsis, revolution and liberation', unlike most other demonstrations at the time was 'very ecstatic and very relaxed'.

As a gathering of the tribes, The Albert Hall reading was memorable yet much of the polemicism buckles under the weight of hindsight. For Johnny Byrne it was the end of the genuine feeling of an alternative culture. 'Everything as far as I was concerned went downhill after that, even if some saw it as the seed of such things as *International Times*.'

Adrian Henri too felt it the end, rather than the beginning of something: 'The fact that we never read and were, literally, waiting in the wings, was symbolic. I felt at the time I wanted poetry to become "overground". ' For McGough it was almost embarrassing. Patten, closer in some ways and easier with people whom Henri and McGough would steer clear of, but always, 'slightly on the edge of it all', simply felt indifferent. 'Counter-culture is not an expression I would ever use. It didn't really affect me.'

What did affect them was how the Beat Generation made poetry out of their own lives, the boundaries between life and art gradually becoming eroded. For the poets, writing in one's own voice and in the way one breathed was liberating; poets read their poems out loud in bars, and art was no longer confined to the galleries. But subliminally, even when Ginsberg said 'Liverpool is at the present moment the centre of consciousness of the human universe' in 1965, Adrian Henri and others knew he was talking about The Beatles.

The Beatles' success coincided with a change of government in Sixties Britain. The Conservatives had fallen, supreme power now resting with a pipe-smoking Yorkshireman who wore a tartan-lined raincoat and represented a constituency near Liverpool. His was a 'New Britain' of 'dynamic action', that was both 'expanding and confident'. He talked up a 'purposive Britain, forged in the white heat of technological revolution.' The Harold Wilson Age despite its indications of austerity, was to deliver instead a period of unrivalled hedonism and frivolity. Newly Socialist Britain in 1965 is not remembered for 'driving dynamism' but for short-term extravagance, the emphasis placed on the informal and immediate. Such was the hallmark of Swinging Britain during pop's peak years of 1965-1967, with the unashamedly libertarian Roy Jenkins, 'the apostle of the Permissive Society', playing an unlikely if thrusting roll as Wilson's reforming Home Secretary. Bob Dylan had gone electric and the Byrds had released 'Mr Tambourine Man' fusing Dylan and the Beatles at a stroke. London had become the centre of the fashion world where the new designer Mary Quant defined a new Mod look for girls: Op Art mini-dress, PVC 'kinky' boots, coloured tights and cropped hair as modelled by Jean Shrimpton and Twiggy.

In Liverpool, no one was more associated with this changing hedonistic climate than Roger McGough. The Liverpool poet with The Beatles' connection met Bob Dylan at Allan Williams' Blue Angel club in Seel Street after Dylan's legendary gig at the Odeon in London Road. Together with Clive Goodwin, (later to edit *Black Dwarf* before dying in mysterious circumstances in Los Angeles in 1977), McGough briefly entered the world of show business management. He had discovered an all black girl singing group called The Poppies. Mike McGear remembers them well. 'They were beautiful, not quite black, quick witted and sexy. There was only one slight drawback – they couldn't sing!'

McGough and McGear had seen Dylan's show at the Odeon and were highly delighted to bump into him later coming out of the Blue Angel draped around two of The Poppies. After pleasantries were exchanged, Dylan, McGear, the Poppies and their 'new manager' all headed off to the Adelphi Hotel for drinks. Everything went well until The Poppies launched into an impromptu 'Da Doo Ron Ron', which, according to McGear, immediately persuaded McGough against the heady world of show-biz management, 'although Bob seemed to love it'.

In the dandified spirit of Baudelaire, McGough kept a close eye on fashion: Thelma, now running a boutique called 'Monika', made unique and brightly coloured shirts for him. Adrian Henri, whilst working on *The Entry Of Christ Into Liverpool* would repaint him from corduroys to Flower power via Italian Beatle suits, the ultimate sartorial accolade coming years later from the legendary performance poet John Cooper-Clarke, who disclosed to McGough that he had always been his 'fashion-guru'.

The period was a purple patch in other ways for McGough. He and Thelma – in the words of Heather Holden, 'the fashionable middle-class girl who didn't muck in' – were enjoying a pleasant lull in their frequently stormy relationship. Still unmarried, they had moved to 6 Huskisson Street, in the heart of now fashionable Liverpool 8. *Summer with Monika* was to be published by a local press run by Wendy Harpe, Thelma having designed a cover entirely of pink hearts. McGough had also been commissioned to write a play for the Everyman Theatre. Typically it was called *The Commission*, and was about someone being commissioned to write a play. Scaffold too was successful, but most importantly for McGough who always considered himself a poet first, his poem 'Let Me Die A Youngman's Death' had demonstrated his ability to write a mature poem both technically sound and metaphorically original. Both funny and sad, it was above all, a poem that would 'stick around'.

Resting at Number 87 in a recently published BBC anthology of the nation's favourite hundred poems, McGough winces somewhat at the 'constant good tumour' pun in the second stanza, but still holds the poem in high affection, still includes it in his readings, acknowledging wryly his early obsession with death:

> Let me die a youngman's death
> not a clean & inbetween
> the sheets holywater death
> not a famous-last words
> peaceful out of breath death

The opening stanza reveals McGough's controlled incantatory register before inserting three acceptably comic verses where the defiant speaker goes from 73 in a red sports car, to a 91 year-old gangster, finally being banned from the Cavern at 104 and slaughtered by his mistress:

Let me die a youngman's death
not a free from sin tiptoe in
candle wax & waning death
not a curtains drawn by angels borne
'what a nice way to go' death

During the mid-sixties, Andy Roberts had gone to a concert at the Arts Theatre in Cambridge, billed as poetry and jazz. Fascinated by the idea, his conclusions were similar to those of Adrian Henri's concerning the uneasy fusion. 'The reality wasn't very good because the music wasn't specific to the poetry, poets were fighting the music all the time.'

Renewing his musical association with the Liverpool poets in Edinburgh, Roberts gradually perfected his often intricate and 'poet-specific' style of accompaniment whereby the music became 'a carpet for the poem to walk on, without examining how good the pattern is' (no pun intended).

In alliance with the new Scottish poets such as Alan Jackson and Pete Morgan and the veteran poet/singer Hamish Henderson, open-house poetry and music sessions based on the Liverpool model were held every afternoon at the Traverse Theatre in Edinburgh. Heather Holden remembers long sessions at Deacon Brodie's Tavern and Greyfriar Bobby's, sleeping on floors until Pete Brown introduced them to the Reverend David Logan and his wife Betty in Leith:

Betty was on dexedrine so she never slept, and she stayed up all night eating chocolate, she was great and the vicar was great; we'd come home at three or four in the morning and stay chatting with his wife for hours.

Attitudes here to poetry were also changing. George Macbeth, still part of The Group, had chaired the 1964 poets' conference at Edinburgh, warning participants not to misbehave as 'we'd had a bad press and as we all wanted a full scale conference next year we mustn't jeopardize our chances.' Macbeth, reverting to the tight control of The Group's Friday night sessions reported his chairmanship as ' much more serious and worthwhile than the previous day's'. Shortly afterwards, Macbeth's ideas decidedly changed. Answering John Schofield's questionnaire regarding features of the current scene, a newly long-haired Macbeth replied, 'the rise, development and improvement of public poetry reading as an art form. The return to humour, experiment and gut energy as criteria of impact.' When asked in a later interview by Tom Davis about poetry depending on rhythm he gave Adrian Henri as an example.

Henri, still at the Art College in Liverpool was finding his relationship with Arthur Ballard rapidly deteriorating:

I was much more interested in American painting and pop-art than French painting and wanted to do assemblages. Arthur didn't really approve, but what was very interesting about Arthur was he had a very good eye for people. In the department were myself, Don McKinlay, Maurice Cockrill, Sam Walsh – Roger did some part-time work there – Henry Graham did some liberal studies and the conceptual artist Keith Arnatt taught there. So he was good at putting a team together, but on the other hand was totally out of sympathy with what they were doing. But he could see that it was good, and he could see it was different and it was original.

Ballard's problem with Henri was that he became increasingly irritated with all his 'extra-curricular activities' and felt he could not carry on working for him. He could not do both. Eventually he would have to choose. One such 'activity' was Yoko Ono. A year before John Lennon met his second wife, Yoko visited Liverpool in 1966. Wendy Harpe of Great George's Art Centre (the Blackie) was running The Bluecoat Chambers, had given Mark Boyle his first English exhibition and arranged a show for the conceptual artist John Latham. Someone had told her that Yoko Ono, hardly known outside of America, wanted to do something in Liverpool. Henri, due to his interest in the New York performance scene, wanted to be involved:

> She did these performance pieces, one of which, a famous one where she wore this dress and invited the audience to come up and cut pieces off it, ending up pretty much naked really. Then she did a bandage piece, and I got recruited to do the bandaging, so she had this microphone underneath this thing and I turned her into a mummy. There's a photograph of me doing this. Then after the show Mike Evans and I took her off to O'Connor's Tavern. She was very sweet. I presented her with a plastic chrysanthemum.

O'Connor's Tavern, presided over by the ever-beaming Jimmy Moore, whose holidays were an annual visit to Lourdes and Liverpool F.C.'s European games, was the final venue for the Mersey Poets. Windowless and smoky with an eerie sepia light, it was more like a bar in Harlem. It was here in the upstairs room that Maurice Cockrill remembers a defining moment in the attitude and spirit of the live readings of those times:

> These serious Liverpool heavies just suddenly turned up completely out of the blue. One of them [Charles Connolly] had just been released after doing a lot of time concerning this notorious murder at the Cameo Cinema in Wavertree. And there they were in the bar about to watch a poetry evening! Everyone thought it wouldn't happen, they won't get

up and do it, they'll chicken out. But Adrian got up, did his usual jokes and Mike Evans did his bit and the gangsters took it.They all laughed. Adrian and Mike won them over and then they left. Looking back, that took so much courage and professionalism. Imagine if that had been in some soppy Hampstead venue? There'd have been ructions.

Cockrill, something of a poet himself, before establishing himself as a major painter, has always respected Mike Evans as a musician, performer and a writer of deceptive poignancy.

After meeting Henri at Rhyl (through the Chet Baker album), Evans had been a regular visitor to Liverpool, coming over initially for a Lee Konitz gig at the end of the summer of 1958. For a while he rented a room for ten shillings a week in 24 Falkner Square ('which could be generously described as a wardrobe') during the Half Moon Club days. In the early sixties Evans was studying economics at the Regent Street Polytechnic in London, one of the very few people to be privy to what was happening at both The Cavern in Liverpool and The Marquee in London:

I saw the Beatles in their that last phase of playing at The Cavern regularly. We were all jazz snobs at the time because Rock'n'Roll in England was Cliff Richard and Adam Faith, so when this girl Josephine I was going out with said, come and hear the Beatles down The Cavern I was negative about it. Anyway she eventually persuaded me to go down there and I was absolutely amazed – like knocked out – because here was this band with these weird looking guys playing old Rock 'n' Roll, the kind I'd always liked – Chuck Berry and all that kind of thing – and incredibly loud.

Evans enthusiastically passed on the news about what was happening at the Cavern to Henri – who was immediately interested – and Joyce, who was not, her reply being, 'The Beatles, aren't they that group with that awful John Lennon who used to be at the Art School?'

In parallel was the scene centred around Alexis Korner, at The Marquee in Wardour Street, five minutes walk for Evans from the polytechnic in Regent Street. He began taking saxophone lessons from Dick Heckstall-Smith, whom Evans was introduced to by Pete Brown. 'Dick was in Alexis's band and this weird guy from the L.S.E. Mick Jagger would get up on vocals, so I was watching all this, and at weekends I was watching all this other craziness going on in Liverpool'.

Neither scene knew about the other, nor at the time did they seem to want to. Evans remembers asking Lennon whether he was aware of the rhythm'n'blues scene in London. 'And Lennon said, no what's that? And I told him about the

Marquee, and I said there was a big two-page spread about it in the *Melody Maker* last week. And he said, oh I don't read the *Melody Maker*, that's for jazz snobs, I read the *N.M.E.*'

Bands were now playing at Hope Hall, most notably The Clayton Squares who were assembled by a certain George Roberts, one of the many 'new Brian Epsteins' springing up on the scene. Evans, returning a guitar there that he had borrowed from Sam Walsh, was recruited on the strength of this and the fact that he owned a saxophone. Arguably the best group to miss out on the Mersey Beat boom were The Roadrunners, who at one point George Harrison rated more highly than the Rolling Stones. Their leader Mike Hart had been involved with Adrian Henri's Happenings and was widely regarded as the most talented singer/songwriter in the city. John Peel would later produce his solo album *Mike Hart Bleeds* but sadly he was someone who could never 'take a break'.

Drink was a major problem that would bring about the self-destruction of an artist who could sing well, play and write an original lyric. Adrian Henri remembers a later gig at The Roundhouse:

> Mike was staying with Paul McCartney in St John's Wood. He was still in The Liverpool Scene at the time, but we were all staying elsewhere. He got so drunk that he ended up smashing his guitar up in the dressing-room afterwards, then went on to Paul's with the ruins of it in his hands.

1966 saw Roger McGough becoming more actively involved in television, his picture even appearing on the front of the *T.V. Times*. Playing the narrator in an A.T.V's *Saturday While Sunday*, he was awarded that year's most promising newcomer award. This meant missing the Nottingham Poetry Festival organised by the progressive Trent Bridge Bookshop. This large-scale weekend event featured sound poets, concrete poets, jazz-poetry and new poetry of every kind. Patten and Henri were invited to read. Here they met Edward Lucie-Smith.

Impressed by a piece Henri had read called 'The New Our Times', Lucie-Smith asked if he could use it in an article in *Encounter*. Henri readily accepted, thinking Lucie-Smith an unlikely person to be interested in anything he was doing, but aware of him, both as a poet and art critic. When he returned the magazine it contained a letter inquiring, 'have you ever thought of somebody doing an anthology of poetry from Liverpool?' Henri replied, he didn't think there would be anyone daft enough to do it. But he was wrong

Edward Lucie-Smith was as unlikely a champion of the Mersey Poets as Brian Epstein had been regarding The Beatles. Born in Kingston, Jamaica he had obtained an M.A. from Merton College, Oxford, and had taken over the chairmanship of The Group from Philip Hobsbaum in 1959. Writing to the poet Fred Grubb, Hobsbaum felt that 'Lucie-Smith seemed the obvious person to act as my successor as chairman. He had shown himself highly articulate, was making a name as a poet and had recently shown a propensity towards writing critiques in unobtrusively elegant prose.' When Hobsbaum left London, The Group moved premises to Lucie-Smith's flat in Sydney Street, Chelsea. Anyone who lists one of their recreations as malice cannot be completely orthodox, and part of Lucie-Smith's character has always been anti-the-perceived wisdom-of-the-time. Having resigned from The Group in 1965, looking for something new, he had met Donald Carroll. Carroll, an American with advanced ideas about publication and marketing, had the then idealistic, and to many, 'lunatic' notion of serious contemporary poetry published in a way that could be commercially successful. Despite much evidence to the contrary Carroll was convinced that with the right poets it could be done, and was willing to risk his partner, George Rapp's money in trying. There was one problem – he had no idea who the 'right poets' were. Discussing the dilemma, Lucie-Smith asked whether Carroll had heard about these chaps from Liverpool? 'And to be honest I hadn't. But Ted felt they might be just what I was looking for.'

To Adrian Henri's utter astonishment, a further letter said they would like to do a book, which Lucie-Smith would edit, broadly as a record of a life-style containing poems, prose and photographs. Lucie-Smith's research interrupted The Group's meetings, known as 'Lucie's Fridays'. The acerbic (but essentially sound) Fred Grubb remembers him returning after a sojourn saying he had recently discovered some poets in Liverpool, 'which was met with bland indifference by the Group. Then it was back to Leavis.' To complicate matters further, shortly after Lucie-Smith had started work on *The Liverpool Scene*, featuring not only McGough, Henri and Patten – although they were given prominence – but also Pete Brown, Spike Hawkins, Henry Graham, Mike Evans and Heather Holden, a much bigger fish was becoming sold on the Mersey Poets.

McGough had been recommended to the editor of *The Times Literary Supplement* by John Willett, leading to a publishing deal for his first book, the clumsily titled *Frinck, a Life in the Day of, and Summer With Monika*. It also brought him to the attention of Tony Richardson of Penguin Books. Richardson, aware of Patten's work, was keen to publish the two Liverpudlians as part of the pioneering Penguin Modern Poets series, but wanted a third person who would complement their work rather than rub against it. Harry Fainlight was discussed but felt unsuitable. Richardson rang Patten asking whether there was anyone else in Liverpool. Patten replied 'there's Adrian', who quickly responded with a bundle of poems that were deemed appropriate. The book was put to bed.

Rapp & Carroll were meanwhile publicising their book as if it was a record. A long way from Leavis, they had posters, stickers and badges, and were planning a big launch party at The Cavern for 3rd March. The band The Almost Blues were hired, trainloads of journalists shipped up from London, there were television crews, hundreds of bottles of champagne, and on Carroll's instructions, Henri was to invite – free of charge – that year's intake of Art College beauties. This proved too heady a mix for some of the journalists; marriages broke up in an explosive farrago which Henri, McGough and Patten were oblivious to, as they were wanted for interviews.

Because of the way the book was being marketed, there was an enormous amount of newspaper publicity, followed by highly favourable reviews by like-minded critics such as George Melly and Ray Gosling, perceiving the book largely as a social phenomenon. 'It was a funny No-Man's Land kind of book, Henri adds, 'about a northern city as much as it was about poetry. It got very sympathetic reviews from those kinds of people, and was totally rubbished by the literary press, but by then it had acquired an energy all of its own. Then two months later came the Penguin book'.

The hardback *Liverpool Scene* (recorded live along the Mersey Beat) that Donald Carroll felt would be such a winner still stands out as something of a curiosity piece. Designed by Lawrence Edwards, the book is clearly representative of the typopgraphy and graphics of the time. Its front cover variously depicts The Beatles, Henri peering through stacks of Campbell's soup cans, a long-haired girl called Ingrid, and three red word-balloons featuring Batman in the goalmouth with an Ee-Aye-Addio banner, the opening quotes of 'Let Me Die A Youngman's Death' and Spike Hawkins's 'Pig' poem. The back of the book more sedately makes eleven lines of Allen Ginsberg's quote about Liverpool being 'the centre of the consciousness of the human universe.' George Melly perceptively pointed out that by substituting 'the Young' for 'the human universe' the comment loses much of its hyperbole.

In his later book *Revolt Into Style* Melly describes how

> the provincial Underground became public property. The pop poets were published and appeared on television and were attacked and defended from within the ranks of traditional culture. They reaffirmed their treaty with older poets of protest like Adrian Mitchell and Christopher Logue. Finally, and logically, Henri and that honorary freeman of the Liverpool scene, Pete Brown, went truly pop and formed

and led straight Underground pop groups. The Liverpool adventure was at an end.

Dedicated to The Beatles (without whom &etc), *The Liverpool Scene* made Roger McGough feel somewhat uneasy:

> We were in a dilemma. We could sense all the excitement, and we could see that it might be a good idea commercially, but we didn't want to be packaged as a group. We were all poets; we were all separate – we just met together. But even today, we're still grouped together. At festivals, people still seem to want a Liverpool poet.

Lavishly illustrated with 'urban-wasteland' photographs by Philip Jones-Griffiths, Lucie-Smith's introduction favourably compares the Liverpool writers with Rimbaud and Baudelaire where 'the poem is no longer an artifact, or a commodity, but a service; it is an agent rather than an object'. It singles out Henri as the central figure of a group of artists and writers sharing one another's ideas, contrasted with the overall segregation and consequent enfeeblement of English poetry at this time. The defensive, negative postures and attitudes of a sheltered literati are contrasted with 'the poems in this book written by people who are more interested in life than in literature'.

Lucie-Smith argues well, although at times driven with a defensiveness implying that someone needs to plead on the Liverpool writers' behalf. Much of the poetry is at best uneven; many poems a draft away from more tightly edited versions to appear later. He acknowledges the sentimentality, coarseness of texture, carelessness with details, but is at pains to point out the 'real and pressing situations' in which the poetry is written. He sees them foreshadowing developments bound to take place in literature and society as a whole, and not 'the disastrous effect on the weaker brethren' that John Wain claimed in his pompous account, 'Professing Poetry'. Emphasising how strong tides of opinion create pervasive fashions, Wain felt this led to complacent silliness that seem 'in the climate of the time, perfectly respectable'.

Lucie-Smith's account is further enlivened by Patten, Henri and McGough talking in varying degrees of lucidity. McGough, born in a working-class home where, 'if you're a poet it's something to be ashamed of'. Patten professes no urge to go to London, wanting to be 'independent of cities really, you know'. Henri, contrasting his painting with his poems, tells how ' you can tell whether (people) hate them or not, or if they like them, or laugh at them...' Intriguingly, half-way through the book sits Henry Graham's 'Good luck to you Kafka / You'll need it boss'. The poem (later to become the title of his first collection) was the nearest Graham would come to echo the style of his contemporaries (particularly McGough). Always sceptical of 'the Liverpool

Scene', he stood aloof from it, finding it particularly hard to take anything Henri did seriously.

According to Mike Evans, 'Henry saw a lot of what Adrian did as being very opportunist. The fact that Adrian would mess about with pop groups or do Happenings and all of that, whereas Henry was a painter and a poet and that was it. They had the same roots and enthusiasms about abstract painting, it's just that Adrian went very whole heartedly down the pop art route whereas Henry stayed in the abstract tradition. Adrian was a good self-publicist, but he was also good at publicising other people as well, and people like Henry would obviously resent that because that's not the kind of way they think you should do things'.

Maurice Cockrill also noticed their differences: 'Henry said that what Adrian really wanted to be was a Beatle, but he was too late and he couldn't sing'.

Despite occasional curmudgeonly behaviour, Graham was an original, who could at times be very funny. His ironic 'The Invention' is the last poem in *The Liverpool Scene*; the final three pages taken up with some sharp surrealistic dialogue by McGough. There are some quotes on live readings and audiences, with Henri summing up 'the whole modern tradition [as] writing for your own voice.'

Internal politics within Rapp & Carroll meant that Donald Carroll, who rightly wanted to do a paperback version of the book, was gradually replaced by a much safer pair of hands. Ronald Whiting (his successor), was uneasy about the prospects of 'going paperback'. 'It was the biggest mistake they ever made,' says Henri, 'they did all the work, did all the publicity, then missed out on cashing in'.

It was at this point that Patten made the decision to be independent of the city, the media and the attention. In the spring of 1967 coinciding with the publication of *Little Johnny's Confession* by Allen and Unwin, he moved to Winchester.

Although their close friendship blossomed later in the seventies, McGough admired Patten's decision to move out of the spotlight and write quietly and 'live like a poet'. Despite his abrasive and at times aggressive and mercurial nature, he has often acted as a conscience.

Events were overtaking themselves in Liverpool, Henri announcing at one reading that 'you can't throw a bottle in a pub in Liverpool without hitting a poet'. Patten, alarmed and uncertain about the gathering publicity, was getting angry about the increasing trivialisation. 'If we were having a radio interview – I'd sit there – and someone would ask a question, and Roger would be polite and answer it, and Adrian would be very erudite and answer it, and I'd say that's a fucking stupid question, I'm going to get a drink, and vanish. I didn't want to play along with the media/circus type thing, I was very aggressive to all that, so I buggered off to Winchester'.

He had published a Winchester poet called Pat Waites in *Underdog*, who had become a friend and seemed a good enough reason to go there:

I liked it because it was misty and ancient and quiet; totally the opposite of any kind of public razzmatazz like Liverpool which I'd grown out of in a way. I just didn't want to be involved in a music scene, I just wanted to write and that was it. Maybe I was seen as more of a poet than Adrian and Roger at that time because I wasn't involved with all that kind of world. I wasn't doing anything else but writing. I wasn't standing on the stage fronting a Rock and Roll group or singing Lily the Pink.

Despite his professed aversion to publicity that is exactly what *Little Johnny's Confession* got on publication. Conveniently launched between *The Liverpool Scene* and *The Mersey Sound* much of the brouhaha focussed on the fact that Patten was only twenty-one. Allen Ginsberg, quoted on the dust-jacket, pointed out that Patten was younger than the atom bomb, Lucie-Smith went one further, marvelling at someone so young being able 'to tell so much truth so simply'. The title poem particularly with its combination of dreamlike violence and detachment became common poetic coinage for a generation.

The book (and perhaps his next two), became mandatory cultural currency like an early Dylan or Leonard Cohen L.P. for those that may never read – or certainly would never buy – any poetry again. Opening with the 'Little Johnny' sequence of eight poems that germinated below the skylight in Canning Street, the book is an amalgam of childhood isolation and surrealism in an urban setting, clearly, although not specifically, set in Liverpool. Many of his most famous early poems are here: 'Party Piece', 'Somewhere Between Heaven And Woolworth's', 'Where Are You Now Batman', 'Sleep Now', 'Room' and 'Schoolboy'. When it appeared it was hailed as a masterpiece, winning an Eric Gregory prize (one of the three judges being Ted Hughes). He also received a Pernod Creative Arts Award in the same year.

The book is rich in the celestial and mirrored imagery so long associated with his work. The corruption of innocence where rain acts as a substitute for tears, and where the life of the past is set against a 'new kind of dawn' signifying the beginning of a new kind of consciousness:

Readjusting your conscience
You wake, and
woken you dream

or so it seems
of forests you've come across
and lives you'd have swum through
had you been strong enough.

When interviewed, he described the collection merely as 'a shrinking of ignorant innocence', but went somewhat further in 1992, when in an author's note prefacing *Grinning Jack,* his Selected Poems, Patten accepted that:

A few of the earliest of these poems were written when I was fifteen or sixteen and perhaps ought to have been relegated to juvenilia, but the boy who wrote them would have argued quite vehemently (if not quite accurately) that his poems were as good as many by older poets. As I haven't the heart to dissuade him, I've slipped a few in.

For those not sceptical of the messages and colours of the sixties, 1967 will long be remembered as the apogee of a collective hallucination before it all lost its bloom. It was, and for many still is, the dawning of a new age centred on love and peace. In America, the war in Vietnam, begun by Kennedy and vigorously continued by Lyndon Johnson, had become a catastrophe causing a world-wide sense of outrage. It had also become a rallying call against the values of a society who could preside over helicopters gunning straw villages causing scorched babies, and the grotesque horror of naked helpless children being faced with mass artillery in burning paddy fields and camps. New values were being sought analogous with ideas originally embraced by the Beats. Now they were given added resonance by the hippies, whose flowers, long hair, flowing garments and bare feet represented gentleness and a oneness with both themselves and nature itself.

Swinging London had begat the Summer of Love, the mini-skirt replaced by see-through kaftans; girls jangled jewellery, walked barefoot and bra-less down hot pavements along the Kings Road. Men became dandified, wearing flowered shirts and beads. In June The Beatles crystallised the spirit of the entire period with the release of their seventh L.P. the culturally-defining *Sergeant Pepper's Lonely Hearts Club Band.*

His sensual nature in cultural harmony with his fairground training, Adrian Henri arranged a 'Love Night' at the Everyman Theatre. This saw the emergence of the pink heart, a constant motif in his growing personal imagery. Sadly, 'Our Lady of Haslingdon', Heather Holden, the muse for so much of his early work had left him for his old friend Philip Jones-Griffiths. Another student had caught his eye, provoking the slight but enduring 'Love Is', (recently voted as one of the nation's best loved comic *and* love poems!). A traumatic relationship and a hectic two-year period followed, causing him to almost 'die a young man's death' before the next decade was underway. It was during this period that Henri assembled around him three of the best local musicians: Andy Roberts, Mike Hart and Mike Evans. Between them they provided the nucleus for The Liverpool Scene.

Both Evans and Hart were at a loose end as The Clayton Squares and The Roadrunners were by now defunct. Evans had been gigging in Germany and Spain in various spin-off bands and remembers going up to Edinburgh in the summer of 1967 when loose formats and scratch bands were the order of the day, making the Happenings and 'Events' seem like paragons of professionalism. 'We were on at The Traverse Theatre and they'd put on the chalk board outside, 'The Liverpool Scene' after the book because that was the catalyst. And the name stuck.'

The beginning of the band coincided with the publication of *The Mersey Sound*, and Henri happily acknowledges: 'it couldn't have been better timed – 1967, the Summer of Love, *Sgt Pepper* – the whole thing. And if you had actually tried to work out a better time for it you couldn't. It definitely did ride on the crest of that wave.'

On a crest of a wave himself, but not domestically, Roger McGough and Thelma had parted company. She found it particularly difficult in accepting his constant touring with Scaffold and he had taken brief residence and refuge at 64 Canning Steet.

Scaffold were going through a lean period, and after some remote unrewarding gigs McGough would question the validity of what he was doing. Defensively he insists 'it was just a way of life, it didn't affect my poetry, I was always writing.' Michael Joseph decided to publish *Summer with Monika* in tandem with *Frinck*, his first and only novel.

His Scaffold years were a double-edged sword; people had heard of him, rare for a poet, but often they weren't sure why or how. Often they simply felt he had something to do with The Beatles, or in one doubly ironic case – 'wasn't his brother in Marmalade?' This ambiguity is hardly surprising. Managed by Brian Epstein, who had secured them a recording contract with Parlophone, the summer of '67 saw Scaffold sinking rather than swimming on the crest of a wave and at the point of splitting up. This coincided with the return from holiday in California of Paul McCartney besmitten by much of the West Coast's cultural eccentricity, particularly the adventures of Ken Kesey and his Merry Pranksters. Shortly before the Magical Mystery Tour, McCartney went into the studio to produce an album called *McGough-McGear*. To give his brother every possible chance of success, McCartney hired an all-superstar line-up including Jimi Hendrix, Graham Nash and Dave Mason.

The album was a flop but has subsequently become something of a valuable collector's item solely due to the famous itinerary of musicians. In many ways it was an uncomfortable time for McGough, who kept his head down, knowing his place. 'My problem was not being a musician. So although I knew I was in the presence of heavies, I didn't know why: the language they spoke and things that entranced them I didn't appreciate.'

Back again with Thelma, and now living in Parkfield Road in Sefton Park, the couple stayed briefly at 7 Cavendish Avenue, the home Paul McCartney shared with Jane Asher in St John's Wood. Thelma felt the most notable thing about the house was 'the large jar of grass on the mantlepiece for anyone to dip into, and the mirrored Indian cushions Jane had bought on Portobello Road'.

McGough was seriously tempted by television. *Saturday While Sunday* had been the first TV work for actors Timothy Dalton and Malcolm MacDowell, and director Jim Goddard, who still remains a friend. He was establishing a media track record. He also had the opportunity to finish Joe Orton's final script for Dick Lester that The Beatles were considering. McGough was felt to be the man for the job but turned it down as it would have meant leaving Liverpool and 'not working with John and Mike'. Then salvation occurred. Written by Mike McCartney as a thank you to his brother for a Nikon camera, 'Thank U Very Much', released in October 1967 rescued Scaffold, peaking at number four in the charts a month later.

It was an extremely happy family gathering that met on New Year's Eve at Rembrandt in West Kirkby, the house Paul McCartney had bought for his father Jim. For once both brothers had something to celebrate: Paul, his engagement to Jane, and Mike, a hit record of his own. Understandably boosted by Scaffold's unexpected end of year success, John Gorman was in even more festive spirits than usual. Unfortunately the girl he was with became so 'tired and emotional' that she fell out of a second-floor window. This meant an ambulance, with Gorman ending up at 'another party in the hospital.' The previous year he had stolen a bottle of rum, 'so I'd well and truly blotted my copybook – I wasn't allowed to go to their parties anymore'. The incident has some similarity to the incident involving John Lennon's vicious beating of local D.J. Bob Wooler at Paul's twenty-first. McGough witnessed this four years earlier, when the McCartney code of behaviour had been so markedly violated. He has a strong family ethos himself, endorsing theirs: You're welcome here, as long as you behave in the right way.'

At the end of 1967, Brian Patten, himself later to become a source of McCartney family disapproval, was living quietly in Winchester. He had gravitated towards artists and students at the city's College of Art including the sculptor Heinz Henghes and the young Brian Eno. Writing prolifically and with passionate intensity, Patten avoided tours and other forms of publicity simply to promote his work. 'That was their bag – we're just different people that's all – different poets'.

In one remarkable late autumn day, in a damp dark room in Winchester, Patten wrote 'The Projectionist's Nightmare', 'A Small Dragon', 'You Come To me Quiet As Rain Not Yet Fallen', and 'You Better Believe Him'. It could hardly be described as a mere visitation – more a case of the muse moving in as a lodger. It never happened again. 'I think it was to do with a huge, strange upheaval in one's life, a massive change, but the sort of change or gamble that you have to fight for.'

Despite omitting much of his best work from *The Mersey Sound* to go into *Little Johnny's Confession*, Patten still managed to pick up favourable reviews from the poetry establishment including the *T.L.S.*

Oblivious to all perceived wisdom, comment and criticism, Patten was now ferociously writing the poems that would further establish his growing reputation, the work that would make up the influential and best-selling *Notes To The Hurrying Man*. He was living cheaply on bits of this, bits of that – 'just lived as cheap as I could really. Like a poet.'

The End of the Sixties

During 1968 the comparisons between Patten, McGough and Henri were at their widest. McGough had become a regular on A.B.C's *The Eleventh Hour* and was gigging extensively with the revitalised and more musically orientated Scaffold. Their stage humour was very different from their songs. 'Our songs certainly brought financial success and made us household names', McGough acknowledges, 'but it also misled audiences. Mums and dads came along and we weren't providing what they wanted. We were never a musical knockabout act like The Grumbleweeds, but that was what so many people thought we were.'

Mike McGear has other regrets. 'The big thing at the time on telly was Batman, and Roger had written a lovely parody, "Goodbat Nightman". We went to Brian [Epstein] in his NEMS emporium and said, we've got this great idea and we've got to do it now. The Batman phenomenon is going to be even bigger. He hummed and ha-d and wanted us to do other things. It didn't come out until the end of the Batman mayhem. The record didn't reach the audience it should have done.'

Making the bat metaphor literal, McGough's poem playfully re-evokes A.A.Milne's children's nursery rhyme:

> They've locked all the doors
> and they've put out the bat,
> Put on their batjamas
> (They like doing that)

With the T.V. programme's theme to the fore, Henri chose another route – dedicating the piece to Bob Kane (the creator of the strip) and local band The Almost Blues, he directly echoed Adrian Mitchell and the spirit of the counterculture:

> Help us out in Vietnam
> Batman
>
> Help us drop that BatNapalm
> Batman
>
> Help us bomb those jungle towns
> Spreading pain and death around
> Coke 'n' candy wins them round
> Batman

Concluding Henri's *Love Night* at The Everyman, the poem became the 'Bat-Rave' featuring everyone concerned. This event became the first gig for The Liverpool Scene. The original line-up was Henri as the poet, Mike Hart on vocals and guitar, Evans on tenor saxophone, Roberts on lead guitar, supplemented by Percy Jones on bass, and drummer Brian Dodson who virtually recruited himself. 'Things were very casual', Evans remembers, 'we'd get booked out to places as a band with no name really so every time we got a gig we started calling ourselves The Liverpool Scene because people were calling us that anyway'. 'Batpoem' became a staple part of their act, featuring strongly on their first John Peel-produced album, *Amazing Adventures Of*.

All this was anathema to Patten. His amazing adventure was writing poetry in his 'Steppenwolf' existence in a quiet town in Hampshire as far away as possible from the increasingly self-preening, heart-shaped, eyebrow-fluttering mood of the times. Never 'that far from it' as far as he was concerned, his 'celluloid companions' in 'Where are you now, Batman?' are not some convenient manifestation of pop-art, but are given an eerie provenance by hanging ominously and 'aimlessly about the streets'

With no way of getting back;
Sir Galahad's been strangled by the Incredible Living Trees,
Zorro killed by his own sword.
In the junk-ridden, disused hangers
Blackhawk's buried the last of his companions;
Rocket Man's fuel tanks have given out over London.
Though the Monster and the Ape still fight it out
In a room where the walls are continually closing
No one is watching.

The poem ends with the enemy of old age approaching, Patten's first image from 'Little Johnny's Confession', in its hands, the machine-gun 'dripping with years'.

In marked contrast to Patten, Henri used everything published in *The Mersey Sound* for his own book, *Tonight At Noon* that came out in 1968. Patten kept his 'Little Johnny' poems separate. McGough, shrewdly mixed his better known poems of the time, such as 'Let Me Die A Youngman's Death', 'My Busconductor', 'At Lunchtime' and 'Sad Aunt Madge' with shorter poignant, wistful pieces such as 'On Picnics', 'Vinegar' and 'Fallen Birdman'. In this way, *Summer with Monika* – despite the unnecessary encumbrance of the unconvincing *Frinck* – reached the public fresh and complete. Although at times fey and sentimental and almost too ready in its exploitation of puns, it has a thematic wholeness, a continuity of language and lightness of touch chiming perfectly with the prevailing mood and colour of the times:

there's someone in the bathroom
someone behind the door
the house is full of naked men
monika! don't you love me anymore?

The most enduring and musical of his earlier books, McGough, aware of its limitations, felt it worked. 'I was pleased with doing it and it gave a lot of people pleasure and I was able to write something throughout which I knew was good and fitted the style of the times.'

Not without some degree of emotional profundity, the book has at times an edgy resonance that may almost have been too close to home:

away from you
I feel a great emptiness
A gnawing loneliness

with you
I get that reassuring feeling
of wanting to escape

In *Revolt Into Style*, George Melly saw Liverpool 8, with its pubs and meeting places as small enough to: 'provide an enclosed stage for the cultivation of its own legend. A figure both charismatic and catalystic was needed to bring it all together. An eclectic Scouse equivalent to Apollinaire. In this case a bearded, pear-shaped, bespectacled one.

Melly has long felt that 'what Adrian does best is paint. It's also what he does least. It reaches fewer people and he is obsessed with communicating. He is generous though in pushing others. He is a formidable entrepreneur'. In this way, disregarding jibes about being a jack-of-all-trades, master of none, and being on top of any passing bandwagon, a Rock and Roll band(wagon) was the logical next logical step for Henri. 'I'd worked with Roberts, and it was around the time The Roadrunners had split and Mike Hart was writing all these solo songs and didn't have an outlet for them. Everyone knew he was a wonderful R&B singer. And Evans who was a sax player had done a bit of singing with the Clayton Squares, was also at a loose end wanting to do something more than just blow in a blues band; so it just came together.'

The original concept of The Liverpool Scene was something of a movable feast featuring a hard core of musicians and fringe members that in the early stages

'Let me die a youngman's death' – Roger McGough in St James' Cemetery, 1964
(Photo by Peter Philip)

'Into the Mirror has walked' – a *Daily Mirror* leader on 'Poets of the new sound'
(Saturday, February 25, 1967)

'A meeting of beards' – Adrian Henri with Allen Ginsberg in Holland Park, 1967.
'Friar Tuck disguised as Sergeant Pepper meets the Baal Shem Tov disguised as the
Maharishi, William Blake providing the sunshine for both.' – Mike Kustow
(Photo by Philip Parkin)

'You sing – I'll play' – Henri and Andy Roberts on tour with the Liverpool Scene, 1968

theoretically included McGough (but not on the upright bass!). This fluidity incorporated Henri's and Evans's poetry and local jazz musicians, leading to a performance at the Everyman called *Revolution, Revolution, Revolution,* with Adrian Mitchell and Christopher Logue.

By 1968 it was a settled six-piece band, but Hart's self-destructive nature again came to the fore. The week their first single (his song) 'Son, Son', and first album were released, was the week he chose to leave. This coincided with the launch of Henri's first collection *Tonight at Noon*; his one-man show at the I.C.A.; and to complete the picture, a play about Apollinaire he had co-written with Mike Kustow.

Talking about the project, Kustow helps throw some clear light on the character to become such an obsession for Henri:

Researching the play we came across photographs of Alfred Jarry's original puppets for Ubu. Very grotesque and aggressive. The Ubu in Adrian's series of paintings and drawings is diminutive, almost bewildered, a dumpy solitary on wide empty Rhyl beaches or trapped in Liverpool traffic like a creature from outer space deposited in our world and trying to find his bearings. Inside that fat body, a deft gentle soul struggling to get out.

Outwardly Henri himself was having no such problems. Without Hart in the band meant vocal duties shared between himself, Roberts and Evans with his own 'I've Got Those Fleetwood Mac, Chicken Shack, John Mayall, Can't Fail Blues' providing the poet with a rabble-rousing vehicle to close the set. Gradually he moved more into the spotlight, and being known as a poet, his was the name booking-secretaries usually recognised:

It was never my intention that it was my band, but very often we would arrive at places billed as 'Adrian Henri and The Liverpool Scene', and if people wanted to do an interview for the *Melody Maker* they tended to interview me.

The Institute of Contemporary Arts (the I.C.A.) began in London's Dover Street in 1949. Founded by the poet and critic Herbert Read, and the surrealist painter Roland Penrose, it rejected 'good taste' for subculture, irony and immediacy, anticipating pop imagery in a foppish Baudelarian way. As its reputation became consolidated it was here that Henri's and Kustow's play *I Wonder* was staged.

It was a momentous week in an already eventful life. It also brought some late belated happiness to Arthur and Emma Henri. For Emma, it vindicated the indulgence she had shown towards her eldest son. For Arthur, so long unsympathetic, it was a great few days in London, his son the toast of the town.

The whole Henri clan was out in force. Sadly this would all soon change.

By the end of 1968 Henri had the world at his feet. *Tonight At Noon* (published by Rapp & Whiting) established him as a new, vital and eclectic force in British poetry. Less allegorical than Patten, less witty than McGough, the book was the perfect antidote for the at-times overt ephemerality of Patten and adroit whimsy of McGough. An inventive, spontaneous and energetic collection, its rough edges are offset by an unassailable charm and raw passion that he would never be able to quite recapture.

With its seminal cover combining Lawrence Edwards' imaginative design over Don McCullin's defining photograph; Henri to the fore in P.V.C. mac and Lennonesque cap, it resembles an L.P. sleeve rather than a book of verse. This was reflected in the sales. Much longer than both Patten and McGough's first collections at nearly a hundred pages, it contained all the poems he had made his reputation with, including 'Galactic Lovepoem' written for the new woman in his life, Susan Sterne:

> Warm your feet at sunset
> Before we go to bed
> Read your book by the light of Orion
> With Sirius guarding your head
> Then reach out and switch off the planets
> We'll watch them go out one by one
> You kiss me and tell me you love me
> By the light of the last setting sun

Borrowing freely from Apollinaire's practise of Automatism, writing from the unconscious mind where one word suggests the next, *Tonight at Noon* – often comically, often in a deceptively visionary way – presents a world in reverse in which habits and principles are turned upside down, where:

> Tonight at noon
> Supermarkets will advertise 3d EXTRA on everything
> Tonight at noon
> Children from happy families will be sent to live in a home
> Elephants will tell each other human jokes
> America will declare peace on Russia
> World War 1 generals will sell poppies in the streets on
> November 11th
> The first daffodils of autumn will appear
> When the leaves fall upwards to the trees

Roger McGough, despite his essentially diplomatic nature occasionally ran into controversy with his poetry, 'At Lunchtime' entering Hansard, after a

Conservative M.P. had complained about 'the type of things school children were asked to read in text-books nowadays'. Reluctantly, McGough also had to accept that Scaffold's first political song 'Yesterday's Men' could not be recorded. Prime Minister Harold Wilson said he found it personally offensive so it had to be binned. Previously he had named 'Thank U Very Much' as his favourite record. 'It's quite an achievement to have written both a Prime Minister's most-liked and most-hated song', McGough ruefully acknowledges. To counter this setback, after reworking the lyrics to an old rugby song, Scaffold struck gold with 'Lily the Pink'. So in the same month as Henri's great week, the poet Roger McGough found himself Number One in the hit parade.

Much of the fuss that accompanied the success of 'Lily the Pink' focused on Mike McGear. There was a surfeit of 'Beatle Paul's kid brother hits No1 spot' headlines, McGear himself uneasy about overtly commercial songs agreeing with Gorman's choices only if the B-sides reflected the trio's theatre-humour-poetry side. Norrie Paramour (with Tim Rice as his asssitant) produced the record. Their musical director was ex Manfred Mann guitarist Mike Vickers who invited Cream's bassist Jack Bruce to one of the sessions. McGear, a fan of Cream, gave Bruce permission to ad lib at will:

> When he heard Lily in rehearsals Jack said, quite honestly Mike, the only thing I can do on this song is 'bum bum......bum bum'. As he was absolutely right, I left him to it.

At the end of a hard-working and positive day, 'Lily The Pink', with Jack Bruce, Graham Nash on back-up vocals, and lots of added bass drum thud, was in the can.

Scaffold also recorded another song around this time called 'Promiscuity'. Co-written by McGough and McGear with the Liverpool poet Sid Hoddes and recorded by EMI, the witty calypso whose lyric began:

> Promiscuity, promiscuity, it isn't a sin or a vice
> I don't even think it's good for me,
> I just do it because it is nice.

was considered too risqué – even in the late sixties – so the track stayed on the shelf.

Adrian Henri had encountered Susan Sterne in the by now time-honoured way – she was one of his students. Originally from Leeds, Henri met her just before push came to shove with Arthur Ballard at the Art College. Talented but committed to current avant-garde methods, she very quickly became a square peg in a round hole, finding herself completely out of step with her tutors at

Liverpool. All except one. Shortly after Joyce Henri moved out of the increasingly ramshackle 'open house' at 64 Canning Street, Sue Sterne moved in. The Henris' marriage had been an amicable arrangement for some time, but when Joyce acquired a boyfriend – someone Henri did not get on with – the difficulties became insurmountable. One of them had to call it a day, and this time it was Joyce.

McGough too was on the move again. Boosted enormously by the sales of 'Lily the Pink', he found himself for the first time with enough spare capital to buy a house of substance. Backing on to Princes Park, containing a tree-filled convent, Victorian street lamps and paving stones, Windermere Terrace is the urban oasis its name suggests. At forty-five degrees to where Ullet Road meets Sefton Park, its 387 acres only broken on the skyline by the tower of the distant Mossley Hill church, the terrace looks directly at the park's elegant cottages ownees acting as keepers' lodges. The terrace's jewel in the crown is Windermere House.

Originally built for Sir Joseph Paxton, a Palladian villa with white stucco facade and neo-classical columns, 'McGough Towers' is one of the finest Victorian houses in Liverpool. Visible from any passing bus, it stands self-confidently gazing at Sefton Park's well-designed terrain. McGough feels that he must have been making some sort of a statement after eventually deciding to buy it. 'Maybe it was the nuns' – one apocryphal story has him turning up carrying a suitcase full of money in full view of the sisters. Regardless of its beauty, with French windows practically opening on to Princes Park, the vast entrance-hall made it a difficult place in which to live. Ways were tried to divide it, but ominously none with any lasting success.

Brian Patten also found himself in more elegant surroundings, moving to Notting Hill Gate. Despite his disclaimers about cities in *The Liverpool Scene*, he had left Winchester for London after the publication of his second collection *Notes To The Hurrying Man*. The second book was even more successful than the first, which was clearly situated in, although not about Liverpool. The new volume was far less place-specific. This was hardly surprising, as Patten himself was less place-specific. Earlier themes were broadened; urban cameos replaced by what the critic Richard Holmes described as 'visionary anecdotes'. Patten's reputation as a writer of metaphysical fables begins here. The tone is less strident, the poems both direct and ephemeral, with his fascination for the telepohone as metaphor first evident. Patten treads with a deceptive maturity in the shadowy borders of magical realism. A bird finds its way into a cinema screen, a fashionable guru tells his media audience to 'think of governments, chewing gum, ping-pong balls, wars, Queen Elizabeth coronation cups, anything', and a timid dragon is found in the woodshed, nesting and fading away in the coal:

If you believed in it I would come
hurrying to your house to let you share my wonder
but I want instead to see
if you yourself will pass this way

The most famous of all his urban parables, 'A Small Dragon' is a modern classic, an early example of what critic, poet and Booker Prize nominee Martin Booth noticed, as 'the kinds of ideas that Patten developed and made his own... no one could write as he did. He was a phenomenon, original and unique.'

Not all of the book works. At times its 'other-wordliness' becomes almost laboured and contrived. Patten himself felt the poetry was starting to get 'too abstract, too quasi-mystical'. One of the last poems, 'Ode On Celestial Music' brings things down to earth somewhat, the protagonist grumpily realising what a 'filthy trick' it was when: 'It's not celestial music it's the girl in the bathroom singing.'

The spacy allegorical tone of *Notes To The Hurrying Man*, complete with white 'psychedelic' lettering on the cover, meant it became staple reading for the'counter-culture'. Patten knew many of its leading players during his frequent visits to the infamous flat at Cranley Mansions in South Kensington, housing at any given time Johnny Byrne, Spike Hawkins and the notorious Thom Keyes. Jenny Fabian remembers the scene in her book *Groupie*:

Spike introduced me to Johnny Byrne and Thom Keyes. Keyes was absolutely unbearable. He treated Johnny and Spike like shit. He treated everyone like shit. As the days went by at Cranley Mansions he became so spaced out on methedrine who knows what was really speaking. He was a real little fuhrer. But it was his place: you couldn't tell him to piss off.

Byrne had met the seventeen years old Keyes in Liverpool through his interest in beatnik literature. 'He was the only beatnik I knew who drove a sports car. He'd come through Christ College, Oxford, and when he came to London he would go to the Casanova Club where he had a gambling account.' Steve Abrams, later to found SOMA (The Society Of Mental Awareness) remembers Patten at Cranley Mansions, and also the film actor David Rook, who 'had lots of beautiful girls around him. And an otter that lived in one of the bath tubs. Cranley Mansions was a completely mad place. When Keyes was at his worst he had a sign up about who could be admitted to the house: there were four people, nobody else. Me, Patten, Roger Vadim and Marlon Brando.'

Keyes, who would die half way up a mountain in Bolivia in 1995, became something of a hero for Patten who remembers the time and the place with some affection. 'I liked Thom a lot. The flat was amazing. It was a bit like an ocean liner full of misfits all adrift on drugs. I never lived there, just stayed over some nights. Thom was pure Hollywood. He should have been born there instead of the outskirts of Liverpool.'

As so often before: his background, his school days, the Liverpool poetry scene, the music scene, Patten also felt 'on the edge' of the 'counter-culture'. 'I was never at ease with it, I never dressed up in hippy clothing for instance.' He was beginning to get to know the area around Holland Park and the Gate, soon moving to Ledbury Road in the (then much shabbier) part of Notting Hill.

McGough was also in London, this time with Scaffold, surprisingly (to some) at the experimental Open Space Theatre run by the iconoclastic Charles Marowitz and Thelma Holt. Still riding high with 'Lily The Pink', the public face of a coin whose other side was double-faceted enough for the trio to perform the *Puny Life Show*, without any musical diversions whatsoever. Tim Rice had worked on 'Lily the Pink' as Norrie Paramour's assistant whilst writing *Joseph and his Technicoloured Dreamcoat*. He still has a receipt from those days: 'Scaffold – Dinner at Speakeasy – £6.16. 6d'. He later produced *Fresh Liver* for them at Richard Branson's studio in Oxfordshire, always naming McGough as one of his favourite poets. McGough's growing reputation caused him to become briefly involved with a lucrative, if uncredited project, inevitably connected with The Beatles.

American company T.V.C. had made the cartoon film of *Yellow Submarine*, but had serious problems with the writing. Originally scripted by a Chicago-based writer, it was re-written by Eric Segal, but was still too American. It needed to be 'Liverpudlianised' – McGough was seen as the man for the job. 'They sounded like good Jewish boys from New York, the language, the jokes, so I had to start all over again.' McGough wrote the beginning of the film, and more interestingly 'The Sea of Monsters' sequence, one of the film's highlights. It was an exciting time for McGough, then much influenced by Paul Ableman whose *Tests* and *Green Julia* were formative regarding many of the elliptical 'two-handers' prevalent at this time. He never saw his 'job' with Scaffold impinging on the poetry. He had been a teacher. This was different; 'more far-reaching more fun', and he felt lucky to be able to do it. But it was still just another job.'It wasn't a question ever of making a choice – it happened to you and it was great – you don't think, shall I make a choice?'

Working on the B.B.C's *The Eleventh Hour* with Scaffold, meant McGough had to write a poem each week about the weekly news. Many of these went into his next collection *Watchwords* and fare least well in a disappointingly slight book that Cape stopped reprinting at McGough's own request in 1983. The exceptions are the family poems 'Snipers' and 'Soil' – in which, almost as a metaphorical afterthought, understated emotional weight is given, when:

> One coldbright April morning
> A handful of you drummed
> On my father's waxworked coffin

the sinister overview asserts:

> we've avoided each other a long time
> and I'm strictly a city man
> anytime to call would be the wrong time
> I'll avoid you as long as I can.

Few of the poems match up to the coherently mosaic narrative and melancholic wit of *Summer with Monika*. 'My Busseductress' falls flat compared to its famous sibling poem, and where the earlier book's flirtations with whimsy are regularly curtailed, 'The Act of Love' is a rare exception in the later collection:

> The Act of Love lies somewhere
> between the belly and the mind
> I lost the love sometime ago
> Now I've only the act to grind.

Fronting The Liverpool Scene was having an adverse effect on Henri's writing too. *Tonight At Noon* revealed a de-mythifier crystallising Henri's personal iconography in which Alfred Jarry and James Ensor would mingle with jazz musicians, artists and friends, and where cultural references would be juxtaposed with Omo packets, supermarkets, the topography of his neighbourhood, fairground souvenirs and the inevitable schoolgirl underwear. *City* however, written mostly on tour with the band as a long journalistic poem, unfortunately generally misses the mark. It is far too pleased with its globetrotting bohemian milieu. The 'room' sequence at the end of part three appears vapid set against Patten's biting intensity in his poem of the same name, much of its itinerant, apostolic nature and sentiment making it an unmissable target for Wendy Cope's later parody 'Strugnell in Liverpool', which is dedicated to 'Allen Ginsberg, Charlie Parker, T.S.Eliot, Paul McCartney, Marcel Proust and all the other great men who have influenced my writing':

> waking early
> listening to
> birdsong watching
> the curtains brighten

like a shirt
washed in Omo
feeling the empty
space beside me
thinking of you

going
up
stairs
again
and
getting
dressed

think-
ing
of
you

With the exception of a North West Association Writers on Tour where Henri met Nell Dunn – leading to their later collaboration *I Want* – 1969 was entirely taken up with the band. 'Bread on the Night' was released by R.C.A, and 'Adrian Henri's Talking after Christmas Blues' – his only poem to come entirely in one block – was published with accompanying music by Turret Books. An early gig in London was a poetry marathon at The Roundhouse in Camden. It was a volatile and typically disorganised gathering of poets and musicians. Charles Causley, an unlikely participant, remembers the sheer presence of Henri at that time. 'He was very strong on stage. And funny.' Causley has further fond recollections of Henri defusing one potentially volatile situation between two pugilistic and drunken poets by imploring them to 'mind the instruments! They're not paid for yet!'

The five-piece, now featuring 'The Entry of Christ into Liverpool' as a performance piece, played the Bath Blues Festival, touring in an old battered van on the same line-up as Led Zeppelin. Andy Roberts remembers Bradford as a favourite gig. 'There was one particular curry house we used to visit that had a weighing-machine and we would regularly weigh Adrian before and after the meal. Sometimes he had actually put on as much as a stone after the meal and his usual ten pints. He was definitely a big lad in those days.'

Henri used both his size and that of the crowd to telling effect in their next gig after the Bath Festival that summer at the first Isle of Wight festival. This marked the return to the country after some years, of Bob Dylan. Sunday 31st August, or 'Dylan Day', ended with 'the voice of the generation' flying back by helicopter to John Lennon's new mansion in Weybridge. It is remembered by Rock archivist and biographer Brian Hinton as 'starting with the Liverpool Scene getting things underway at mid-day with overweight, bearded Liverpool poet Adrian Henri (bounding) about the stage with remarkable energy. "Let's see if we can wake Bob Dylan up from here", he yelled. And he went into a number about an American rock'n'roll group who died when a soda fountain exploded in New York, drowning 200 people in soda ice cream.'

It was easily the biggest gig that The Liverpool Scene had played. 'We did it for £100 which was top money for us then', Andy Roberts recalls, 'it was a very folky line-up – Julie Felix, Tom Paxton and Richie Havens – and we had an early slot. As the crowd was so large, Adrian decided he was going to be even larger. He became incredibly energised, barrelling about the stage, it was a totally outstanding Henri performance.' So much so that the Pathe News film clip of the festival featured The Liverpool Scene almost as if they were the 'second act' on the bill. 'And that was because of Adrian,' Roberts asserts, 'he does have this Mister Showbiz side to him, he goes for it and doesn't care whether he makes a prat of himself or not. It doesn't always come off but more often than not it does.' Mike Evans felt that Henri's strength as a performer in the band was his phrasing. 'He's not a vocalist at all, he can project, but he can't always pitch and can sing out of tune if he's not careful. But because he's been brought up on jazz and rhythm and blues he's got the phrasing and the feel for it, and he makes it work – which is great.'

Working individually with Henri has always been a different experience for Roberts compared to working with McGough and Patten:

> With Roger it's more like a rhythmical punctuation around the words, and with Brian – who is much more ambivalent about music – it's like being handed a piece whole and then having to make something out of it. Even though Adrian's never played anything more than a washboard – it really is like working with a muso, so his pieces become riffs on the words.

Granada T.V. whose programme *Scene at 6.30* actively promoted the poetry scene, gave the band a series of six shows which got them both favourable viewer response and increased visibility, enabling them to work out of Liverpool more often. After the Isle of Wight, they toured America in September. In New York they encountered St Adrian Co, Broadway and 3rd, which Henri based a record sleeve design around, but shortly afterwards things started to go wrong.

A combination of bad management, exploitation and naivety caused the band to return to England with a debt of £5000. They recorded one more disc,

The Liverpool Scene, the last track of which, the twenty-minute long 'Made in the USA', the best thing they ever did. The album was made in three days, a relaxed and unforced fusion between words and music. The band however was disintegrating and it became their least successful record. The only thing that could have kept the Liverpool Scene together was its recognition. It never happened so they had to call it a day. Andy Roberts felt that 'Made in the USA' is one of the best tonal poems ever recorded by a group – largely due to the writing chemistry between Henri and Evans – and still harbours regrets that it never reached the audience it should have done.

The decade was coming to an end. Or rather, wearing thin. In June, nearly half a million people camped in the open air for four days in upstate New York. The Woodstock message through Country Joe and the Fish, rang out loud and clear: 'There ain't no time to wonder why, whoopee, we're all going to die!'

In July, the first men walked on the moon. The Sixties had made it into the future. Harold Wilson's 'white heat of technology' had been forged. Society had been changed 'in one bounding leap'.

Wilson's once favourite group, Scaffold performed at The Royal Gala commemorating the opening of the second Mersey Tunnel, Her Majesty telling McGough that she would love to stay' but simply had to catch [her] train'. 'Why don't you catch the next one?', was the Lennonesque reply.

The trio, at their most raffish by the end of 1969 (even Gorman looked dandified), were in New York playing The Bitter End club. They appeared on a David Frost network spectacular with Diana Rigg, later performing on the Mike Douglas Show in the unlikely company of Douglas Fairbanks Junior. The trip culminated in some hair-raising scenes with groupies at the notorious Chelsea Hotel. Despite such apparent hedonism, times were wearing thin for Scaffold too.

Meanwhile in a studio in North London, the decade's most famous and creative catalysts agreed to temporarily bury their now much heralded differences. The Beatles met in September 1969 at Abbey Road to record together for the last time.

The Seventies

'...nobody's particularly eager to take my albatross...'

The Sixties are sometimes described as 'three guys having the best party in the world, and everyone else trying to find out the address'. January 1970 sat there like the guest who had discovered it all that little bit too late. The carnival was over. All that remained was detritus for those the celebrations had left out. There were violent anti-war protests in Whitehall when B-52s bombed Ho Chi Minh's trail in South Vietnam. In America, U.S. police had to intervene to stop 'bussed' black children being attacked by whites. In Britain, Rolf Harris was top of the charts with 'Two Little Boys', Mick Jagger was fined £200 for possession of cannabis, police raided an exhibition of John Lennon's lithographs in Bond Street, and Ringo Starr recorded 'Sentimental Journey'.

In April The Beatles officially broke up. Two months later, a Conservative government led by Edward Heath was elected. To Philip Larkin, writing to Kingsley Amis , the fall of Harold Wilson, was not 'an important failure':

Fuck the whole lot of them I say, the decimal-loving, nigger-mad, army-cutting, abortion-promoting, murderer-pardoning, daylight-hating ponces, to hell with them, the worst government I can remember.

One of the earliest critics of the Sixties was John Lennon. Talking to *Rolling Stone* in 1970, the years of change and counter-cultural rebellion were seen by him as little more than a fancy-dress parade.'Everyone dressed up but nothing changed.' This view is shared by Brian Patten, who positively acknowledges the social freedom the decade gave him in breaking free from a class system that sought to suppress those it had failed or had been unable to educate. But he could never identify with the hippies and communal living. He loved the beautiful women with flowers in their hair, was glad to have known a further flowering and greater trust in humanity, but felt the sixties became a gigantic clothes-show, where 'some joined in, some sat round the edges, some stole the silver and all left without paying the bill'. As the period wound down he felt its values were as false as its discarded fashions. He saw a future in which communal workshops ended up as listed companies, in which protest songs would be regurgitated as piped muzak and the beads and kaftans relegated to attics where they would become parodic uniforms for future children.

Despite such disclaimers, the beginning of the new decade was a particularly happy period in Patten's life. Shortly before leaving Winchester, he read at Dartington, near Totnes in South Devon, where he met Leonard and Dorothy Elmhurst who had rebuilt in visionary fashion the entire Dartington estate.

After the reading, the Elmhursts asked Patten to stay with them. 'I thought it was this old couple taking me to a little cottage, and it turned out to be this marvellous mansion.' Patten subsequently visited Dartington a great deal, living part of the time in the boathouse at Sharpham, the country estate of the philosopher and philanthropist, Maurice Ash. Here he would write 'One Reason For Sympathy', 'Going Back and Going On', and 'Frogs In The Wood'. It was his first experience of a more elevated, cultured way of life, of which he was to see a great deal more over the forthcoming years.

Living in Ledbury Road near Portobello Market, shortly afterwards, 'twenty-four and dreaming', Patten went to a friend's photography exhibition. It was here that he met Mary Moore.

Daughter of the world famous sculptor Henry Moore, unlike anyone he had met before, she became the most central and in many ways most defining relationship of his life. An only child and a late arrival for the Moores, she was taught to draw by her father before she could read and write. Friends from Cranbourne Chase, the progressive boarding school in Dorset she attended, remember her as full of energy, charismatic, headstrong and something of a leader. Her romance with Patten lasted until 1975. Most of it was spent in Holland Park, one of the smartest parts of London. The couple also stayed at the Moores' family home in Much Hadham and their holiday villa in Tuscany. An infinitely more rarefied world than Wavertree Vale and the cold-water flat in Canning Street, it was mostly a period of reflective contentment for Patten.

His first poem for her, 'Early in the Evening' was soon followed by the poems that went into *The Irrelevant Song* charting the early days of love. His next collection, the stronger *Vanishing Trick* dealt with the end of it. Both books established Patten as a love poet tangled up in the bitterness and unsettling nature of love. The relationship had positive creative benefits for Mary too. Talented and skilled as an artist, she collaborated with Patten in a new area for him, that of children's books. 'Mary got something of a rough ride from some of the other students when she was at college', Patten claims, 'because of who her father was, but she had great natural talent for drawing, and as an illustrator was probably better than Henry.'

Inspired by a toy elephant that he rescued from the River Dart in Devon, Patten published *The Elephant and the Flower*, a story that led to three others, all beautifully illustrated by Mary Moore: *Jumping Mouse, Emma's Doll* and the classic *Mr Moon's Last Case*. Uniquely, the last drawing in *Emma's Doll* is something of a collaboration between both Moores, Henry giving his daughter a deft helping hand in 'tidying up' her original sketch. The broken doll became a metaphor for their partnership which would lead to the stoical irony of a poem such as 'It is Time to Tidy Up Your Life', with Patten accepting that:

You must withdraw your love from that
Which would kill your love.
There is nothing flawless anywhere,
Nothing that has not the power to hurt.
As much as hate, tenderness is the weapon of one
Whose love is neither perfect nor complete.

For Roger McGough 1970 was also incomplete. Scaffold's hits had dried up.
Lacking direction and short of fresh stimulus, internal friction was creeping in.
They had recorded *Fresh Liver* on Island Records, which met with mixed
success. The criticism was mild compared to their next and last L.P. *Sold Out.*
In an interview with Tom Davis, McGough went some way to combat this.
'People don't expect us to change – Scaffold make funny songs and poetry
records, they therefore should always do this. I suppose the sound has held us
back as writers by being so successful.'

His present concerns, the ending of one chapter and possible opening of
another, combined with his quixotic nature: cautious and religious, yet
adventurous and controversial were oscillating in the poems that would form
After the Merrymaking.

In 'On having no one to write a love poem about' the image of a rose in a litter
bin inside his head makes him wait to give it to the first girl who smiles at him:

it's getting dark
and i'm still waiting
The rose attracts a fly

   getting dark
two groupies and a dumb broad
have been the only passersby

      dark
i chance a prayer
There is a smell of tinsel in the air.

The tinsel turned to confetti, when after years of to-ing and fro-ing, McGough
and Thelma finally got married. The wedding was in a registry office and
therefore not officially recognised by the Roman Catholic Church. In some
ways it was never 'officially' recognised by McGough either.

For the atheist Adrian Henri things were looking good at the beginning of the
new decade. Within months his life could have been subtitled, 'Four Deaths and
a Heart-Attack'.

64 Canning Street had been the Henri's home since early 1963. Originally owned by Don McKinlay's mother, it was where Allen Ginsberg, Ted Joans and Robert Creeley had all stayed, and a place where Mike Evans, Mike Hart, Maurice Cockrill, Andy Roberts and Roger McGough had at one time or another all laid more than their hats. Maurice Cockrill remembers McGough's room as being easily the tidiest.

Roger has always been Mr Nice Guy, always impeccable, always neat and tidy. If he had a problem – and he had plenty around that time – he would always make light of it. That Liverpool thing of not allowing any public suffering. Roger could always see some funny angle and would never unload it on to anyone else.

The Henris' had the whole of the top floor as a flat/studio where Joyce would cook her 'potatoes with everything' meals. The standard of the cuisine fell when she moved out in 1968.

Due to the nature of the occupants and the various comings and goings, the house became increasingly chaotic. Maurice Cockrill inherited Mike Hart's old room. 'Mike had wrecked it completely, he'd painted it all pink with a roller on everything – the chairs, the cupboards, the lot! But I was going through a bit of bad phase myself and one night in a drunken rage really trashed it. I always remember Mike Evans saying 'the way Harty left that room looked like Habitat compared to the way it looks now'.

Henri, who fondly recalls Mike Hart's pink footsteps on the landing, concurs:

There was something about that room. Bad kharma maybe – definitely something. I remember Sue Sterne and I having to wait in the hall for over an hour one night until Maurice decided there was nothing left he wanted to throw out.

Cockrill later moved to Huskisson Street, his parting shot, making a huge snowball, covering it in bright blue powder paint – Yves Klein style – and leaving it outside the front door. 'Maurice always had a good sense of imagery', Henri acknowledges.

Despite the anarchy and camaraderie, Henri was becoming increasingly disenchanted with 64 Canning Street. He wanted a place that could truly be called his own. Looking around, he chanced upon 21 Mount Street.

Situated north of Chinatown, opposite the Institute School, joining Hope Street and parallel with Rice Street where Ye Cracke is still situated, Mount Street is both central and inviolate. Having done the initial negotiations, Sue Sterne completed the move whilst Henri was touring in the States.

On May 13th 1970, Henri's maternal grandfather Albert Johnson, whose gleaming black boots and shiny silver watch chain were such vivid images for him as a boy, and whose allotment he used to visit regularly, died in squalid circumstances at 17 Sydney Buildings in Birkenhead. Three days later, his wife Frances, a long-time invalid, followed.

Henri was to write dramatically about visiting them shortly before they were hospitalized, a photograph of the house taken by Sue Sterne, becoming the cover of *Autobiography* published in 1971. His mother Emma, suffering from heart problems for years, and irrevocably shocked by the nature of her own parents' demise, died herself within less than a month. Arthur Henri who had participated so actively during the family celebrations of November 1968, having relied so much on Emma, went to live with his daughter Christine in Cheshire. 'And he seemed to be alright for a while', Henri felt, 'then suddenly another phone-call.'

Henri's world was falling apart. The loss of his immediate family compounded by the break-up of the band left him feeling empty, low and hurt. Having painted nothing and written little other than material for the band, his three-year investment hardly seemed to amount to very much. Never short of self-belief, some seeds of doubt crept in as he started to question for the first time every move he had made since leaving the school he began teaching at in Preston.

Worse was to follow. Having toured Norway with *Henri and Friends*, he went to the Edinburgh Festival in August, where it soon became apparent by his constant struggling for breath that something was seriously wrong. He was advised to see a doctor, who told him, 'you're going to go straight to bed, and you don't get up until I tell you.'

Seriously overweight, he had had a mild heart attack. Jumping off stages, and drinking twelve pints of beer every night had taken their toll. He needed absolute rest, no drink, restricted liquids, a very strict diet and medication. He was told that on no condition was he to go out of the house for six months. For someone so sociable this was difficult. No longer a 'Rock and Roll star', he had to learn to become housebound. It was time to take stock and reflect.

Thanks largely to Susan Sterne's supportiveness, his family and friends, radio messages from D.J's such as John Peel and Bob Harris, and his own determination to lose at least five stone, he pulled through. In the poems that would make up *Autobiography* a dichotomy emerged that would reappear in future work. The essence of the book was a personal and at times guilt-ridden reaction to the changing times. It also drew a line under everything he had done before, becoming a turning point and a fresh start. Originally meant as a political book, the only way he could write it was about me and my inability to [be that political], and say in very forceful terms just what I meant. There's only a bit of the book that's left from the original intention. I'm a very political person, so it does come out, but only obliquely.

Adrian Mitchell, when asked if he felt the Liverpool poets had 'sold out' responded in characteristic terms:

It's not a question of selling out. I usually associate that with politics and it's not as if Adrian, Roger and Brian started off as political poets. Except they were against the bomb like the rest of us. They've always been more concerned with entertainment. Entertainment is a good thing. I wish they were much more political but they're not and that's that.

Picking up on this in *Conversations with Poets*, some months later, Tom Davis put it to a more sombre-looking Henri, that the choice facing him can only be two-fold: be commercial and reach a lot of people, or be a mandarin in a movement and maintain your integrity. Henri rebuffs this 'unforgivable English sin' of popularity by saying that there's no good reason why you can't do both. 'It's difficult, but that's no reason not to try. I'm not prepared to aim at doing anything less.'

Opening with the sad visit to Sydney Buildings, *Autobiography* is in four parts: the early years, portraits of his family, his student and early teaching years, a poem for Liverpool 8, and his move to Liverpool. There is the pivotal 'A Poem for Summer 1967' and pieces about the summer of 1970 and his relationship with Sue Sterne. It is an approachable, benevolent and generous book. If not carrying the attack of *Tonight At Noon*, it happily steers clear of the excesses and repetitions that undercut the energy of *City*. Concluding ruminatively, Henri reflects on the biggest influence of his life, his ever-supportive mother Emma:

after the empty years between
suddenly given
the literary
lion's share
but who
to share it with?

ending with a silence of a very different kind:

the lion sleeps
confused, exhausted.
the dark outside echoes to his cries.

After The Merrymaking also represents a similarly timely return to form for McGough. Without recapturing the fizz of *Summer With Monika*, the collection reasserts McGough's skill at making words do what he wants with them. The ingenious 'tennis poem', '40-Love', a staple part of many live readings, and the audaciously theatrical 'The Newly Pressed Suit' combine idiosyncratically in the pervading mood of love and infidelity: the end of the revelling, the passing of time. In a typically disquieting but more sepulchral image the speaker in 'Head Injury' whose eyes bob like 'dead birds in a watertank' tries to say:

...Have pity on me, pity on yourself
Put a bullet between the birds.
But instead can only gurgle:
You kiss me then walk out of the room.
I see your back.
I feel a colour coming on, mottled, mainly black.

As Linda Cookson points out in her study of Brian Patten, (published by the British Council in 1997), the early seventies, from *The Irrelevant Song* (1971) to its successor *Vanishing Trick* (1976) represent his most sustained achievement as a love poet. With both his earlier collections in their fourth and fifth impressions, *The Irrelevant Song* sees the beginning of Patten's highly resilient line, that both avoids obscurity and gives his images clarity and purpose centred around poems such as 'The Wrong Poem' all too aware of the 'temporary' nature of love. The collection also has a number of notable poems that stray from this theme. 'Interruption at the Opera House' was later performed by the great mime-artist Lindsay Kemp, and 'Albatross Ramble' became a hilarious vehicle for Patten himself at future gigs with the all-purpose band Grimms:

I rush into the corridor and shout:
'Does anyone own an albatross? Has anyone lost it?
There's an albatross in my room!'
I'm met by an awkward silence.

It also marks the beginning of Patten's cynicism about the intelligentsia. During his time with Mary Moore he was often in the company of people he describes as 'lords and ladies of politics' and was rarely comfortable:

I wasn't sure it was the place I wanted to be. Mary was much stronger than me but neither of us where what you'd call socialites. We'd just flit in and out of it all. Mary was always her own woman with some very strong views to match.

Brian Patten got on well with Henry Moore who found the Liverpool poet a refreshing change from some of his daughter's previous boyfriends, identifying perhaps with his own northern working-class roots.

Patten also briefly became friendly with David Hockney just before the artist left for America. He would often visit him at his studio fascinated by the way Hockney would arrange and rearrange his famous and fashionable sitters. During this period he and Mary would holiday in Italy attending the decadent festivals at Spoleto where weirdness was carried to the utmost extreme. Picking up on this perhaps in 'The Literary Gathering', Patten himself became

Like a dumb canary let out of its cage
I'd found another cage.
It did not suit me.
In my beak the invitations melted.

Wanting 'to explain away any song' he felt a growing identification with other poets, who, to paraphrase Christopher Logue, 'were all one poet – just as all wars are one war'. Some he knew personally: Robert Graves, Pablo Neruda and, perhaps most like-minded of all, Stevie Smith. Patten once confided his fear of flying to Stevie, who responded 'It's not the flying that's the problem Brian, it's the landing'. Like Robert Frost whom Patten has always regarded as a stabilising influence, Smith became one of a select group of poets to command a special place in his heart. Not all peers admired her, Stephen Spender letting it be known to Patten that he felt her work was frivolous, bordering on doggerel. In response, Patten asked 'who can quote a line of Stephen Spender's?'

Flying in the charts with Scaffold at the end of the sixties had been 'Urban Spaceman' by the equally eccentric Bonzo-Dog Doo-Dah Band. Featuring Neil Innes, Legs Larry Smith and Vivian Stanshall, they met Scaffold on Top of the Pops, hit it off, and ended up doing a show together at The Dome in Brighton. McGough remembers it as a happy occasion:

They were great, they had some of the things we didn't because they were musicians, but we had the same sort of interests and the same wackyness, and it seemed common sense to do some things together. We decided to form this group called Grimms: Gorman, Roberts, Innes, McGough, McGear and Stanshall.

After Scaffold, McGough found Grimms a great relief. He particularly enjoyed working with Neil Innes, who looks back fondly on the fusion: 'I don't know what attracted the Scaffold to the Bonzos; we were incredibly anarchic which was something probably shared by the Scaffold as well. Hence Grimms, this leap in the dark.'

Musicians Zoot Money and Mike Giles joined them for their first gig in Corby in Lincolnshire. A second booking soon followed at Greenwich Town Hall with Keith Moon from The Who guesting on drums. A tour was arranged adding a slimmed down rejuvenated Adrian Henri, and surprisingly, Brian

Patten who felt: 'I joined Grimms because maybe I just wanted to get out of the house for a bit. I'd been on my own too long. Maybe I just wanted to get back in with the lads.'

Their manager John Gledhill remembers Grimms as being 'the good old days when everybody was in it. There were about a dozen people on stage. It was a very looseknit show; it got slicker later on.' McGough understood comedy, having honed his observations skilfully and economically; Grimms was tailor-made for him. For Henri too it was something of a godsend, although disenchantment set in as it became increasingly London-based, but it did get him back into music and touring.

'The three of them', remembers Neil Innes, 'mixed up with the nonsense music we used to do and John Gorman's clowning made for a really good evening. None of us knew what was going to happen, we didn't know whether comedy, music and poetry would sit together. But it did. Especially with a pint of beer in your hand.'

Andy Roberts takes a slightly different view, feeling that with so many front-liners it was impossible to keep it going on a regular basis, and was never wholly satisfying for anyone:

It was hopeless, for example, to expect Brian Patten to get involved with a show where he was only on stage for a quarter of an hour and having to match up to some very high-powered music on the one hand and some very up-front humour on the other.

Patten also had to cope with the increasingly out-of-it Viv Stanshall (around only for the earliest shows) throwing beer cans at him from the wings. Grimms suffered at times from having too many chiefs. On good nights it was mould-breaking, on bad ones, shambolic. It was nothing if not varied, and at times a contender for one of the most seriously 'dumbed-down' adult shows ever to hit the road. Given Patten's ambivalence to music – which Roberts feels is due to the amount of music already within the poetry – the guitarist recalls the poet in direct counterpoise to this:

Brian was great in some of the sketches, particularly the side-stepping pig sequence with John Gorman playing the part of the pig. He also came up with some brilliant theatrical allusions similar at times to Marcel Marceau. Brian does have a very strong sense of theatre. He would come on in white-face as an introduction to the show and once wore this 'Brian Patten wig' he'd found which he would pull off – not quite as vicious as the thinking behind 'The Right Mask' – but pulling off his own hair – it was very effective.

Patten was starting to discover what would become his real performing forte. His voice had always been unusual and distinctive, now it was taking on an air of both other-worldliness and authority. He was beginning to crack it now as far as readings were concerned, so much so that his contributions on Grimms albums such as 'Albatross Ramble' stand out as highlights in an increasingly extempore set:

> I didn't just read poems in Grimms, I helped create the shape for it as well. Often I would begin it or create the structure of the show. I had stories that were enacted out by John Gorman, or mimed by Lindsay Kemp when he joined us occasionally.

Grimms was a personal breakthrough for Patten who had always less at ease with mixed performance. Hearing him on the records is hearing him purge his personal devils, communicating to audiences with what Peter Porter later called 'that little touch of moonlight'. In his stoned-sounding introduction to 'Albatross Ramble', Patten almost toys with the audience:

> This is dedicated to everybody who's ever woke up in the morning... and it's called 'Albatross Ramble'... and it's about waking up in the morning... almost a black comedy.

Patten then gives vent to the voice Adrian Mitchell describes as having 'all the colours of a melancholic alto sax'. He laughingly interrupts himself on 'nobody's particularly eager to take my albatross' with 'an absurd line, never mind', milking the pause after 'I'm met with an awkward silence' with an audacity that Noel Coward may have approved.

Grimms produced three albums, the third, *Rockin' Duck*, far less self-conscious than its predecessors, demonstrating thematic control and fusion, a belated taster of what might have been. Musical highlights include Andy Roberts' sublime 'Songs of the Stars' and one of McGough and McGear's best songs, the powerful 'Take It While You Can'. The humour, too, sounds less in a time warp when McGough is to the fore, most notably in his 'sound effects' piece 'FX' ('in his mind's eye he saw the thing coming towards him / half man, half beast, half pissed'). After three years of touring – mostly on university campuses – Grimms broke up. Henri was the first to leave, then Mike McGear dropped out – literally – after a fight with Patten on the tour bus in Manchester. The two never got on according to McGough: 'Brian was always getting at Mike, and Mike was always getting at Brian. Then one day Brian just let him have one.'

In March 1973, *The Oxford Book of Twentieth Century English Verse*, edited by Philip Larkin was published. As Larkin expected, it caused a storm of controversy. He had set out to produce an anthology of poems rather than poets, celebrating the large emotions which can erupt in ordinary lives, and the small ones which can become tumultous in their own way. In *A Writer's Life*, his fine biography of Larkin, Andrew Motion highlights the 'virtues' Larkin wanted to affirm: truthfulness, lack of pretension, traditional formal skills, attitudes which help us both to enjoy and endure. Rank invention, references to other writers, technical high jinks, obscurity: these are the vices he wished to exclude. In his short introduction, Larkin concludes that in making his selection, he felt material fell into three groups:

> Poems representing aspects of the talents of poets judged either by the age or by myself to be worthy of inclusion, poems judged by me to be worthy of inclusion without reference to their authors, and poems judged by me to carry with them something of the century in which they were written'.

The poet Fred Grubb quarrels slightly with this assessment, feeling Larkin's real aim was to create a picture of a century. 'A sort of historical panorama reflecting its moods and occasions, rather than value-judgments of poets by amount of selection or inclusion.'

When the book appeared on March 29th, only a few positive views (Auden and Betjeman) were aired, although Martin Bell defended it in comparison with what he felt was Yeats's bizarre earlier effort. Donald Davie in *The Listener* was particularly hostile. Larkin, according to Davie had showed 'positive cynicism', misrepresented Modernism, and produced 'the perverse triumph of philistinism, the cult of the amateur, the wrong kind of post-modernism, the weakest kind of Englishry.' Under the heading 'Larkin's Choice', Davie particularly challenges Brian Patten's inclusion in the anthology. 'Portrait of a Young Girl Raped at a Suburban Party' was quoted in full, with the following comment:

> That's it. That's the poem. At no point, by not one of the many ways available has imagination entered, penetrated, opened up, transformed...
> How Patten got to the point of thinking this sort of thing is a poem is a good and appalling question.

Initially daunted, Larkin, realising he had supporters as well as detractors, started to enjoy the clamour. He wrote to Patten: 'ignore them. The scissor-men (a veiled reference from 'Ode on Celestial Music') – are everywhere.' Larkin wrote off the reviewers as jealous or unperceptive time-servers, taking great pleasure from the letters he got from total strangers saying how much they liked the book. 'Davie does seem to be dancing up and down rather', he wrote to Martin Bell. 'I hope he isn't going off his chump.' Larkin continued his Davie-mockery, sending Kingsley Amis the following ditty in 1976:

Davie, Davie, give me a bad review,
That's your gravy, telling chaps what to do.
Forget about style and passion
As long as it's the fashion –
But let's be fair, it's got you a Chair
Which was all it was meant to do.

Notable amongst those omitted were David Jones, Seamus Heaney (which seems incredible) and John Fuller. Fuller was later to say that he 'didn't mind being left out but Larkin had Roger McGough!' It is arguable that McGough was Larkin's personal favourite of 'the Liverpool Lads'. The two poems chosen however do him few favours. 'If Life's a Lousy Picture, Why Not Leave Before the End' did not even make McGough's Selected, and 'My Cat and I' is a good example of the fey whimsy so often levelled at him. Henri's 'Mrs Albion You've Got A Lovely Daughter' identifies the period in which it was written to far greater effect. How seriously Larkin took them is open to debate. Some 'in the know' say hardly at all. But who is 'in the know' when it comes to Larkin? He did admit later that the last thirty pages of the book in which they were included with such notables as Derek Walcott, P.J. Kavanagh, Peter Redgrove and, ironically, Douglas Dunn – who takes a swipe in his poem 'The Clothes Pit' – 'were not impressive'. This (to Larkin) confirmed his argument: the influence of the modernists had been a bad one.

Larkin's argument against the modernists had been expressed, not to say overstated, three years earlier in *All What Jazz*, a collection of his jazz reviews. Pound, Charlie Parker and Picasso – 'the mad lads' – he insisted, had destroyed art's traditional broad 'pleasure-seeking' audience.

This point however seems lost on Peter Porter whose distaste for poetry audiences is apparent in a rather patronising recorded conversation, 'the Poet in the Sixties: Vices and Virtues', in Grevel Lindop's *British Poetry Since 1960* published in 1972:

> I've found that the only really popular style of poetry is the Liverpool cabaret type poetry. That goes down pretty well. There's a tremendous fondness for anything soft and squashy.

Lindop himself in the same book naively takes exception to a remark made by Henri concerning the part an audience can play in the organisation of poetry. Lindop's chapter 'Poetry, Rhetoric and the Mass Audience: The Case of the Liverpool Poets' does however, perceptively contrast the reading styles of Patten and McGough:

> McGough's style is very attractive... 'his act' is meticulously controlled: the moods of the poems are carefully varied, McGough keeping an entirely straight face through even the most comic ones. Patten on the

other hand seems both more spontaneous and less relaxed. He appears moody, even inarticulate between poems, and the audience is excited, probably, not only by the enormous passion with which he reads (or rather intones or chants) his poems but also by the suspicion that at any moment he may be going to pick a quarrel with someone.

Henry Graham, more sceptical even than Patten of the Liverpool Poet tag, in what Yankel Feather had christened his disdainful 'high presbyterian way' had nonetheless also been active in the poetry world, publishing *Good Luck To You Kafka / You' ll Need It Boss* with Rapp & Whiting. The collection was generally well reviewed. Discussing his second book *Passport To Earth*, the poet Edwin Brock stated how Graham's poetry 'differs from the others by coming out of his head and being a good deal more subtle than Ee-Aye-Adio'.

The years 1972 to 1975 were crammed with a series of small tours, residencies, publications and events for the three writers, local humorist Peter O'Halligan capturing some of the mood and flavour of 1973's Edinburgh Festival in an article for *The Liverpool Echo*:

Adrian Henri was there. He'd been out shopping and bought a pair of rainbow coloured woollen trousers, watched by a girl called Frances dressed in a school blazer and looking as if she had just stepped out of one of his early poems. Roger McGough was clutching his latest book *Gig* – 'it's not out until October – about a super-group on the road, the groupies, wild parties, sex – all that kind of stuff.'

Brian Patten was reading at The Traverse Theatre bar in the afternoon, and wouldn't hear of having his photograph taken. 'I don't want you making money out of me', he stormed. 'He's a very nervous person', an admiring female fan from Holland Park explained. Patten said I could take a picture in the evening when Mary arrived.

O'Halligan shared the attic in 32 Canning Street with Patten in the early sixties, remembering the intensity with which Patten went about his writing, insisting even then that he was not writing poems 'for future critics to fondle'.

Back at base Henri had become President of the Liverpool Academy of Arts. He later toured with various musicians, undertook a residency in Coventry and further reading tours in America and Canada. In 1972 Cape had published *I Want*, his collaboration with Nell Dunn. Describing a love affair that lasted over fifty years, and written in the voices of Albert Hodgkin and Dolly Argyle – although at times clearly self-referential, the book is tender and harmonious, with Henri demonstrating a sympathetic ear for dialogue and competence as a prose writer. That same year he won £2000 in the John Moores Exhibition for the first in a series of paintings of meat. *Autobiography Part 1* was dramatised by the B.B.C., followed by *Yesterday's Girl*, a play for Granada.

The relationships that have filled his life were becoming increasingly crammed and complicated. Susan Sterne had been having such a bad time at the Art College that she took up photography. She felt that she could not always offer herself as a continually supportive companion to someone whose artistic intentions and achievements were so constant and diverse. 'Somehow she would never let herself do things', Henri stated. 'There were fights because she felt I was shoving her into things, even if it was her own one-woman show'. Their artistic differences gradually made the relationship unsustainable,'we slowly grew apart so she moved out. And Frances moved in.'

Frances Hambidge was one of the few scholarship pupils at the prestigious Howells School for Girls in Denbigh.Talented, determined and impressionable she became smitten with Adrian Henri after he had done a reading and talk at the school. After much goading and some encouragement from her friends she plucked up enough courage to write to him. They began meeting and corresponding for eighteen months until Frances came to Liverpool University to study philosophy. John Willett, who got to know all Henri's girlfriends on various holidays to his home in Normandy, describes Frances as 'bright as paint, she should have become the first woman football commentator, such was her knowledge of the sport'. Soon she was living with Henri in Mount Street, a somewhat delicate situation further complicated a year later by the powerful presence of another student with whom Henri had been corresponding on the same course.

For someone so urban, the early seventies found Adrian Henri in surprisingly bucolic surroundings. Invited to spend the summer in a cottage owned by writer and lecturer Derek Anderton, Henri, with his £2000 prize money, had both the time and the means to accept, thus discovering the Shropshire village of Much Wenlock. One morning, whilst walking with Frances after a hangover, he made another discovery – a hedge. Writing in July 1973, Henri says:

> In the 1930s the Surrealists cultivated certain 'magic' places. When I went to stay in Much Wenlock I was expecting to find something there: I didn't know what. What I found was a deep hedge along a disused railway cutting. This very ordinary bit of English hedgerow has occupied my time ever since. I've tried to make the painting as botanically accurate as possible; like my earlier meat paintings they are not 'composed' and could be (and in many cases are) carried on laterally on another canvas.

An artist constantly at the mercy of his own creation, Henri has always been fiercely deterministic and uninfluenced by tradition. Having taken on areas he had so vilified in the fifties and sixties, he found a fresh leitmotif, a new direction, making common cause with the writings of A.E.Housman and the Victorian paintings of William Davis.

In a letter to Davis, referring to his 'Corner of a Cornfield', John Ruskin had said, 'it seems to me you might have sought over more landscapes for miles together, and not stumbled over anything so little rewarding...as that ditch and wheat field'. So as Henri walked out one morning, he 'stumbled' across this hedge in Wenlock and thought 'I want to paint that'.

The mid-seventies, a fallow period for his painting, culminated in the beautiful *Homage to William Davis*. Henri particularly liked the startlingly modern and uncomposed nature of the Liverpool artist so admired by Ruskin. Starting from studies of Ashfield Hall Gardens in Much Wenlock, he was not only signifying the potency of gardens and hedgerows – as Davis had done with ditches and wheatfields – but moreover was consciously attempting to recreate that shallow sensual space so honoured in the past by the Pre-Raphaelites. Taking on landscape meant taking on the whole tradition that goes with it, Henri's paintings in the seventies entering what George Melly referred to as his 'big seed-packet' period, buying one himself twenty years after his first purchase with Mary the flower-seller's daughter. If his work was becoming more orthodox, Henri's personal life was not.

Carol Ann Duffy was born in Glasgow in 1955 and grew up in Stafford. From the age of fifteen she knew she wanted to be a poet, and sent poems to Bernard Stone at Turret Books who gave her generous early encouragement. Having met Henri after a Grimms gig in 1971, she corresponded actively with him before being accepted at Liverpool University to study philosophy. As Frances Hambidge was still in Henri's life, things were strained to say the least but gradually – as the two women became drinking buddies, then friends – an amicable arrangement ensued. This 'menage-a-trois' horrified Arthur Ballard but amused most of Henri's other associates in Liverpool 8, now centring on The Grapes in Egerton Street with its flamboyant landlord John Meakins. Despite her youth, Carol Ann's direct, combative and highly charged personality meant that she fitted in immediately. She had a profound effect on Henri:

> I've always had this tendency to over-intellectualise – the working class guy showing off his learning – so whenever I meet someone like Brian or Heather or Carol Ann who seem to arrive fully-formed, their spontaneity acts as a corrective to what I do. She was obviously talented, and was always going to make it as soon as she found the right direction.

Carol Ann happily replaced Frances Hambidge in Henri's affections, learning a great deal from him about creativity itself; how to live the life of an artist on the developing reading circuit, and how to deal with pressures and survive. They shared a great deal of art together during the seventies. Once Duffy did find her own direction towards the end of the decade she became one of the defining voices of her generation. Comparing her favourably with Larkin, Vernon Scannell would later describe her as having that 'rare ability to modulate from the rough demotic to a language of lyric intensity'. Her rise in the poetry world throughout the eighties would prove unstoppable. Like Henri's other girlfriends, she became a great friend of John Willett's, who claims he owes her his life after a Sunday outing to the mouth of the Somme:

Stunned by lunch I became unbelievably sleepy which of course affected my driving, but Carol Ann kept me awake by continually talking about her childhood in Glasgow and we were all able to make it home.

It was during this fertile period in his career that Henri first tutored at the Arvon Foundation at Totleigh Barton in Devon. Set up by John Moat and John Fairfax, who after working with fifteen school children at the Beaford Centre in 1968, chanced upon a pattern of creative learning and living that they felt had to be pursued. The thatched farmhouse and surroundings at Totleigh Barton proved favourable to their ideals, 'the Arvon experience' subsequently changing many lives. Henri has been one of its longest serving tutors finding similar sensory images around the River Torridge to those he had experienced in the hinterland of Much Wenlock in Shropshire.

His work has never laid claim to any central diktat or dogmatic attitude. His move to Liverpool itself in 1957 was random and spur of the moment, the tutelage he received from the wideboys at Rhyl Fairground as equally formative as Richard Hamilton's artistic concerns and innovations at Durham University. Flying in the face of cultural supremacism he has constantly allowed the element of chance to dictate the next move. Occasionally his subversive twists and turns have meant lost compasses and blind alleys, but this has never deterred him from venturing into areas previously unmapped.

Following a tour of Germany with McGough and Patten where they were billed as 'The Little Poor Poets' there followed a reunion reading in Liverpool to a packed audience of 500 people in St George's Hall. For those present the most memorable moment was arguably when Patten streaked across the stage to add 'some point' to a love poem that Henri was reading.

'If we are being honest with our words', an unrepentant Patten said later, 'it seems to me that we should be honest with our bodies.' Asked why he left early,

Patten replied, 'I didn't really want to hang around too long because I was only wearing a pair of boots.'

Discounting streakers, Henri's serendipitous career is perhaps best exemplified during the years 1973-1979. Often in partnership with Carol Ann Duffy, he embarked on a multiplicity of mixed-media events, commissions and assignments. Even at his most paradoxical, when easy associations were at times denied, his unrelenting 'popular modernist' crusade meant inclusiveness was the essential value, audience always the governing criteria.

The art historian Peter Davies in his section on Henri in *Liverpool Seen* was at pains to point out his 'open-ended response to culture in its broadest guises, [continually avoiding] 'the pitfalls of precious formalism and both academic and avant garde convention.' Edward Lucie-Smith takes a similar view, seeing him as provincial and international but not metropolitan, shrewdly picking up on Henri's continual knack of going over the heads of 'the great and the good':

He takes supposedly difficult and esoteric concepts, and turns them into common currency. The people who remain baffled are (those) who regard it as their task to analyse the modernist achievement, then to filter the approved components out to the mass.

George Melly has compared his collages to the great German Dadaist Kurt Schwitters in their use of discarded detritus and his instinct for composition and found imagery. In an art review of this period Henri declared that 'Happenings consist of what you couldn't stick to a canvas – people, smells, perishable objects, places', and that 'poetry consists for me of a means to say something that would be impossible to paint'. Thames and Hudson published *Environments and Happenings* launched at Claude Gill Books in Oxford Street, with 'Window Event', featuring at least two former lovers and something of a passing influence from Mark Boyle.

Still felt by many to be 'the poet of the three' (irritatingly so for McGough and Henri), Brian Patten had appeared at the 'Poetry Gala' at the Royal Festival Hall in February 1969 with Basil Bunting, Ted Hughes, Christopher Logue and Stevie Smith. He found himself in equally auspicious company at the same venue in May 1972. The Poetry Consortium – an unlikely alliance between the Poetry Society, the Greater London Arts Association, the London Poetry Secretariat and the National Book League – were staging 'A Festival Of Poetry with Music'. This event included Patten and Adrian Mitchell reading with Stephen Spender and Pablo Neruda, music coming from the folk group Lindisfarne. Several of the audience heckled Neruda, shouting abuse of a political nature at him until one was struck forcibly with a shoe.

Heinz Henghes, the sculptor in Winchester to whom Patten dedicated *Grave Gossip*, visited him in London shortly before he prematurely died. Patten would later write about Henghes in 'Friends' and 'The Last Gift', Patten's answer to Henghes question about the meaning of *Jumping Mouse* forming the epigraph of the later poem:

> Patten: '[It's] about a mouse that gets eaten by an eagle.'
> Henghes: 'Poor mouse.'
> Patten: 'No, the mouse becomes part of the eagle.'
> Henghes: 'Lucky mouse. Perhaps I'll be that lucky.'

Derived from an Indian folk-tale *Jumping Mouse* is set in a magical animal world, and is described by Charles Causley as a 'small masterpiece'. Encouraged by this success Patten began work on what was to become one of his most acclaimed works, the award-winning children's novel *Mr Moon's Last Case*.

Set in fictional Steelborough, clearly evoking the gaslit fifties streets of his childhood, the story interweaves between allusion and narrative with freshness, vivacity and a coruscating edge. It tells of an ex-policeman, Mr Moon, about whom Patten found he knew less and less as the book progressed. Woven seamlessly into the text is Mr Moon's dogged and well intentioned pursuit of Nameon, a dwarf in search of his own real world. In the preface Patten brings to light a newspaper account of a leprechaun sighting in a Liverpool park:

> Within twenty-four hours [it] had spread like wildfire, the park in question besieged by over two thousand children. A sports match was cancelled, fights broke out, a first-aid tent doubled as a base for lost children, traffic round the park was thrown into chaos, and dozens of policemen and members of the St John Ambulance Brigade spent hours trying to cope with the situation. Although they succeeded in clearing the park, they could not convince the children that the leprechaun did not exist.

His belief in the probability, if not the certainty of, another world is prefigured by an account of an older boy in his street continually interrupting other children's imaginative games, trying to convice them that the only world they would ever know was the one in which they existed. Patten watched the boy become increasingly ostracised, staggering between two worlds, but 'wished him no luck whatsoever' as he had caused him to question the creatures of his imagination. That iconic place of his alternative childhood world, the Magnet Cinema, introduced to him by Lizzy Graham (to whom the book is dedicated), is re-imagined in Steelborough. Other locations are further afield. Typically in Patten's shoreless spectrum, Norton Bay is based on Seaton Carew in the north-east, where in January 1974 freak tides revealed prehistoric forests and other strange archeaological finds under ancient peat beds. All much closer to 'Frieda's Room' and the domain of what may or may not be uncovered.

The book received a special award from the Mystery Writers of America Guild in 1977. With at times a staccato simplicity, both melancholic and absurd, the worlds of imagination and discovery were described by Margery Fisher in *Growing Point* as pictorialising in prose what is 'always exact and reverberant'. Creatively Patten was going from strength to strength. The Everyman Theatre in Liverpool premiered his children's play *The Pig and the Junkle*. He recorded an L.P. with the jazz singer Cleo Laine, and with greater intensity and conviction than ever was finishing the collection of poems that would establish his reputation even further.

Roger McGough, too, felt something fruitful for his writing had arrived as the seventies struggled to replicate the good times of the previous decade. Performing much less, he had been awarded a Poetry Fellowship at Loughborough University. He told Tom Davis:

> I write every day and revise everything. I hadn't used to, I think I'm more conscientious now than when I first started writing. The Loughborough Fellowship is very useful because it means I can have long periods to be alone and write.

Cape had published *Gig*, his fourth single collection in six years, a book largely based on notes McGough had made whilst on the road. The title proved to be something of a misnomer. Few of the poems were about life in a band, although a sense of being on tour does come across in the poems about towns: Huddersfield, Cardiff – 'Sure as eggs / is eggs is eggs is eggs is eggs' – and Bradford, but the slightness that marred *Watchwords* was again apparent. 'Out of Sequence' has the unblinkered integrity he would be so true to in later collections, but although much of McGough's wit and ingenuity is visible in the syntax of the 'shu f f f ling' eggs in 'the failed reveller', opening lines such as 'lying in bed of a weekday morning' merely irritate. On reflection, the best thing that can be said about *Gig* is that it contains one of the best poems he has ever written, and one not picked up on in generally poor reviews.

McGough spent a long time working on 'The Identification', but given his playwright's ear for various imagined states and voices, he had the nervous formality of the speaker's voice immediately:

> So you think it's Stephen?
> Then I'd best make sure
> Be on the safe side as it were.

Based on the bombing of the Abercorn restaurant in Belfast, where many children were killed, McGough was moved by a father being interviewed after identifying his son. Amazingly, the great American poet Robert Lowell had drafted something from the same identification, but never published it. On the same page of McGough's original draft is an early version of the playfully erotic 'Framed' published nearly ten years later and a very simple ditty, illustrative of the many-mindedness of his writing. For three stanzas 'The Identification' reads like an inventory of schoolboy's things: sweater, scoutbelt, handkerchief; then the mood changes pushing the narrative forward with a minimum of fuss:

...Cigarettes?
Oh this can't be Stephen.
I don't allow him to smoke you see.
He wouldn't disobey me. Not his father.

But the penknife and the key on the keyring were his, so it must have been him. The tone then becomes confessional, and in language that both reveals and hides, prompts a form of apostasy:

I think I know what happened
...about the cigarettes.
No doubt he was minding them
for one of the older boys.
Yes that's it
That's him.
That's our Stephen.

The long periods 'to be alone and write' were not totally realised at Loughborough. The donnish oasis was in reality yet another place to get to in an already overcrowded life. Still in both Grimms and Scaffold, working as a presenter for Yorkshire Television's children's programme *Focus*, with his home-life in disarray once more and his mother ill with Parkinson's disease, much of the seventies was one problem after another for an increasingly washed-out looking McGough.

In 1972, his first son Finn was born, followed two years later by Tom, closely followed by 'The Rot':

Experts came to treat it.
Could not.
The Rot could not be stopped.

Part of McGough's original attraction to Thelma Monaghan had been an almost forbidden quality about her, flying in the face of everything he had ever been brought up to believe in. Maurice Cockrill felt 'Thelma could be difficult, but if she wanted something she'd always get it. She was an operator, a natural beauty with a lot of sex appeal who always knew her worth. She wasn't intellectual but she was intelligent, a good dresser, stylish like a dark Debbie Harry.'

Her continual resentment of his time spent away from home meant that the relationship, so often vexed, had become impossible. His depressed state was made worse by increasing feelings of guilt concerning his mother who was in a nursing home in Waterloo, looked after by his sister Brenda.

Early in 1974, Edward Heath, constantly at odds with Britain's powerful trade union leaders, had called a General Election centred around the slogan 'Who Governs Britain?' and built on a set of decidedly shaky assumptions. It was an ill-judged move, which allowed Harold Wilson to form a minority government in April of that year.

This did little to improve McGough's frame of mind, by now somewhat out of place amongst the scientists and technocrats at Loughborough, whose purple track-suited athletic activities gave rise to his light-hearted collection *Sporting Relations*. The poems for his next collection, despite the disarray of his life were generally whimsical and assuagingly droll. Typical is the scrupulously observed 'Conversation on a Train' where the poem reimagines for itself a meeting between McGough and two Welsh girls, Shirley and Mary who had been to 'Paris last year. Didn't like it. / Where', they wonder:

> are you from now?
> Oh aye, diya know the Beatles then?
> Liar!
> And what do you do for a living?
> You don't say.
> Diya hear that Mary?
> Well I hope you don't go home
> And write a bloody poem about us.

Grimms, now decidedly more poetry/music-led than rock-led, was obliged to record one more album, but the constant strain of touring was showing and by the mid-seventies the band were practically defunct. Scaffold, surprisingly, got a late, albeit too late, chance of another top ten hit. Paul McCartney produced the *McGear* album in the summer of 1974, and at the end of the session offered a T.V. booking for Scaffold. McCartney suggested they try 'Liverpool Lou' done in their instantly recognisable way. Once again, McCartney's skill at putting the right interpretation on the right song was evident. But Scaffold's time was up, McGough now echoing some of Patten's sentiments, 'it was great fun doing *Top of the Pops* and touring with The Hollies, The Yardbirds and Manfred Mann, but I felt outside it. I've never been a musician and I knew I was on borrowed time.'

So was his marriage. Thelma had moved to a separate part of the house with their two young sons. McGough took in lodgers, spent some days so much in the doldrums he could hardly be bothered to get up. His residency at Loughborough over, he was working part of the time as a presenter for *Book Tower* for Thames Television and writing a play, *The Lifeswappers,* for a series jingoistically called Plays for Britain. To some extent his moods were buoyed by regulars and friends at the booming Everyman Bistro. Here he would see Adrian Henri, Sam Walsh and John Hewson. He was also spending more time in London. He would stay either with Patten – who he was now getting closer to, or with Jim Goddard his old friend from *Saturday While Sunday*. He was seriously considering a permanent move to London, but had too many problems in Liverpool that could not be left behind.

The political climate was altering in the mid-seventies. Having lost three general elections out of four, Edward Heath, rooted in liberal conservatism, an advocate of working relations with reasonable trade unions was ousted from leadership of his party by a politician far more stridently radical and devoted to restoring the class war. Since 1951 when Winston Churchill came back to power, the post-war socialism and welfare consensus had been accepted. Margaret Thatcher, who defeated William Whitelaw (Heath's preferred choice) for the leadership of the Conservatives in 1975, was under no such illusions. The winds of change were back, but blowing in another direction. The following year Harold Wilson resigned for reasons that have never been adequately explained. Speculation was rife but probably unwarranted. Wilson had never been the same since the Sixties; he made way for an older man – James Callaghan. The government, under pressure from all sides, looked tired, low on both energy and ideas.

Roger McGough was feeling exactly the same. Looking through his desk at Windermere House around this time he uncovered a diary entry made shortly after he bought the property in 1970 – 'if you can't fight, buy a big house'. Now he needed to sell it. No longer 'Scaffolding' or 'Grimmaging', but continually on the move, his marriage irreparable and mother seriously ill, racked with guilt, his growing friendship with Brian Patten had never been more important. 'I'd always enjoyed Roger's company', Patten says, 'but we became much closer after the breakdown of his marriage. Roger has had a smooth life – he doesn't take many chances with his life – and it was around that time that I introduced him to Victoria.'

McGough met Victoria Rothschild at a party given by John Brown, then on the staff at Cape. Despite being the daughter of Lord Rothschild she had always been her own woman and was teaching at St.Mary's College in London. She had just finished a relationship with William Waldegrave, later a Cabinet Minister in two Tory administrations. Like McGough she was looking for someone. Unfortunately the relationship was doomed from the start: 'Docker's Son Leaves Wife And Children For Millionaire's Daughter' read one headline. They did give each other some good times and affection, however, at a time when it was most needed. It lasted about a year and they lived together in Holland Park, the part of London McGough was now gravitating towards. Through Jim Goddard he joined the Chelsea Arts Club in 1977. 'London didn't really work out for Roger at first', Adrian Henri recalls, 'he wasn't sure what to do for the best. I felt he should come back to Liverpool, and for a while that's what he did.'

The poems that were beginning to take shape during this period were as diverse as usual: from the sinister 'The Lake' where

in livingrooms, anglers dangle their lines
on patterned carpets, and bemoan the fate
of the ones that got away.

to the droll humour of 'Take a poem Miss Smith', and 'Missed' which borders on a disproportionate mime of his own situation: 'out of work / divorced / usually pissed / he aimed / low in life / and / missed'. McGough was generally able to stand behind his own feelings. Only in the title poem, 'Holiday on Death Row', his next and best collection since *Summer with Monika*, did he finally drop his mordant guard allowing more scope to his anger and pain.

The years 1976 and 1977 are largely remembered for one exceptionally hot summer, the Queen's Jubilee, the Sex Pistols and the beginnings of Punk Rock. For McGough, life back in Liverpool was little better than in London. He had close friends such as Henri, Maurice Cockrill (now renting the ballroom at Windermere House) where McGough first introduced him to muesli – 'this new health food' – and John Hewson. 'Hewo' had just opened Kirklands, Liverpool's first successful wine bar, so a whole new scene was opening up in Hardman Street, but for McGough, with Thelma living in another part of the house, and most of his work in London, it was all naggingly incomplete. Then salvation arrived at a bus stop in Ullet Road.

Yorkshire-born Hilary Clough was studying at Liverpool University. Her car had broken down and whilst waiting for a bus, not knowing they were on strike, she got talking to a fashionably dressed man whom she tacitly recognised. The bus never came. They walked to the Philharmonic Hotel in Hope Street. She made the man laugh at a time when he needed to. He asked her out and that night they went to The Everyman Theatre where she met Adrian Henri, still the epicentre of what was becoming the fag-end of 'the Liverpool Scene'. More than any temporary release from his depression, she was the turning point for McGough, a source of strength and comfort, helping him through the added pain of his mother's death. She also provoked his decisive move to London by going there herself to study for an M.Sc. at Chelsea College of Science. McGough followed. They got a flat together in Fulham before eventually settling at 70 Portobello Road.

Adrian Henri became 'the one that stayed at home' as Mike Evans and Maurice Cockrill soon also moved to London. 'Obviously you miss having people around', Henri reflects.'When Maurice Cockrill moved to London that was a blow because he was the person I was spending most time with then as a painter. In the same way having Roger around meant you could talk about your writing – when people who you've been associated with for a long time are suddenly not around anymore then it definitely leaves a gap.'

Entirely at ease in both New York and Paris, Henri and London have never gelled. 'It's hard to say why really, it's not bad experiences and it's nothing to do with being a writer – you can be a writer anywhere – and I realise I miss out on a lot of things. It's just that I now find that whenever I go there, I do what I have to and find myself back at Euston Station as soon as possible.'

City Hedges published by Cape in 1977, with its greater emphasis on form and metre was the natural distillation in language of where he had headed with his painting. Cross-fertilisation at its height, his pictorial themes at their most lyrical, his poetic imagery was at its most structured. Unfortunately, it did not quite come off, the Housman influence generally not a good one. Many of the poems take on an uncomfortably sonorous tone, seem uncertain of their own voice, few matching the authority, energy and precision of 'Metropolis', Henri's fine tribute to the influential surrealist poet David Gascoyne. The collection strives too hard, is self-conscious, rarely striking the natural resonance of 'Don't Look' (written at Totleigh Barton), and the two poems for Carol Ann Duffy, the tender filigree 'Butterfly', and 'Evening Song':

> I will come to you when the light has gone
> When the sea has wandered far from its shores
> And the hedges are drenched in evening
> I will come to you when the light is gone

With hindsight, the book is transitional in the canon of his work with its concentration of lyrical and other concerns, its fond sense of reporting back and evocation of memories. It became the template for future collections but generally failed to make up for the disappointing *The Best of Henri*, which Cape had previously published as something of a filler. *Out-takes* would have been more appropriate. The book is perhaps most notable for the photograph of 'Ruby Keeler', Henri's living room art-nouveau mannequin seen with him on the cover.

Holiday on Death Row had the opposite effect for McGough, bringing him an entirely new readership as well as satisfying the old. Divided into a dozen twelve line stanzas, written partly at Mary Moore's studio in a manner not normally associated with McGough, the title poem demonstrates his all too rare excursion into describing dramas of personal feeling. His characteristically demotic use of language is still in place, but the omission of pronouns and connectives give it a hurried, sinister sense of nervousness:

> Wife want life of own.
> Husband want life of Wife.
> Husband hire hitman.
> Hitman hit wife.
> Wife hit back.
> Hit, hitman run.
> Wife run harder.
> Hurt hitman.
> Hurt hitman hit Husband.
> Tired Husband hire second
> hitman to fire first hitman
> Fired hitman retire, hurt.

James Callaghan's Labour government was heading for a similar fate. Instead of going to the country in 1978 with a seven-point lead, Callaghan fatally hesitated, the upshot being the notorious 'winter of discontent'. The entire workforce appeared to be on strike. Picket lines blocked hospitals entrances; in Liverpool it was reported the dead were going unburied, and bin bags filled the streets under the noses of news cameras and in the eye of the media. After years of consensus the electorate had collectively made its mind up against Labour.

Situated in Church Walk, Kensington at the back of the church of St Mary Abbots, Bernard Stone's bookshop was not only the headquarters of Turret

Press, it functioned as the de facto centre of literary London. Beaming behind thick spectacles, glass in hand, Stone was to the sixties and seventies what David Archer had been to the thirties and forties with his bookshop in Parton Street. It was here that the American poet and adventurer Ben Wright found himself in 1974. After a reading from his recently published collection *What Next*, Stone suggested the American poet should meet Brian Patten. Wright felt that Stone was working on the assumption that two such 'bolshy unmanageable madmen would either destroy one another or find solace in each other's company'. Wright had seen a recent *Vogue* magazine article featuring a fey-looking Patten complete with poodle haircut. The person he met was hardly precious. They went drinking together, usually in the Prince of Wales in Notting Hill Gate, and became friends.

A devoted admirer of Robert Graves, Wright had long been privy to the 'Graves Gossip' surrounding the poet's home in Deya in Northern Majorca, this being another secret corner of other-worldliness the two had in common. Patten had met Graves and become friendly with his sons Tomas and Juan whilst working on a childrens' book on the island. Wright became enamoured of Patten's work as well as his unpredictable company, seeing in him the tradition of what Allen Ginsberg called the 'vatic' poets at the fountain-head of fable-making and prophecy:

> At times he really hits it, that essence of the romantic poet, of seeing the universe in the cry of a skylark – someone as great as Claribelle Alegria calling 'Angel Wings' one of the greatest lyrics in any language! But then he fucks himself and makes a joke out of it – it's only me – then there's a shuffle and jive. Roger's the same. All the Liverpool poets – 'because I will completely shoot myself in the foot then do a pirouette as I have this uncanny ability to grab failure from the jaws of success'. It's that Charlie Chaplin-slapstick, self-mockery thing – Roger's P.C. Plod slouching off towards Bethlehem Avenue – he's in the whole tradition of English literature! At times it's like that magic realism of Borges and Marquez, that messianic vision. And these guys get real close.

Patten, who would have seriously failed exams set on his own poetry, was letting the disparity between his and Mary's backgrounds and aspirations show. He was coming to another phase in his life, his most important relationship doomed. It ended in 1975, presaging his fourth book, the critically acclaimed *Vanishing Trick*. Writing about the collection in *The Times Literary Supplement*, the poet and novelist D.M. Thomas described it as:

a truthful and tender sequence of poems about the death of love; but also about the drive into oneself, that painful lonely experience involving the shedding of false images of oneself created by other people.The poems write in a very assured way about being diffident and vulnerable.

Other reviewers were equally positive, Martin Booth in *Tribune* commenting: 'he is the master poet of his genre, the only one continually and successfully to 'ring true.' In his account of British poetry from 1964-1984, *Driving through the Barricades*, Booth notes 'as [Patten] grew older so did his poems... Patten was taking his audience with him. The girl at the teenage party has become the civil servant who resigned her job to love and follow a concert violinist. The (small) dragon has metamorphosed into adaptations of Aesop's fabulous animals or a scientist's regeneration of the dodo.'

Until the recent publication of *Armada*, *Vanishing Trick* stands as Patten's richest and most rewarding collection. It provides more than its fair share of reverberative coinage:'You ask for a poem / I offer you a blade of grass', 'And a fountain empties itself into the grass','It felt like a warm planet', 'I need a drop of blood for that / a drop of unclouded blood'.

'A Blade of Grass' is one of Patten's most anthologised poems. In a different context it could be a paradigm for creative oneness, an extended metaphor for the imaginative sensibility in its entirety. Its genesis is a simple question – 'you ask for a poem' – but the asker is offered a blade of grass which 'is not good enough'. It progresses with a strange truncated vividness as if the poem itself is reminding Patten to obey subliminal instructions regarding his true ethical imagination. All his familiar personal cliches are in place: 'absurd', 'of my making' etc. – in fact it is hard to read the word 'poem' aloud without pronouncing it 'pome'. What the poem asks, it answers in its own un-manipulative way, finally asserting how:

A blade of grass
Becomes more and more difficult to offer,

And about how as you grow older
A blade of grass
Becomes more difficult to accept.

Soon after the book came *Vanishing Trick* the record. Produced by Mike Steyn for Tangent Records, it is one of the most defining versions of poetry set to music. Featuring Patten reading seventeen poems from the collection on side 2, it is most notable for eight superbly worked versions of his poems as song on side 1. Selected from *Vanishing Trick*, *Little Johnny's Confession* and *The Irrelevant Song* with musical settings by Mike Westbrooke, Neil Innes and Andy Roberts, and loving vocals shared between Linda Thompson, Norma

Winston and Linda Peters, it is a vividly compelling evocation of Patten's darkly sensuous lyrical gift. The folk music legend Richard Thompson is featured on guitar on 'After Frost' and 'Embroidered Butterflies' (both from *Vanishing Trick*) on a record all the more exemplary for its inclusion of three pieces from *Little Johnny's Confession*. There is Norma Winstone's stunning reading of 'A Creature to Tell the Time By', the musical items concluding with the overlooked 'Seascape' and the seminal 'Somewhere between Heaven and Woolworth's' (with Patten's moonlit voice somewhere between the verse) on a hit record that never saw the light of day.

Things were changing in the poetry world. Despite their advancing years, the Liverpool poets had had little trouble since 1967 in maintaining their 'enfants terrible' status. In the mid-seventies however, on the back of Punk Rock a whole new wave of strident poets came through the door that the Mersey poets had opened. Punk bands performed in small clubs, often using poets as supports or M.C.s. The pioneer was Salford-born John Cooper-Clarke, whose rapid fire delivery and extraordinary mid-sixties Dylan-as-beanpole appearance gave him prominence outside the poetry world. Other styles and performers evolved: 'Ranters' such as Attila the Stockbroker; passionate social commentators like Joolz; the cabaret-orientated comedic skills of Henry Normal, John Hegley and others centred around the new London venue 'Apples and Snakes'. In parallel, and sometimes in association with, came the black poetry scene of rap, dub and hip-hop. Prominent were Linton Kwesi Johnson, Benjamin Zephaniah, Grace Nichols, Jean Binta Breeze and Lemm Sissay. All owe some debt to the Mersey Poets as well as Mike Horovitz and Adrian Mitchell for opening doors and creating space for them to fill.

In contrast, two other young poets appeared on the scene, both attracting controversial attention and some notoriety. In 1979 Craig Raine, a graduate of Exeter College, Oxford, quickly followed his successful first collection *The Onion Memory* with *A Martian Sends a Postcard Home*. With his vitalised similes, metaphors and vigorous transforming imaginative effects, the book received much acclaim, the fine poet James Fenton crediting Raine and his like-minded contemporaries as founding an entire new school known collectively as the 'Martians'. Soon afterwards followed the flamboyant aesthete Jeremy Reed, whose later concerns with drug culture and cross-dressing obscured the early plaudits he had received from such alumni as David Gascoyne and Kathleen Raine as being the (almost) lone inheritor of the surrealist tradition.

Adrian Henri in typically resourceful manner continued his adventurous way as lone survivor of the Mersey poets in Liverpool. He had been President of the

'The way things were' – Henri and McGough as seventies' fashion victims,
this time sharing the same seat of a bus.

'The Right Mask' – Patten unusually upstaging McGough and Henri after a Grimms gig in the early seventies.

'Over their heads' – Patten and McGough searching for words at the end of the seventies.
(Photo by Nick Taylor)

'Not fade away' – Adrian Henri at 21 Mount Street in 1990.
(Photo by Neil Marsland) (Photo of A.H. on wall by Don McCullen, 1968)

Liverpool Academy of Arts since 1972, and at the risk of further 'poacher turned gamekeeper' accusations, in 1978 became president of the Merseyside Arts Association. A long-standing critic of how public money concerning the arts was misspent, he now took the opportunity to use his status in the public dimension. This became a ritualisation of what he had been doing in the sixties. He obtained the required funding to start 'Henri's Hope Street Poets', a monthly series of readings in The Everyman Theatre foyer. This consisted of himself as M.C., Carol Ann Duffy, Sidney Hoddes, two other local poets and a regular guest reader. The guests included Norman MacCaig, Christopher Logue, David Gascoyne, George MacBeth, and a poet Henri had increasingly come to admire, W.S. Graham.

Born in Greenock on the Clyde in 1918, Graham had published his earliest work in the forties, romantically wooed and wed fellow poet Nessie Dunsmuir, before moving to London, later establishing his reputation with *The Nightfishing* published in 1955. The couple later settled in Madron near Penzance where Graham became friendly with the equally heavy drinking abstract painter Roger Hilton. They were both renowned for their fractious temperaments and consumption of whisky. When Sydney Graham came to Liverpool to stay with Adrian Henri he brought his own time-scale with him: 'He never wanted to eat when we did, but then around midnight he'd say "Have ye no got anything to eat in the house?" ' Henri and Duffy were due to visit Paris whilst Graham was in Liverpool, and after a heavy night's drinking desperately needed some sleep. 'About three in the morning there was this knock on the bedroom door, and there was this childlike figure in the doorway in winceyette pyjamas – it was Sydney – "I don't seem to be able to find the whisky bottle".'

Faber published W.S. Graham's *Collected Poems* the following year, when McGough, also an admirer, met him after a reading he and Patten had given in St Ives. McGough was invited to Madron for 'afternoon whisky'. He noticed the discrepancy between Graham, a master of his craft, and the comparatively affluent painters of the area. Here was a poet, greatly admired by Eliot, whom Seamus Heaney had described as looking towards the end of the century and beyond, unlike his friend Dylan Thomas whom Heaney felt represented the end of an earlier tradition. McGough remembers the meeting with Graham as 'one of those all too rare poet's days'. 'A Visit to the Poet and his Wife', published in *Waving at Trains* three years later, in some ways described that afternoon:

To set the scene: A cave
in Madron, Cornwall.
On a warm September afternoon
Mr and Mrs W.S.G. are 'at home'
to admirers bearing distilled gifts.

In May 1979 Margaret Thatcher's admirers had elected a Conservative government. Most people in the arts were alarmed, Philip Larkin being the predictable exception. 'Her great virtue', he told one journalist, 'is saying that two and two make four, which is as unpopular nowadays as it always has been.' A new hubristic and nationalistic era was afoot. Shortly before it got underway, Brian Patten published his fifth collection of poetry in twelve years.

Until the publication of *Grave Gossip*, with its somewhat sinister cover showing Patten in a telephone kiosk, left hand pressed hard against the glass, his reputation as a poet had been progressively enhanced by each collection. Although the new book was his most diverse and wide-ranging, it was in certain respects the least convincing. There are many good poems: 'The Right Mask', the natural successor to 'A Blade of Grass', 'Burning Genius' irony of the highest order, and 'Waves', a masterful vignette:

And the one throwing the lifebelt,
Even he needs help at times,
Stranded on the beach,
Terrified of the waves.

However, too many of the competing elements in his complex nature seem to be at odds: the impulse to love and be loved, countered by the yearning for solitude; the continued fascination with telephones and communicating with people, contrasted with anthropomorphism and pick'n'mix fables. More assured and authoritative is the deftly lyrical elegy for Stevie Smith, a poet whom Larkin credited with having 'the authority of sadness'. Persuasively, and not by the usual routes, it asks:

Must she always walk with Death, must she?
I went out and asked the sky.
No, it said, no,
She'll do as I do, as I do.
I go on forever.

And having knocked on these doors moves from doubt through to celebratory approval with:

Stevie elemental

Free now of the personal,
Through sky and soil
And fire and water
Swim on, Blake's purest daughter!

'We don't need no education, we don't need no thought control', Pink Floyd sang as the decade's final number one. Few could have imagined the impact of an event that would shake the world less than a year later as the new 'selfish' decade was beginning to get underway.

The Eighties

'...a city in need of Ambassadors...'

In Britain, only pre-dawn travellers immediately heard the BBC Overseas Service's announcement that John Lennon had been shot outside his New York apartment. Two hours earlier, Mark David Chapman surrendered his signed autograph book, his .38 calibre revolver, and was taken into custody. The shock, when the rest of the country awoke on Saturday December 9th, 1980 had the quality of releasing a vast simultaneous emotion for all those still in thrall of the Beatles' music. There was suddenly something very urgent to talk about for anybody who still held those times as a refuge from the recent decade where both violence and lassitude had gained so much currency. Not since John Kennedy was assassinated had so many stangers spoken, so many old friends rung each other reminding themselves about where they were when they first heard Love Me Do or who they were in the summer of 1967. Above all perhaps they reminisced about that inclusive spontaneity and mosaical joy of *Sergeant Pepper's Lonely Hearts Club's Band*, countered by that feeling of where-did-it-all-go-wrong on watching the concert on the roof. Not for some time had so many stretched their memories for affectionate anecdotes concerning John, Paul, George and Ringo.

On Sunday in Liverpool over 30,000 people filled the plateau of St George's Hall. Appropriately so, as its designer Harvey Lonsdale Elmes was only twenty-three when it was built, and the neo-classical building is perhaps the finest example of Liverpool's belief in the possibilities of youth. But there's always one though isn't there? In this case a drunk in the Crown Hotel, in sole blissful charge of the city's characteristic sarcasm: 'I could understand it if it was Ken Dodd'.

Across the same arena Adrian Henri remembers John and Paul, Stuart Sutcliffe, Rod Murray and Thelma Pickles, with their carnival floats built for Allan Williams's Mersey Arts Ball in the summer of 1959. In the labyrinthine streets off neighbouring Whitechapel, Mathew Street had never known a Sunday quite like it. Beneath Arthur Dooley's overhead sculpture, honouring 'Four Lads Who Shook the World', wry and tender images – straight out of one of Henri's poems – came alive in the form of love notes attached to the damp walls, flowers in the dirt blowing across littered streets.

Carol Ann Duffy found herself drawn to Mathew Street where 'huge crowds of people standing silently around' provoked her to write 'Liverpool Echo' a sonnet which took its name from the local newspaper:

Pat Hodges kissed you once, although quite shy
in sixty-two. Small crowds in Mathew Street
endure rain for the echo of a beat,
as if nostalgia means you did not die.

Inside phone booths loveless ladies cry
on Merseyside. Their faces show defeat.
An ancient jukebox blares out Aint She Sweet
in Liverpool, which cannot say goodbye.

Here everybody has an anecdote
of how they met you, were the best of mates.
The seagulls circle round a ferry-boat

out on the river, where it's getting late.
Like litter on the water, people float
outside the Cavern in the rain. And wait.

Adrian Henri remembers being

woken at seven in the morning by a friend ringing to tell me the news,
fell asleep again, and really thought I'd dreamt it. When I woke up later
I put the radio on and they were playing Beautiful Boy and one of the
lines stuck in my head about 'crossing the street' [and being busy]
'making other plans' which struck me as being particularly ironic on
that particular day.

A year later Henri was asked to write a poem for a John Lennon Memorial
Concert. Describing 'a year in the life' after this publically tragic event, the
resulting 'New York City Blues', published in *Penny Arcade* in 1983, is one of
the best poems of his career. The stoicism of the opening lines:

You do not cross the road
To step into immortality

is undercut immediately by a dash of nostalgia:

An empty steet is only the beginning

and then through unobtrusive imagery – 'a dead flower, a faded letter' – the
poem understates even as it deftly affirms the Lennon quote:

Life is what happens to you
When you're busy making other plans

then recoils delivering a snapshot of current attitudes: riot vans, angry embers of summer, ghost guitars, before producing the freely imaginative penultimate stanza:

Meanwhile, in the Valley of Indecision,
We rehearse stale words, store up expected songs,
Celebrate sad anniversaries.
Flowers and flashbulbs. Cold pavements.

By now Henri and Duffy's own relationship was also colder. Carol Ann, graduating in 1977, had already had two of her plays performed, and published a pamphlet of poems. The well-crafted monologues and social criticism channelled through a variety of sensibilities and fantasy lives that later would establish her reputation, were now beginning to emerge.

Henri had recently published *From the Loveless Motel*. The cover photograph taken by Sue Sterne depicts a white-jacketed Henri in a hotel phone lobby – in this case the Holiday Inn in Liverpool. (The actual 'Loveless Motel' is situated on Highway 100 near Nashville.) The bedrock poem in the book is 'Wasteland' originally part of series of 'Debris' poster/poems commissioned by the Walker Art Gallery. The Eliot imagery so effective in 'New York City Blues' is over apparent and crowded here – 'stirring dead leaves / round rotting treestumps / ...heaps of broken images' – whether intentional irony or not. 'The Blues in Rats' Alley' is a more convincing example of his rebarbative qualities:

Think we're in Rats' Alley where the deadmen lost their bones
Where the vandals smashed the windows and they took the telephones.

Few of the poems – many thumbnail surveys and verbal collages from his continually adventurous life – have the confidence of 'Autumn Leaving', his goodbye to Frances Hambidge. Owing much to deconstruction, and something of a collision between the old and new, the book's balancing of gravity and wit, of literal-mindedness and myth-mindedness is at times all too misty-eyed in its execution.

Undeterred, Henri moved into a new area of productivity almost immediately. He became the first Writer-in-Residence at the Tattenhall Centre in Cheshire, where the poet Gary Boswell, then a student on the course, remembers Henri's welcome approach to writer-in-the community work, holding court and running up tabs in the nearby Bear and Ragged Staff.

The project was set up by Mark Fisher, later to become the Labour M.P. for Stoke Central. Son of a Tory M.P., Fisher's background had been in freelance writing and film. With his gift for people and talent for raising money he transformed what was a fairly run down affair into something vital and dynamic. Inadvertently he introduced Henri to writing for children, an area in which Brian Patten had enjoyed great success.

As Henri was now working with children and finding it stimulating, he began *Eric the Punk Cat.* Named after Eric's the 'new Cavern' in Mathew Street, it was published in 1982 by Hodder & Stoughton. Illustrated by Roger Wade Walker, it gave Henri some of the best poetry reviews he had ever received.

1980 passed relatively quietly for both Patten and McGough. Patten was working on a book about the great nineteenth century Northamptonshire poet John Clare and preparing a selection of his own widely praised love poems. McGough, finally divorced, was settling into his new life in London with Hilary. Prolific as ever, he was editing *Strictly Private,* an anthology of poems for teenagers that would be both contemporary and approachable, an antidote to Palgrave's Golden Treasury, and ' without the Ghost of Critics-Past peering over [anyone's] shoulder'.

In 1981 McGough undertook a reading tour of Germany with Henri and Andy Roberts. Patten declined the invitation. He and McGough had other ambitious plans of their own. They were each becoming the brother they neither had, Patten, the infuriating but lovable crazy kid brother, McGough, the sensible yet other-wordly elder one. 'We stick up for one another against other people', McGough asserts,' and I suppose we feel we've earned the right to slag each other off when the situation demands. Sometimes we do it in public and people are quite surprised, sometimes shocked.' Ben Wright takes it further:

> It's the strongest bond I know. Brian thinks Roger should have been a priest – he has the hands of a priest – Roger brings the best out of him, he's the guy he looks to, while Brian acts a kind of Pan-like conscience to Roger. It's an incredible friendship.

They had decided to collaborate on *The Mouthtrap,* a play about poets and poetry. It played to capacity houses at the Tricycle, and then The Lyric in Hammersmith, transferring successfully to Edinburgh featuring the two poets with the actress Helen Atkinson-Wood. Neither was totally satisfied, however, Patten going as far as to say:

> It was a very bad play. Thankfully none of it exists. We wrote it together and there were some good ideas, but I was never comfortable with my own acting and it needed a good director'.

McGough agrees:

> It was daft having the two of us play ourselves. The dialogue and some of the theatrical devices were fine but you can't quite match each other's passion for an idea, and Brian was never quite happy with it. I think it only appealed to people who knew our work and what we were doing. In a sense a bit like *The Mersey Sound.*

McGough was writing the macabre 'The Birderman' which appeared in *Waving At Trains* published by Cape in 1982, the inspired verb 'ledger' supplied by Patten. Snatches of dialogue from *The Mouthtrap* however do still occasionally crop up at unrehearsed and impromptu moments:

> Patten: 'Should I do "Angel Wings" or "Albatross" tonight?'
> McGough: 'I think "Albatross".'
> Patten: 'What's wrong with "Angel Wings"?'
> McGough: 'Nothing Brian They're both good.'
> Patten: 'Don't you like "Angel Wings"?'
> MGough: 'Yes I like it. Do "Angel Wings" – it's good.'
> Patten: 'Mmmm... you don't think "Albatross"ll work then? '

Waving at Trains was a worthy successor to *Holiday On Death Row* in the now familiar 'what you see is what you get' McGough vein. Poems such as 'You and I', 'What My Lady Did' and 'Noah's Arc' show an increasing attention to more regular forms, whilst 'Rainbow' is a rare and tender love poem. The book is an adroit balance between the insouciant and the sinister, perhaps why John Betjeman went on record as saying 'I'm also sold on Roger McGough'. Two poems stand out: the title poem and the 169-liner 'Unlucky for Some'.

> I'd been watching this television programme called Chelsea Girls about old women in a hostel, so I started to hear more voices in monologues; one of the poems was thirteen lines, another twelve, so I thought – ah! – thirteen lines, thirteen poems. Each section opens and closes with the same line ('What do I do for a living? Survive.' 'It's the addicts I can't stand.' 'I'm no good, that's what I've been told.').

Written in double space in similar fashion to 'Holiday on Death Row', it relies less on the telegraphic syntax and nervous impatience of the earlier poem whose hurriedness was heightened by clipped and contracting words. Here McGough uses a much more elastic word arrangement, intricately shaped yet casually conversational. The defiant tone of the voice artfully circumvents the poem enhancing its colloquial ease with the nonchalance of:

> If you keep on the move, time soon passes.

> Things are better now, with me new glasses.

The dangers of sentimentality are great, but McGough successfully avoids it. There are few better examples of what Elizabeth Jennings has cited as his 'concern about people and society fused perfectly with his love of language':

Would you like to see me dance?
I'll dance for you. I dance in here
all the time. The girls love it.
Do you like my dancing? Round
and round. Not bad eh? For my age.
I always wanted to go on the stage.

The opening lines of the collection's title poem ask three rhetorical questions:

Do people who wave at trains
Wave at the driver, or at the train itself?
Or, do people who wave at trains
Wave at the passengers? Those hurtling strangers,
The unidentifiable flying faces?

The voice then becomes more perfunctory, more plainly descriptive, the train compartment a storage space of conjecture, concluding that (the wavers) probably 'continue their walk' feeling 'that their love has been returned / Because they have not seen it rejected'. In the beautiful final verse McGough, echoes Larkin in tone, but offers the reader a purely pantheistic and accordingly much more affirmative image:

It's like God in a way. Another day
Another universe. Always off somewhere.
And left behind, the faithful few,
Stuck out there. Not a care in the world.
All innocence. Arms in the air. Waving.

It was to be McGough's last book for Cape. His first editor, the current theatre critic Susannah Clapp had left, and Cape's poetry list was waning. Although they did their best to keep him, McGough moved to Penguin whose poetry editor Tony Lacey, had published his children's books.

Brian Patten had also acquired a new love. This was a remarkably composed black cat called Wiz, later the subject of his poem 'Inessential Things', who had recently entered his life. He had also bought a house in Brook Green in Hammersmith, and was revisiting the Graves family at Deya:

I was originally told about Deya by the artist Paul Hogarth's wife, and first went there around 1967. I'll always remember first seeing Graves. He was walking down these village steps carrying a basket of fruit, dressed in what looked like pyjamas. He had a straw hat on, and I thought – yesssss!

Occasionally he would go there with McGough who had become friendly with the poet and pipes player Ronny Wothan, a resident in the village.

Sometimes they stayed at the house occupied by Graves's last muse, the fourteen year old girl eponymously used in 'Operation Julie', the world-wide drugs investigation centred around Howard Marks, (a resident and subsequent guest at Patten's fiftieth birthday party held on the island in 1996). Both Patten and McGough have given readings in the beautiful ampitheatre built there at the instigation of Tomas Graves.

In 1983 Penguin published a follow-up book to *The Mersey Sound* with an appropriately punning title. *New Volume* 'is a selection by the poets of their recent work (it) is as direct, provocative and humorous as its predecessor' claimed the blurb. But whilst still showing social concerns, the new anthology 'reflects the broadening of each poet's characteristics and style to reveal a maturer, more sensitive perspective'. Whatever the spin, they were getting older.

There is an air of stoicism about the three faces that stare from a corner of Kirklands' Wine-bar in Liverpool on the cover of *New Volume*. Henri, no longer the tubby beatnik or overweight Rock star, presents a benign semi-professorial look: wire-rimmed glasses instead of the dark frames, a greying, trimmed beard replacing the bushy earlier model. McGough, throughout the seventies electing for most hirsute options – long hair, beard, sideburns, droopy moustache – is now clean shaven, receding; greying too but (like Henri), neatly colourful. Patten, Medusa-haired, less gamin-like, is much the same as ever (his only fashion concession in the seventies, a 'semi-Afro' around the time of *Grave Gossip*). He stands behind Henri and McGough, leaning slightly, staring beyond them and out into the vast unknown.

New Volume is as strong, if not a stronger, selection than its predecessor. Yet despite some early success at the Edinburgh launch and a full-scale UK tour, as an anthology it never made any really big waves. A constant source of irritation for all three writers has been the assumption that 'they were the ones who did something in the sixties' and that is where they still remain. *New Volume* did little to rectify this. *The Mersey Sound* kept on selling.

1983 was particularly busy for Carol Ann Duffy, who had moved out of Mount Street, acquired a writer-in-residence post for East London schools, been awarded a C. Day-Lewis fellowship, and won the National Poetry Competition all in that year. 'Whoever She Was' (the winning poem) appeared in her first full collection, the critically acclaimed *Standing Female Nude* published by Anvil in 1985.

Henri, newly smitten by Lis Burgoyne, a student from Wallasey doing a dissertation on his work, had seen his novel with Nell Dunn, *I Want,* adapted and performed at the Liverpool Playhouse, and had published *Penny Arcade*. His best collection since *Autobiography*, the continued use of what Eliot referred to as 'objective correlative' – linking language directly to actual objects rather than the use and extension of metaphors – makes it a hard book to quote from, yet an easy one to experience. The sense of travel and contrasting landscape, whether Germany, Canada, Hollywood or New York, Cheshire, Devon or Liverpool, is cohesive and no more lyrically effective than in the Audenesque villanelle 'Aubade' with its concluding stanza:

Time will not stop: your careless hand will tear
The faded snapshot, all that was left to show.
I mourn for something that was never there,
The scent of roses in the morning air.

The visual qualities of 'Harbour', the autobiographical running phrases and narrative skills of 'Cat' are also exceptional. He poignantly returns to the 'Talking Blues' style he so successfully hi-jacked in the sixties, this time in response to the widely reported riots in his neighbourhood in 1981, when Liverpool 8 became Toxteth and Henri responded with 'Adrian Henri's Talking Toxteth Blues':

Well, I woke up this morning, there was buzzing overhead
Saw the helicopter as I got out of bed,
Smelt the smell of burning, saw the buildings fall,
Bulldozers pulling down next door's wall.
    Toxteth nightmare...
        yes...
        ...city with a hangover.

Many blamed the riots on the unacceptably high rise in unemployment resulting from the vindictive monetarist policies being pursued by the Thatcher government. Despite much alarm and disaffection within her own ranks, Thatcher had struck a chord with the British electorate in a way no other political leader had since Winston Churchill. Buoyed by her recent triumph in the controversial Falklands War, she had been returned in 1983 with a huge majority. Even some of those who detested her politics grudgingly respected her as someone 'who said what she believed, and believed what she said'. Certain Marxists even went as far as portraying her as a true class warrior. She was a Radical and a revolutionary, not a Tory, (they said), who had stolen the Left's clothes. Labour's earlier election of the 'other-worldly' Michael Foot as their leader, himself a covert admirer of Thatcher's fighting qualities, did little to improve their standing. To the electorate, Labour no longer looked serious about office. Their manifesto in 1983 was regarded as the 'longest suicide note in history' as Thatcher swept everything before her in the eighties, her most sustained opposition coming from Edward Heath and other disenchanted Tories. Labour looked divided and hopelessly dated. They needed to change or else face political extinction.

Ironically, in oppressive and philistine times the arts often flourish. The Thatcher years saw art as prerequisite for status, and it saw theatre as something best handled by the entrepreneur. Whilst the Mersey poets were working together again in the subsequent *Gifted Wreckage* and *It's For You* tours, a new success story in Poetry was happening in the north-east.

Neil Astley, a former employee at Dove Cottage in the Lake District, had started the much-needed Bloodaxe Books. 'Poetry with an Edge' was its slogan (complete with a hatchet-brandishing Eric Bloodaxe logo). Its mission was to publish overlooked poets of outstanding ability, its first title, *Tristan Crazy* by Ken Smith published in October 1978. An LP record of Basil Bunting reading from *Briggflatts* made a small profit, and new authors including Sean O'Brien, Peter Didsbury and Helen Dunmore were added to a fast-growing list. Astley's judgement proved remarkably sound and Bloodaxe's reputation as a publishing company, genuinely working for readers and writers, was soon established. It quickly expanded bringing with it an increasing range of street-wise, urban, feminine, political and ethnically mixed attitudes and sensibilities.

As times became more deregulated so did the muse. The success of Bloodaxe and subsequent claims of an alternative poetry capital in Huddersfield were quickly countered by *The Penguin Book of Contemporary Poetry*. Edited by Andrew Motion and Blake Morrison and published – against cries of cultural supremacism and elitism – in 1982. The book contained only twenty writers taking issue with Al Alvarez's *The New Poetry* of twenty years earlier. The implication of that book, despite its influence, fighting talk and attack on 'gentility', argue Motion and Morrison, was that it confused gravity of subject with quality of achievement. Motion included himself in the twenty writers but gave generous account to their selected poets in a volume leading with the influence of Seamus Heaney, but also celebrating among others, Tony Harrison, James Fenton and Paul Muldoon. The hostility that it generated only went further to underline the poetry scene as even more riven by factionalism than twenty years earlier when the Mersey Poets had seemed such a problematic group.

Tongue in cheek as ever, all three in the mid-eighties were enjoying huge success in the growing market for children's poetry. Henri was awarded the Book Marketing Council's Children's Choice Award for *Eric the Punk Cat*, McGough's *Sky in the Pie* became a best-seller, winning the coveted Signal

Award for children's poetry and he later received a Bafta award for his T.V. play *Kurt, Mungo B.P. and Me.*

Brian Patten's first book of poetry solely for children, the slangily insouciant and anarchic *Gargling With Jelly* was hailed as a breakthrough in the genre, an all-time classic, later adapted as a play, and reviewed in *The Times Educational Supplement* as 'a kind of poetic version of *The Beano*'. It would be wrong to assume that it was all laughs. Patten has long held genuine respect for the genre. 'Poems written for children retain their freshness. The best have a sense of wonder, mystery and mischief.' He consciously included a number of thoughtful, serious poems. 'Looking for Dad' deals with divorce, and 'The Newcomer', a poem to become justly famous among ten-year-olds, went on to win a £1,250 in 1997. Unfortunately it was plagiarised by a thirteen-year old girl who had to return the money much to the embarrassment of the judges.

Patten was typically phlegmatic. 'I am happy that she found the poem of enough interest to draw attention to the issues. Perhaps she will go on to write some really good stuff of her own, and good luck to her. If the judges did not spot it, tough luck on them.' The poem spoke of 'something new' in the river, the trees, the warren and the whiteness:

> Throughout the animal kingdom
> The news was spreading fast –
> No beak no claws no feathers,
> No scales no fur no gills,
> It lives in the trees and the water,
> In the earth and the snow and the hills,
> And it kills and it kills and it kills.

In December 1984 Philip Larkin turned down the offer of the Poet Laureatship ('Think of the stamps! Think of the stamps!'). Larkin was 'sorry to disappoint' but happy that 'Mrs Thatcher [had been] very nice and understanding about it all'. Ted Hughes was allocated the burial space in Westminster Abbey instead. Larkin himself faced up 'to the inevitable' a year later, shortly after Robert Graves died in Deya, aged ninety.

During the winter of 1984-85, Brian Patten gave a reading tour of Indian universities before making a rare and brief excursion into academia, accepting the post of Regent's lecturer at San Diego University in California. Henri returned to Hollywood and New York with Lis Burgoyne dedicating a series of notebook poems to her called 'Holiday-Snaps'. Roger McGough built a smokescreen and stood in front of it.

135

The political backdrop focused on the miners' strike. This proved a turning point for relations between government and trade unions. It also became a benchmark for splits within the Labour movement, and how the Left would deal with what was becoming the Thatcher legacy. Following their reverses under Heath, for the Conservatives defeat was not an option. The miners were the last redoubt of an old attitude. Their leader Arthur Scargill, whose alarmingly powerful sense of destiny was matched only by Thatcher's herself, eventually became another scalp alongside the Argentinian leader General Galtieri in the Tories' continuing political domination.

For Labour it was another divisive disaster, their new leader Neil Kinnock appearing at times almost as hapless as his predecessor and they slipped further out of the political reckoning. It could be argued however, that the Conservatives had been doing some of Labour's work for them. By eliminating Scargill, they removed a major embarassment for the middle-of-the-road brand of socialism that Kinnock and his new breed of rising stars and political managers – who included Gordon Brown, Tony Blair and Peter Mandelson – were trying to advance. It may take time but the sea change that James Callaghan was so aware of at the end of the seventies could happen all over again. Next time it could be in their favour.

For Brian Patten much of the eighties had been miasmatic. His publications had been sporadic and had met with mixed success. His selected Love Poems with its Puck-like sketch of the author by Jo Brocklehurst, had been reprinted in 1984. *Gargling with Jelly* was an unqualified success, but he had been dissatisfied with *The Mouthtrap* and *New Volume* and as yet had not followed up the uneven *Grave Gossip*. His health was poor and he was spending more time than ever in the Prince of Wales, where McGough too had become a 'key regular'. He had been involved in a series of relationships – some serious, some less so, most disastrous – was approaching forty, and still showed no outward signs of settling down. It was during this period that Patten's 'reputation' for recalcitrance grew. Everyone seemed to have a story: broken-hearted girls, drunkenness, fights with night porters, or pursuing Greek fish and chip shop owners out to avenge their wronged daughters. Whether outbursts of temper, prolonged sulkiness, or spurned alcoholic women signing the pledge, someone had heard something. For the lad himself, 'a lot of the eighties was a lost period that I don't really want to go into. I suppose the best I could say about it was I was re-inventing myself. I just wished I knew into what.'

Yet the horror stories are equally matched by accounts of unexpected generosity and kindness, his humility and almost coy politeness; the time he devotes to children and the disabled, the courtesy he has always shown to the elderly. 'He's like Pan', says Ben Wright, 'all he needs is a pipe. I haven't checked his feet out, but I'm sure they're cloven. He's a loner, a play-actor, but he's got a heart the size of a house. That guy can be be the most generous guy in the world.'

Patten remains indifferent to what is said about him, taking an ambivalent stance even when it comes to poetry. 'It's a diary of a life. And I don't give a fuck. It's as simple as that. What people make of it is up to them. I imagine there are poets who start tidying up their past after a while. I don't want to be one of those poets.'

1986 was a good year for Roger McGough. Hilary gave birth to his third son Matthew and they got married. It was his first church wedding, (with Patten officiating as best man). He published his eighth collection (for adults), and first for Penguin, *Melting into the Foreground.*

The broad, energetic furrow ploughed by Bloodaxe Books and the equally eclectic Carcanet Press meant there were more poets publishing than ever before. The effect of the Women's Movement meant a flowering of many voices newly bestowed with a permission to give vent to feral imaginations. Liverpool was no longer seen (if it ever was) as a poetry centre. In 1980 Neil Astley had edited *Ten North-East Poets* followed two years later by Douglas Dunn's *A Rumoured City*, featuring new poets from Hull including Sean O'Brien, Pete Didsbury, Douglas Houston and Frank Redpath. Throughout the eighties the influx of diverse new voices such as Ian McMillan, Selima Hill, Matthew Sweeney, Kathleen Jaimie, Jo Shapcott, Glyn Maxwell and Simon Armitage had completely transformed and displaced any existing orthodoxy. As the times got stranger so did the poetry.

In this tougher era McGough's *Melting into the Foreground* could have looked hopelessly dated, at best quirkily irrelevant. He was associated with a period that had long lost its bloom. That the collection stands up so well says much for his constant contemporaneousness, what the poet Kit Wright has called 'Roger's slender, but strong and enduring talent'. As if obeying Philip Larkin's personal instructions to 'make [readers] laugh, make them cry, and bring on the dancing girls', poems such as 'The End of Summer' and 'Happy Birthday' seethe with a cool urgency, the utterly innocent vernacular and simple questing of 'Q' transformed into the bluntest of propositions:

I join the queue
We move up nicely.

I ask the lady in front
What are we queing for.
To join another queue,'
She explains.

How pointless,' I say,
I'm leaving.' She points
To another long queue.
Then you must get in line.'

I join the queue.
We move up nicely.

Concise ordinary images are remade by deft phrasing, witty images and allusions, none better than the gauche drunken party-goer in the collection's title poem whose 'wit [was] wet sand in a sock':

I'd lie low for a while if I were you.
Stay at home for a year or two.
Take up painting. Do something ceramic.
Failing that, emigrate to somewhere Islamic.

The poem McGough spent most time on was the elegy for his Aunt Marge, whom his sister Brenda remembers as 'being absolutely brilliant. She was like a Mary Poppins character, she spoilt us but also related to us in a way most adults can't do. She had a great gift'. 'Hearts and Flowers' took McGough four months to write. 'I wrote nothing else during that time. I was writing and re-writing it because I didn't know where I was going or what was going to happen.' The poem illustrates McGough's craftsmanship better than most. It combines the aphoristic understated narrative of an earthy vignette with the emotional intensity of a lyric as it sets up a portrait of

          Everybody's
Favourite aunt. A cuddly toy adult
That sang loud and out of tune.
That dropped, knocked over and bumped into things,
That got ticked off just like us.

Through carefully selected images of childhood domesticity and play (pontoon, snap, toffees, a card with kisses), it builds to to a stirring climax, achieving a tone that is both immediately recognisable and bound to the demotic whilst longing for spiritual transcendence:

                    From the missal
In her lap, holy pictures, like playing cards,

Lay scattered. Five were face-up:
A Full House of Sacred Hearts and Little Flowers.
Aunty Marge, lucky in cards.

McGough has always remained loyal to his faith, attending church when he can. He has always dealt with it in his own way, Roman Catholicism playing a large part in his life if not in the poetry. He is tolerant of unorthodox life-styles that have at times included his own:

Hopefully I get forgiven. It's complicated and there are pre-illusions and some strength that I draw from it. I've never seen myself as the way I'm often described. I'm not irreverent really and I don't think I've ever been a cynic.

Like Henri, he is frequently asked to sit on various councils, and has often been something of a dignitary. Is he then, he wonders, the person he thinks he is? Like his father, he is not immune to a certain amount of status. No longer the one 'who always had to get back', but nevertheless the one who does the running orders, the professional, organised, and always well prepared.

Brian Patten shares some of McGough's religious conviction but will not accept that his close friend is an organiser:

Roger was always interested in doing things but never organising them. He's still like that. Roger's very good at having other people organise things. He's good at being the President of this-and-that, but not the organiser. He's good at telling other people to organise things, and when they have, he does them. He's not so much the organiser as the man who tells people how to organise. That's the way I see it. I think Adrian would say the same.

Having been one himself for so long, this is highly likely. Henri is aware too, that he has often been seen as something of a 'theoriser'. In the opening chapter of *Environments and Happenings* he talks about moving 'Towards a Total Art'. His own career is this argument's best example. For the past thirty years he had been involved with painting, poetry, music, theatre, television and performance art. As a painter he had been surprisingly prolific considering his work in so many other areas.

The similarly eclectic and unconventional Maurice Cockrill, arguably the most successful of the Liverpool painters since his move to London in 1982, is still an admirer. 'Adrian has a lot of talent for many things, and I think people have often been envious of him. He's always been very informed with an amazing memory. And also very democratic and unpretentious in a kind of modern Wordsworthian way.'

Henri was getting much milage in his live readings (and still does) out of what must rank as one of the most genuinely serendipitous 'found poems' in the language. A 'Report By Organiser' (a certain Frances Massey) concerning a school visit he had made in Buckinghamshire had been 'leaked' to him by a 'mole' in Buckinghamshire Arts. Given the death of shipbuilding, the Toxteth riots, the horrors of the Hillsborough massacre, there is irony, and then some, in 'Book The Writer', a declaration of independence for poets everywhere. It was a 'poem' that never touched Henri's hand:

Mr. Adrian Henri was punctual.

His talk was lively, imaginative and informative – enjoyed by both adults and children.

Unfortunately his personal appearance left much to be desired and did nothing to reinforce the standards of dress and hygiene held within the school.

It also did nothing to improve the image of Liverpool, a city in need of ambassadors.

In April 1986 South Hill Park Arts Centre in Bracknell arranged a major (and later touring) retrospective of Henri's work. It was the ideal place as there were theatrical, musical, video and performance events accompanying the exhibition. To add to this event Alison & Busby published his *Collected Poems*. To put icing on the cake he met a student from Alsace taking a year out named Catherine Marcangeli.

Lis Burgoyne had never moved into Mount Street, preferring her own place at Little St Bride Street. On finishing the thesis on Henri's work, she was accepted on a Drama Course in Manchester.The relationship abruptly ended around the same time as the thesis:

It was certainly something that I hadn't seen coming. It was not through my decision – it just happened – and was consequently quite painful.

Just as painful was Margaret Thatcher's third election victory in 1987 which cast aside British guilt about material advance whether it be socialists with or without money, or paternalistic Tories who were born with it. Her government, so keenly bent on change had done so with more effect than any since Attlee's, but astute left-wingers saw Thatcherism as an effective initiative in the class war, but one at times whose very spokesmen were embarassed by the strident tones of their eponymous heroine. Unnerved that she could be anything but a positive factor in Conservative appeal, and indifferent to the nemesis that hubris often invites she boldly announced that far from seeking election for an interim period, she was going 'to go on and on'.

Joyce Henri whom Adrian Henri had divorced in the sixties was under no illusions. She was dying. Henri recalls:

> Some years earlier she had been diagnosed as suffering from multiple sclerosis, then had an operation which wasn't successful at all, her illness became quite horrific, but fortunately it was relatively short.

Henri and Catherine Marcangeli met again that summer. Then they saw each other the following year. Since then they have been together, but apart, his new love living variously in Strasbourg, Paris, Oxford and New York, studying English and American literature at the Ecole Normale Superieure, teaching at the Sorbonne and at Merton College, Oxford.

After a gap of nine years, Brian Patten, referring partly to the freak storms that had swept across Britain in the autumn of 1987, and partly to his own careworn, disorientated state of mind, published *Storm Damage*. Expectations were high but the book did not live up to them. Lachlan Mackinnon, writing in *The Independent on Sunday* described it as poetry that 'flickers like the last surviving members of a species of butterfly, a sad memorial to its own failed promise'. Patten himself was no less disappointed:

> I was going through a very bad patch, both physically and mentally and I let the poems go without bothering. I shouldn't have let that particular book go out as it was. I should have worked on the poems a lot more – I wasn't interested – and I kind of regret that.

At nearly ninety pages *Storm Damage* is by far Patten's longest collection, but it lacks cohesion and cries out for an editor. There is much to admire in the book. It is fair to say with more care and attention it could have worked. Three of the better poems, 'The Apple-Flavoured Worm', 'The Bee's Last Journey to the Rose' and 'The Complaint' were taken from *Gargling with Jelly*, and generally there is much more humour than in any of his previous adult work. 'The Almost Loveless Alphabet' and 'Hair Today, No Her Tomorrow' are effectively quicksilver performance pieces, the latter arguably his most successful comic poem for adults, whilst the somewhat uneven 'A Fallible Lecture' was to become a regular opener for Patten's developing live set. A reply to Adrian Mitchell's 'The Oxford Hysteria Of English Poetry', Patten's oration begins in 1386 'when a gang of people went for a walk to a place called Canterbury'. Picking up Shakespeare, Johnson, Donne, Milton, and Dryden on the way. 'Then along came John Wilmot Earl of Rochester who wrote satirical poems about dildos which were entering fashionable British society in the 1660s.' Later came the Age of Reason when little of great beauty was written 'because everybody was going about feeling incredibly reasonable'.

It ends, after mentioning 'a shy librarian from Hull' with a Yorkshireman who writes about 'belligerent natural forces and sheep'.

There are narrative poems ('Glue Story','20 Million Flies'), there is satire ('Dead Thick') and social comment ('Aphasia' and 'Job Hunting') that do strike chords, but the sequencing of the book is ragged. Poems such as 'Perhaps' register merely as self-parody and the book is littered with fillers that should have been scrapped. One exception is 'The Cynic's Only Love Poem':

> Love comes and goes,
> And often it has paused
> Then comes back to see
> The damage it has caused.

Patten's disengaged mood is best reflected in 'The Tragedy' when finding a note behind the cooker which reads 'Bastard... I'll not be back again.' His response was:

> I was not even sure whether
> It was addressed to me.
> Perhaps. Pehaps not.
> I neither knew nor cared.
> That is the tragedy.

The tragedy of *Storm Damage* (with its unnecessarily ornate presentation) is that it badly serves some fine poems, none better than 'The Ambush' written for a friend constantly unlucky in love. 'I wrote it for her in a bar in Deya, she'd just split up with her boyfriend and was really low. A couple of days later I met her again and she was with someone else! Bit of a waste of time really.'

Despite this added irony, Patten delivers with 'The Ambush', keeping sentimentality at bay by introducing a torn up 'list of regrets' which gives vernacular lustre to both syntax and setting. Instead of an evocatively poetic image at the centre of the poem, he opts for something far more prosaic:

> Hidden from you, crouched
> Among the longings you have suppressed
> And the desire you imagine tamed,
> A sweet pain awaits in ambush.

And in controlled sensuous language where safe habits 'bend like sunlight under water' Patten sends both reader and subject 'falling heavenwards' in a sub-Dionysian sprawl where

> Once again
> Monstrous love will swallow you.

In August 1987, at the age of fifty-two, death swallowed Joyce Henri. Her former husband begins 'For Joyce Henri, New Year 1988' in typically inclusive fashion:

In 1987
Willy was 40, Roger was 50, I was 55 and you
were 52. We drank fizzy wine at your bedside
knowing you wouldn't see 53.

'The only one who could work the bathroom geyser / singing along with Shostakovich' in 'Who', Joyce had often been sceptical of Henri's artistic preoccupations and visibly drunk at some of his openings but, apart from his mother, was the woman who had shaped Henri the most.

Like McGough and Patten before him, Henri now found himself more and more preoccupied with writing for children:

I do have some regrets about not having children of my own. It has been a fairly selfish life I've led. Having so many much younger siblings has meant that in a kind of a way I've been a surrogate father. I suppose the advantage has been that if I starve through the type of life I've led, then it's only me that suffers.

Henri did not find writing for children any easier, but it did give him the licence to be a nine-year old again, *Rhinestone Rhino*, the most autobiographical of his children's work, based largely on early years spent in 'the children's playground' of Rhyl.

The concerns he had as a painter in the seventies had now infiltrated his poetry, without precluding the emotional associations his heart-on-the-sleeve approach usually warranted. He had been commissioned to write a two-part modern-language version of *The Wakefield Mystery Plays*, to be performed in the grounds of Pontefract Castle with music by Andy Roberts. The added challenge of writing for actors' voices rather than his own became self-evident in his next collection for Cape, *Wish You Were Here* published in 1990.

Two other writers established themselves in the Liverpool literary tradition during this period, both in the field of Drama. Willy Russell and Alan Bleasedale, although different as writers, have much in common. Both are former teachers, and both are firmly rooted in family traditions and have gone on record as having been influenced by the Mersey Poets. Russell's *John, Paul, George, Ringo and Bert* had been a massive success at The Everyman Theatre in the mid-seventies, not only launching Russell, but also singer Barbara Dixon and such fine actors as Anthony Sher, Trevor Eve and Bernard Hill. Formerly a hairdresser, with musical ambitions, Russell had been a regular at the poetry readings at the Green Moose that Patten set up so long ago. He went from strength to strength, having a huge international hit with *Educating Rita* (in which his screenplay was nominated for an Oscar), followed by *Blood Brothers* and *Shirley Valentine*, establishing him as second only to Alan Ayckborn as the country's most popular playwright.

Bleasdale's success came initially with television, his epochal drama in six parts *Boys from the Blackstuff* still regarded as a benchmark for social relevance and Scouse quotability. In 1989 as part of the Liverpool Comedy Festival, McGough, Patten, and Henri were teamed with the two playwrights to do a show at The Everyman called *The Famous Five*. McGough remembers

> Alan and Willy being nervous before the show. But they were amazing – you couldn't get them off the stage – and next year we did it again, this time without Alan, just Willy, and he became the motivating force saying let's do more of it.

Dapper as ever, Roger McGough had acquired a ponytail, an ear-ring and had taken to wearing a baseball cap. Anti-fashion as ever, his stage clothes and street attire the same, Brian Patten had been touring Australia, where in an interview he had hinted at writing about his Liverpool past, having 'started to smell the grave'.

Adrian Henri, still in Liverpool, had become the University's Writer-in-Residence. George Melly had long felt that Henri should have moved to London or at least got a London agent: 'but I suppose if Adrian moved now all the committees would have to close'. He had joined the Advisory Committee for the newly opened Tate Gallery in Liverpool, the following year being awarded an Honorary D. Litt.

Wish You Were Here, Henri's final Cape collection, is a heartfelt, warmly resonant book. Less concerned with anonymous places: hedges, riverbanks, gardens and wastegrounds, we follow our hero through his autumnal years in a far more place-specific way as he shares poignant souvenirs. Featuring one of his own collages on the cover including a photo-booth snapshot of Catherine in the top right-hand corner, it reveals a ripped envelope with the words 'Joyce Henri' written in his distinctive handwriting above the title. Opening and closing with poems for Joyce, the sequencing excellent as it looks backwards at journeys taken, at places and memories, mourns those no longer alive, and looks forwards to future shared moments of love. In the unusually macabre 'Suburban Landscape with Figures' Henri sensually sets up a scene at twilight where it is

Dusk. A suburban street. The smell
of lilacs. A man is walking
a small black-and-white dog.

The poem then drifts in and out of awareness almost flippantly touching on the horror it is unravelling: 'all the nice young men, / the powdered bodies / propped carefully in armchairs, / placed carefully beneath floorboards, / who are not dead but only sleeping'.

The understated narrative is then steered backwards and forwards by the controlled repetition of the seven lines of the opening stanza. Augmented by random items of domesticity – a pan, a gas stove – it stretches beyond mere cleverness, revealing ' a young man's severed head' while deep in the darkness:

shadows gather in the lilacs,
the buddleias.

'Morning, Liverpool 8' is a rare encounter with the metaphor for Henri in which he anthropomorphicises his neighbourhood's terraces as 'half-wake' jaded courtesans in Blackburne Place and Canning Street as they

stretch their balconies;
cast-iron railings, Ionic columns
blink into daylight from
a nightmare of bulldozers,
dripping water, charred beams,
distant dreams of hopscotch,
hoofbeats on cobblestones.

The collection constantly stirs up buried emotions. Sometimes successfully, ('Harbour, 'Cullercoats' and 'The Bell'), sometimes not ('Shadowland', despite its surface energy is surprisingly static). There are moments that encapsulate rare penetrative beauty as in 'Ophelia' where Henri curbs his natural tendency to be too visually descriptive, depicting the painting he would have made, but

you are gone
and the image floats away downstream as shadows gather
in the green-carpeted bathroom. The lily-pads
of the bathmat you gave me remember.

The collection is dedicated to Joyce Henri (nee Wilson) 1935-1987; the short closing poem 'For Joyce', by the repetitive use of the same phrase, affirms a stifling presence:

I don't want
to be any trouble' You'd say,

every day. 'Don't want
to be any trouble.' If you don't want
to be any trouble,
why do you walk into my dreams
every night?

The Nineties

Brian Patten began the new decade with a worthy follow-up to *Gargling With Jelly*, the equally praised and more subversive *Thawing Frozen Frogs*. Also published by Puffin, the same length as its predecessor, and again illustrated by David Mostyn, it contains such reflective gems as 'The River', 'Hide-away Sam', 'Spider Apples' and 'You Can't Be That'. There is the mischievously plausible 'Dear Mum' and one of the best and funniest poems in the language for children (read fast), the show-stopping 'The Race to Get to Sleep' ('It's Matthew! It's Penny! It's Penny! It's Matthew!'). Using his comic powers to their fullest effect (something he rarely achieves with adults), the poem's horse race commentary builds, pauses, finally accelerates again taking audiences of all ages along on the bumpy ride.

A child at heart, certainly on their side, Patten echoes Charles Causley's view that 'children are excellent judges of poetry, even if they can't always express it in language. Patten affirms this by saying 'you owe it to them to do it very well'. Instinctively knowing what appeals to children; what bores them and what most definitely patronises them, Patten told *The Independent* that 'writing for children requires a totally different form, and is technically much more demanding'. To keep his adult work in the public domain, Unwin & Allen published *Grinning Jack: Selected Poems*, with the usual portrait of Patten on the cover. Sales, again, were exceptional.

Roger McGough's fourth decade in the public eye saw Hilary give birth to Isabel, his fourth child and first daughter. His children's book, *An Imaginary Menagerie* – an alphabet of outrageous, mostly fictitious, creatures including the Alivator, the Goodgers (and the Badgers), the hairy canary, and one very naughty vignette in which:

> to amuse
> emus
> on warm summer nights
> kiwis
> do wee-wees
> from spectacular heights

had been greatly acclaimed, with enormous sales and response in schools. He was later asked by The Poetry Society to participate in and compere a tour promoting two leading contemporary American poets.

McGough arrived at Victoria Sation to the sound of tap-tap-tap. Sharon Olds, dressed all in black with white ankle socks, was sitting on the floor surrounded by suitcases hammering away at her typewriter. She looked like a bespectacled Dorothy out of *The Wizard of Oz*, but there the resemblance ends. Born in San Francisco in 1942, her collection *The Matter of this World* published in Britain in 1987, had received much critical attention establishing her as one of the natural successors to the 'confessional' American poets so championed by Al Alvarez in *The New Poetry* of 1962. Many critics felt she rivalled Sylvia Plath in intensity, and Elizabeth Bishop for undiluted nerve.

Also on the tour was C.K. Williams whose fifth collection *Flesh and Blood*, published in this country by Bloodaxe, had won the 1987 National Book Critics Circle poetry award. A protegé of Plath's friend Anne Sexton, he was widely regarded as the most challenging American poet of his generation. Writing in *The Washington Post* Caroline Kizer describes him as 'the most exciting poet writing today, an authentically new voice in American poetry, a voice which couldn't be anything but American'.

McGough, whose voice couldn't be anything else but Liverpudlian, got to know them both well:

> Charlie's one of those urbane, self-assured Americans, well mannered, but things have got to be right. And Sharon was amazing – all wide-eyed innocence, she works on this big campus but feels she'd be happier on a small farm. And her poetry was outrageous and shocking, full of in-your-face sex. We started in Brighton, and what was funny was I started the tour being quite big - trying to get the audience warmed up, and Sharon would come on rather tiny with her glass of water. But as the tour progressed I got smaller and smaller and she seemed to get bigger and bigger. By the time we reached Glasgow I expected her to appear in a kilt! It was a different experience for me. Enlightening. And I was sorry when it ended.

The end for Margaret Thatcher came literally out of the blue. Convinced she was nothing other than a positive factor for the Conservatives, she gave scant attention to a challenge from within her own party by Michael Heseltine and paid the price. Not wanting another 'knight in shining armour', the Tories replaced Thatcher with the altogether more reasonable but over-promoted John Major. He was blooded immediately. The leader of Iraq, Saddam Hussein had decided to take the West on in what he described in vivid language as 'the mother of all wars'. It never quite lived up to that billing, but voyeuristically millions were able to watch the clinical new technology of war on television. Underlining Christopher Logue's statement 'all wars are one war', Adrian

Mitchell kept on reading 'Tell me Lies about Vietnam' with as much verve and passion as ever. And Roger McGough concluded in 'Late-Night News':

A million miles of footage
Countless reels of tape
Twentieth-century history:
Murder, torture, rape.

When we hear the starting gun
We dispatch the nearest crew
Today it's Sarajevo
Tomorrow? A town near you.
So if you wake up screaming
From dreams you did not choose

Remember that you saw it first
Here on late-night news.

Hilary McGough, having graduated at Chelsea had worked firstly for the British Medical Association and then become a researcher for the BBC initially on *You and Yours*, later on *Tomorrow's World*. Her husband strayed into her territory when he was commissioned to write a sequence about the elements, which was published in 1991 in the Channel 4 book *An A-Z of the Elements*, accompanying the film *Equinox: The Elements* produced by Windfall Films. McGough gave the acting performance of his life (picking up a Royal Television Society Award),'becoming' Oxygen:

I am the Kiss of Life
Its ebb and flow
With your last gasp
You will call my name:
    'o o o o o o o'

then Nitrogen, followed by Carbon, Iron, Mercury and Sulphur (echoing Adrian Mitchell's famous 'I like that stuff' – the refrain from 'Stufferation':

Mobsters
got where they got with it...
    Children
play a lot with it...
    Cities
glow white hot with it...
    Guy Fawkes
hatched a plot with it...

moving deftly to Gold ('The one on top'), he playfully toys with Fool's Gold ('All who love you are fools.'), and ends up with the man-made Element 109:

> Now you see me
> Now you...

Adrian Henri also had a new commission. This time to write a poem for the Labour Party's next manifesto based around their new designer logo, 'the red rose' – the flag designated as a thing of the past. Henri came up with 'Winter Ending', his friends blaming him for yet another (albeit narrow) subsequent defeat.

McGough felt it good for Liverpool to be asked to become Chairman of Chelsea Arts Club when approached by Adrian Forsyth. There was also the added cachet of being a poet in an arena usually reserved for artists. He accepted a similar offer of joining the Council of The Poetry Society when asked by Carol Ann Duffy, now felt by such peers as Sean O' Brien to be 'the representative poet of the present day, much as Philip Larkin came to seem for the time between Attlee and Thatcher'.

Out of respect for Carol Ann, and risking being the panjandrum Patten jokingly accuses him of, McGough accepted. He used his time there productively however to move that no member should stay on the Council for more than three years:

> Some had been on it for as long as seventeen years, and were serving their own ends rather than the good of poetry. And poetry's important to me so I got the motion passed. And after three years I left. The job was done. But I do wonder sometimes; am I the person I think I am? That 'melting into the foreground' concept: building a smoke screen, then standing in front of it. Sometimes I wonder

Patten was still deeply immersed in wondering about children. After *Thawing Frozen Frogs* followed *The Puffin Book of Twentieth-Century Children's Verse*. Editing the anthology, Patten arranged the poems in reverse chronological order, simulating a journey back through time. Obvious classics such as Walter de la Mare's 'The Listeners' were included, but slotted in with lesser-known poems by equally well-known authors. Talking about the book in 1991 Patten confirmed his belief that while many poems written for adults age and 'grow creaky as the years pass', poems written for children seem to retain their freshness. 'The best have a sense of wonder, mystery and mischief that their older brothers and sisters often seem to lose.'

Two other childrens' books, *Grizzelda Frizzle and Other Stories* and *The Magic Bicycle,* followed. Discussing his increasing involvement in the genre Patten told one interviewer:

> I am interested in fantasy, but always set the fantastic against realistic backgrounds, so that the everyday is put into another perspective. Reality is not constant. Each child and adult creates his own version of it, depending on his needs.

The reality for the electorate in April 1992, despite 'Winter Ending's' 'bright red roses', was yet another Tory government. Through a series of public relations gaffes Neil Kinnock had snatched defeat from the jaws of victory. 'Nightmare on Kinnock Street' proclaimed *The Sun*. 'Will the last one to leave Britain please switch off the lights.' To his credit John Major, despite such jingoistic assistance, fought a determined and sedulous campaign. Much of the latter part was spent amongst the people standing on top of a battered soap-box. In contrast, Kinnock looked triumphalist and shallow; no one knew what he really stood for. Sadly, this was reflected for the changing Labour Party in the polls.

Despite the election setback, 1992 was another good year for Roger McGough. Penguin had published *You at the Back*, a companion (though much weaker) Selected Poems, and his next full collection *Defying Gravity*. The former, dedicated to Hilary – complete with a school photograph on the back showing McGough, quiff in place at St. Mary's (pony-tail and green glasses in place on the front) – can be regarded as a children's book, despite its comic and occasionally subversive nature, and is mainly for completists.

Defying Gravity, originally published under the Viking imprint, is McGough's best book to date. At 107 pages it is by far the longest, despite a gap of only five years since the publication of *Melting into the Foreground*. Featuring a photograph from the Science Photo Library of an egg being fertilised, and rather slickly packaged, it has the feel of a mini-encyclopedia of McGough, being divided into six sections, beginning with his family – who re-appear in part five – and ending with the bonus of the 'Elements'. Never has the argument for omitting the slighter pieces been greater. Many fall flat or merely clutter an already capacious collection. Although *The Times Literary Supplement* declined to review it – on the grounds that it was merely 'humour' – there was much praise: *The Oxford Times* relished its 'sense of time slipping away', the poignancy of its 'emotional reticence'. Elizabeth Jennings, reviewing for *The Daily Telegraph* asserted that 'deftness does not preclude seriousness' and found 'his deliberately comic spirit most refreshing'.

The best poems are the serious ones although 'Ex Patria' augments his catalogue of successfully funny aphorisms:

O England, how I miss you.
Ascot, Henley, Wimbledon. It's the little things

McGough's ability to turn (a poem) in what David Profumo described on 'the rhetoric of surprise' is most evident in 'Five-Car Family', where after setting up the ballad form with six tightly packed quatrains beginning with:

We're a five-car family,
Got what it takes,
Eight thousaand cc,
Four different makes,

the poem 'drives' straight to the rhythmic pulse of writing, changing up into fifth on the seventh :

Cos it's all about noise
And it's all about speed
And it's all about power
And it's all about greed

And it's all about fantasy
And it's all about dash
And it's all about machismo
And it's all about cash

And it's all about blood
And it's all about gore
And it's all about oil
And it's all about war

And it's all about money
And it's all about spend
And it's all about time
That it came to an end.

Roger McGough was fifty-three when his first daughter was born, the same age his own father died. Initially Isabel's birth produced only one significant poem, but it did seem to change certain long-felt attitudes and hardened others.

'Cinders' sees McGough carrying his young daughter back to the car after a Christmas pantomime performance, and 'hunched against the wind and hobbling', feels he 'could be mistaken for [her] grandfather'. Sensing this, he holds her more tightly, 'Knowing that I will never see you dressed for the Ball'. But he might. On one level the poem is an engaging heartfelt entreaty across time, space and culture. On another, we see a born-again father clumsily fumbling with straps on the baby seat of a car:

Waiting in the wings, the witching hour.
Already the car is changing. Smells sweet
Of ripening seed. We must go. Must go.

Few have ever doubted McGough's natural gifts: his near perfect ear, his wit and verbal dexterity. Even Douglas Dunn granted him his occasional successes, but what has constantly irked generations of critics is, they feel, he has never 'developed' as a poet. Charles Causley is dismissive of such assertions. 'When you've come such a long way down the road, you don't need to go anywhere else.' However, the assumption that what you see is what you get – and that's all you get – frequently belies the juxtaposition of the comical and the serious, a concern for both the absurd and the profound. McGough's prime motive has always been the consideration of a poem's theme rather than its method, the finished work rather than the experimentation. This is endorsed in an insightful review of the 'trickster you can trust' in *Poetry Review*, where, dealing specifically with the title poem – the elegy for his old friend John Hewson, the reviewer asserts '[it] is pure McGough – both ordinary and magical – and is perfect in its way.'

No poem illustrates his achievement better than 'Defying Gravity'. Fraught with terminal symbolism the spacious stanzas open with neatly packed assertions and conditionals, reasoned instructions and stoical resignation:

Gravity is one of the oldest tricks in the book.
Let go of the book and it abseils to the ground
As if, at the centre of the earth, spins a giant yo-yo
To which everything is attached by an invisible string.

Tear out a page of the book and make an aeroplane.
Launch it. For an instant it seems that you have fashioned
A shape that can outwit air, that has slipped the knot.
But no. The earth turns, the winch tightens, it is wound in.

Reaching the third verse McGough's voice changes into the prosaic: 'One of my closest friends is, at the time of writing, / Attempting to defy gravity, and will surely succeed. / Eighteen months ago he was playing rugby,' but then as if reminded of the truth, the tone is let go:

Now, seven stones lighter, his wife carries him aw-
Kwardly from room to room. Arranges him gently

Upon the sofa for the visitors. 'How's things?'
(Open brackets. Condition inoperable. Close brackets.)

As if reminded by the 'armful of bones' of the 'clean and inbetween / the sheets holywater death' McGough recoils, releasing the poem's most imaginative leap:

> Freeing himself from the tackle
> He will sidestep the opposition and streak down the wing
> Towards a dimension as yet unimagined.

And as no one can be replaced and nothing repaired – 'Another day / Another universe' – he is jolted by the recurrence of the poem's most defining image into a parallel universe, prompting one final assertion:

> Back where the strings are attached there will be a service
> And homage paid to the giant yo-yo. A box of left-overs
> Will be lowered into a space on loan from the clay.
> Then, weighted down, the living will walk wearily away.

In the Spring of 1993 Bloodaxe published *The New Poetry*, taking its title from Al Alvarez's blast against 'the gentility principle'. Aggressive and ambitious, with an equally long-winded polemical introduction, it collected fifty diverse and challenging voices either under fifty years of age or unpublished until the eighties, staking its claim as an overview of the new generation of British and Irish poets who had emerged since Larkin. It made no apology for using Alvarez's title for an anthology of poetry 'that is fresh in its attitudes, risk-taking in its address, and plural in its forms and voices'.

A more approachable sister volume, also by Bloodaxe, came out later in the same year. Edited by Linda France, *Sixty Women Poets* traced the flowering of women's poetry since the death of Stevie Smith in 1971, emphasising the links that bind the new generation to older writers such as Elma Mitchell and Elizabeth Jennings. Those featured in both anthologies included Carol Ann Duffy, Helen Dunmore, Selima Hill, Jackie Kay and Jo Shapcott.

So where do the Mersey poets fit in such fervid times? Anyone in London interested enough in 1993 to find out, was given the opportunity in the December of that year.

'They're putting the band back together. They're playing a one-off gig at the Queen Elizabeth Hall – a grand place that, for three scruffy Liverpool lads.' So began Mark Jones in 'The Arts' section of *The Evening Standard*. Titled 'The poets who never grew up', Jones, enjoying his musical metaphor, continued, 'Like other bands, they will still be the scruffy, sardonic Mersey poets we've found so lovable this last quarter of a century.' Anticipating the demographics of the audience he felt you would see '24 years-worth of teachers and schoolkids right down to 1990's teenagers whose literary curriculum has not yet gone so far Back to Basics that there isn't room for "Goodbat Nightman" or "My Busconductor".' 'From the day (*The Mersey Sound*) came out', Jones plods on, 'snotty critics have pitched into them apparently bent on preserving contemporary verse for their Oxbridge lecture rooms. That's fine by the band. It proves their point. Theirs is poetry of the people for the people, by people who know the things ordinary people care about.' 'All that seemed liberating at fifteen,' he concludes sagely, 'is embarassing now.' Having a monster hit first time out is fab. Following it up can be a drag'.

Michael Glover of *The Financial Times*, who actually saw the reading came to a similar conclusion: 'The Liverpool Poets were back. But back to what?' Henri was damned with faint praise; Patten patronised – 'some of his love poems' Glover conceded, 'were very good indeed'; and McGough's work was 'mainly about his relations, [which] is... very different from the mildly subversive stuff of the 1960s, the tics picked up from e.e. cummings; the defiant spurning of syntax and punctuation; the not so daring hymns to free love. What he seems to exude now is a mood of incorrigible optimism and the belief that poetry and what it memorialises is for sharing.'

This humble maxim must have impressed Thames Valley University – if not Glover – who honoured McGough with an honourary professorship that year. He was an academic at last.

At the beginning of 1994 Roger McGough was the captive on *Desert Island Discs*, fending off Sue Lawley's slow lobs with a straight bat his father would have been proud of: 'There you were in Liverpool in 1967, absolutely where it was at. What was that like?' McGough: 'If I'd known I'd have taken more notice at the time.' He corrected the idea that he was ever 'a would-be-poet' and revealed as his one regret turning down the role of the narrator in Willy Russell's *Blood Brothers*. His choice of records included 'La Donna Mobile', Dylan Thomas reading from *Under Milk Wood*, 'Love Me Do', Stan Getz's version of 'Funny Valentine', Marilyn Monroe from the *Blood Brothers*' score, and the sound of Mersey tugs' foghorns – which caused great problems for the BBC's sound department ('Do they have to be Mersey tugs?'). The plaintive sound of the tugs was like bees to honey for the 'incorrigibly optimistic' McGough, and became the 'record' he would take with him. The two worldly goods he chose were *The Times Atlas of the Night Sky* and a big black taxi, in which he would live (becoming the first Liverpool poet to drive) and in which he would count his lucky stars.

The following month Brian Patten received the news that his mother Stella Bevan had suffered a brain haemorrhage. Ironically, it happened on the site of what had been The Magnet cinema, a place that loomed so large in his childhood. Stella's last home had been sheltered accommodation near the Lune Laundry where she had worked for so long.

Patten hurried back to Liverpool, staying for a few days with Adrian Henri in Mount Street. It was the most time the two had spent together for years. Henri noticed some changes:

> He seemed far less self-contained somehow and more open to things outside himself. I felt that in many ways this was very positive. Brian, unlike me, has never needed outside stimulus that much. It's all inside his head. Although what happened with his mother was tragic, without it he would never have written the recent poems which go back to his childhood and are some of the best things he's ever done.

Patten spent hours at his mother's hospital bedside in Broadgreen, but she never regained consciousness and died on March 13th 1994. It was both an unexpected and deeply painful experience for him. 'In the end it seems so small – death – the struggle for life so enormous.' Grieving for her during the next few months struck a rich seam of self-reproach, residual guilt and creativity. It was to produce some of the best poems of his entire career.

Soon after Stella Bevan's death came an equally unexpected but much more public demise. John Smith, who had succeeded Neil Kinnock as leader of the Labour Party, suffered a fatal heart attack. On the grounds of seniority he had been the obvious choice to succeed Kinnock in 1992, though some in the party felt the younger Gordon Brown would have been a better long-term bet. By 1994, Brown's fellow moderniser but 'junior partner', the charismatic Tony Blair, had risen above his close colleague, becoming the party's overwhelming choice. An unashamed admirer of Margaret Thatcher's ability to set achievable – if at times unpopular – objectives, Labour under Blair was likely to head towards 'Thatcherism with Welfare'.

In the early nineties, Comedy had been heralded as the new Rock'n'Roll. Now it was Poetry. There had been some recent positive changes. The Poetry Society had appointed a new director, the vigorous, outward-looking Chris Meade; they had acquired better premises in Covent Garden, and effectively promoted the New Generation Poets, a showcase for twenty of the most acclaimed younger contemporaries. This contentious grouping included the now 'long-established' Carol Ann Duffy, seen as exemplary in re-energising a feminist public voice, the fast-rising Simon Armitage, and Liverpool-born Jamie

McKendrick. Simultaneously, Penguin re-launched their Penguin Modern Poets Series, Volume One consisting of James Fenton, Blake Morrison and Kit Wright. McGough (with Charles Causley, the only other poet to be retained from the original series), was grouped in Volume Four, this time with Liz Lochhead and Sharon Olds.

All three of the Mersey poets were as active and involved as ever. They commanded top fees on the circuit, audiences and book sales still outstanding. McGough's sets were brilliantly organised arrangements from his classy back-catalogue, updated by a seemingly inexhaustible supply of fresh new material. He was constantly contemporary, in some ways meeting (the admittedly overstated) assessment of the Irish poet Sean Trayner, as being 'wittier than anyone else, brighter than anyone else and more intelligent than anyone else'.

Henri's readings played somewhere between Patten's and McGough's. More self-deprecating, right leg constantly twitching, they exuded warmth, feeling and insight, taking audiences gently through his avuncular bohemian life. Patten, with that 'little touch of moonlight', eyes often closed, some of the poems read from memory, one hand thrust deep in his pocket, 'successfully blade-of-grassing' his audiences (to quote Matt Holland's memorable phrase), able to make them cry or laugh at will. At times resembling an ageing corkscrew-haired Artful Dodger , his ability to communicate with an audience whether raucous or *sotto voce* remained formidable.

It was primarily his readings that kept his reputation intact. As difficult as ever to capture in the round, over seven years since the disappointing *Storm Damage*, Patten seemed in no hurry to produce a successor. *Gargling with Jelly* had sold 200,000 copies and following Bob Dylan's nineties' 'Never-ending tour' maxim, he undertook more far-reaching commitments. 'He's impossible to fathom', McGough has said, 'when he's on tour he wants to be back home, when he's at home he wants to be away again. He always seems to want to be somewhere else.'

Many of the places he was visiting were rife with war. Whether the Sudan, Yugoslavia or Macedonia, disintegration was just behind him. For safety he spent more and more time at a house rented by his friend Molly Parkin in the *Under Milk Wood*-like village of Mousehole in Cornwall where Dylan Thomas spent his honeymoon. From being so many people's favourite poet, Patten was being re-assessed in the terms of 'I-used-to-like-him-once'. Not that it bothered him. He has long trusted his instincts, always known he is the real thing, someone who has been a poet and nothing else since the age of fifteen. Nonetheless his admirers were hoping for a strong new collection to reinforce their somewhat wavering belief.

Adrian Henri's readership received a boost in 1995 with the publication of *Not Fade Away*, his first collection for Bloodaxe, and the most cohesive and tightly edited book of his writing career. Due to a recent upsurge in his globe trotting activities, Liverpool had become increasingly merely a part of his milieu. Dedicated to Catherine Marcangeli 'in whatever country we are', the presentation of the book is exemplary. Bloodaxe had long been renowned for their pioneering jacket design and the quality of both print and paper. Reproducing *The Entry of Christ into Liverpool* on the cover was inspired. Before opening it, the book feels right. Continuing the theme of the 'preservation of memories' from *Not Fade Away*, it is described by Carol Ann Duffy as reading like a 'warm, personal book of days', speaking 'with a direct simplicity', 'confronting contemporary realities with a sense of renewed vigour'.

Included in the cover painting's anthology of heroes and friends are John Gorman, Arthur Dooley, Roger McGough, Mike Evans, Joyce Henri, Sam Walsh, Pere Ubu, George and Diana Melly, Charles Mingus, Brian Patten, Pete Brown, Charlie Parker, Philip Jones-Griffiths, Henry Graham and The Beatles. Henri claimed the painting:

> is a kind of visual diary of the years it was painted in because the townscape was finished fairly quickly but the figures were done on the additive principle for two years, and sometimes I had to add beards or change the girls' hair colour or style. People I quarrelled with even got painted out.

Two of those closest to Henri had recently prematurely died. Henri had mourned his former wife in his previous book. Now it was the turn of Sam Walsh.

Having been 'invalided out' of the Art College through alcoholism, Walsh, purely a social drinker in the sixties, had become increasingly reclusive, resenting Henri's celebrity and his own failure at not becoming a more unanimously praised painter. The two did exhibit together at The Hanover Gallery in Liverpool in 1986, but were never able to recreate the shared bohemian camaraderie of the late fifties and early sixties.

'A Portrait of the Artist' is a timeless evocation of that part of experience that happens beyond time:

> In a forgotten attic smelling faintly of soot
> propped against a peeling wall,
> there is a painting,
> wrapped in a moth-eaten rug.

Next to it in a 'battered, dark red portfolio' is where 'the artist kept his dreams'. The poem maintains its feeling of being outside time as the narrative telescopes dreams of paintings of the Pier Head, Ingrid Bergman 'painted as tenderly as Alfred Hitchcock', Michael Curtiz and John Wayne, finally arriving where

there is a final dream
the artist did not dream,
of paintings of Saddam Hussain
and General Norman Schwarzkopf,
huge as war memorials.

The timing, the deft transition from one controlled mood to another could hardly be better. We are taken piecemeal into that unfathomable area where artistic energy touches and transforms human experience. We enter an area where the artist 'looks out of the picture which he has forgotten' from an unfinished self-portrait beneath a rug'. The disparate elements in his studio combine with the 'gleaming, skeleton hand' that he does not see 'painted in the manner of Hans Hoblein', striking a despairing resonance, as it places

an opened bottle of whisky
silently on a table by the easel.

'A Portrait of the Artist' opens the first section in which Henri includes poems for Elvis, Andre Breton, Debussy and – in 'A Brief Reflection on Poetry', involving a blackboard in a Music Room – an adroit vignette for Miroslav Holub, which concludes:

in the silence after the poem
the ghost of a violin
quavers briefly.

Memories and magical places including Normandy and Haworth are preserved in the next two sections, 'Souvenirs' and 'Yosemite'; the fourth section, 'Look Stranger' is the most peopled and most concerned with his, by now well-established personal mythology of place. In it he refers affectionately to the mysterious childhood figure of Uncle Bill who would 'roll home once a week / watched by the Birkenhead moon', neatly preceding the prodigious 'Book the Writer' with the moving 'Poet in School'. It ends with 'Love Story, Bosnia'. Facing the plight of Bosko and Admira, two lovers in Bosnia, 'the sweater his mother knitted for her / [lies] on the grave her mother cannot visit'. There is 'Jessica', a teenage single mother, Henri's most convincing poem to date in an assumed voice, and the cinematic penultimate piece, the eerily effective 'The Grandmothers' in which:

The doctors have decided
to switch off Sleeping Beauty's
life-support machine:

seven desolate dwarfs
wander the back lot of Universal Studios.

Adrian Henri freely admits that if he had not moved to Liverpool in 1957, he doubts whether he would have become a poet at all. Like his heroes Baudelaire, Apollinaire, Ginsberg and Eliot, his poetic imagination has been for the most part city-haunted. Early in 1996 he had his most challenging commission since the Wakefield Mysteries in 1988. This came from the Royal Liverpool Philharmonic Orchestra, to work with the composer Richard Gordon-Smith on *Lowlands Away*, an orchestral piece for soloists and chorus. It tells the story of the loss at sea of Gordon-Smith's great-grandfather Captain Gentry, and the message in a bottle he sent to his wife which was miraculously retrieved remaining in the possession of the family to this day:

A message in a bottle
entrusted to the sea
lost in the vague play
of the waves;
seen once more
then lost from sight
between sky and shore.

In 'Ballad of the Thames and Medway Barges' Henri reinvestigates his famous names poem 'Me' written over thirty years ago.

For:

Aidie Ailsa Agnes Mary
Abergavenny Alice Ash
Asphodel Atlantis Atlas
Beyond the bay where breakers splash

Read:

Paul McCartney Gustave Mahler
Alfred Jarry John Coltrane
Charlie Mingus Claude Debussy
Wordsworth Monet Bach and Blake.

'Write me a storm' was a strange request, but the opportunity to work within the extended forms of classical music and the limitations of the composer's needs, Henri found liberating.

Soon afterwards the boys started 'putting the band back together'again. A tour with Willy Russell and the ever-dependable cross-collaborator Andy Roberts (replacing Alan Bleasdale), was planned. It was to be called *Words on the Run* (*Lads on the Run* by their wives and girlfriends), a showcase for all five talents, oscillating between imaginative mind-games, poetry and comedy to prose, scripted extracts and song. 'The tap-dancing poets and day-glo musicians in full swing as you've never seen them before.'

Having come through yet another difficult and complicated emotional period, Brian Patten was starting to thematically group together a new series of poems. Pieces that had already acquired an audience such as 'The Minister For Exams' and 'So Many Different Lengths of Time', were matched with poems written in response to his mother's death, providing the nucleus for *Armada*, his seventh adult collection and arguably his best work to date.

Discussing the obvious nautical associations such a title invites, and referring directly to the book's powerful opening section, Patten suggested an alternative resonance:

At the moment of death, in the micro-second between being and non-being, perhaps consciousness enters a state that can be called 'armada', in which all an individual's million fragments of memory, all thoughts, all sensations simultaneously weigh anchor and set sail across unknowable space and time.

In Roger McGough's 'Cinders', the poem is a fairytale metaphor illustrating his concern about never seeing his daughter dressed for the ball or being on hand to warn her against wayward Prince Charmings. In Brian Patten's poem of the same title, Stella Bevan 'never went to a ball, ever. / In all [her] years of sweeping kitchens / No fairy godmother appeared, never.' Lying on a hospital bed, far away from any ball or any hint of Prince Charmings, no matter how indeterminate, her drip discontinued:

Life was never a fairy-tale.
Cinders soon.

In Patten's title poem he looks back over forty years to

when everything I was told was believable
and the little I knew was less limited than now,
I stretched belly down on the grass beside a pond
and to the far bank launched a child's armada.

The metaphor extends as physically it disintegrates into a ruination of burnt tissue and twigs, as it penetrates into the distilled essence of his mother's being:

And you, mother, stood beside me,
impatient to be going,
old at twenty-three, alone,
thin overcoat flapping.

Linda Cookson's study of Patten's work notices how the 'thin overcoat flapping', freezes a 'fragile picture of poverty, vulnerability and oppression' in three words. The shifting perspectives of earlier poems such as 'You Come to Me Quiet as Rain not yet Fallen' are now brought to complete fruition. The poem cuts back to the hospital where Patten's hands reach 'out across forty years to touch once more/that pond's cool surface', touching instead transparent Epiphany:

and it is your cool skin I'm touching;
for as on a pond a child's paper boat
was blown out of reach
by the smallest gust of wind,
so too have you been blown out of reach
by the smallest whisper of death,
and the heart burns as that armada burnt,
long, long ago.

During the mid-seventies Patten had read with Pablo Neruda, whose tone he sometimes resembles. He later described Neruda as 'an all time great poet, a man who was bigger than life... a planet in a suit!' In 'So Many Different Lengths Of Time' Patten answers the Chilean poet's 'How Long Is A Man's Life?', the first two stanzas translated from the original by Lucia Graves giving it a transcendental ecumenical quality. Commenting about the poem Patten has said:

'So Many Different Lengths of Time' is now frequently used in memorial services. A lot of people don't even know who wrote it any more. It's really nice when a poem takes on a life of its own like that.

In its affirming way, at variance with so many sonorous paeans on the subject, the poem details the shared experiences of life that immortalise people to those who knew them best. Loosening the knots of grief in the stomach, calming the 'puffed faces' of grief, it identifies wholly with poetry's covenant with the unspoken word:

And on that day he will not have ceased,
but will have ceased to be separated by death.
How long does a man live, finally?
A man lives so many different lengths of time.

Patten's mistrust of and antipathy towards academics is deep-rooted, surfacing in his poetry as long ago as 'Schoolboy' in *Little Johnny's Confession*, and more recently in the rather easily achieved 'Dead Thick' in *Storm Damage*. Far more effective is 'The Minister For Exams' where the somewhat disingenuous protagonist having 'described the grief of Adam when he was expelled from Eden', and written down 'the exact weight of an elephant's dream' finds himself cleaning out the toilets of the 'fat hotels':

Why? Because constantly I failed my exams.
Why? Well, let me set a test.
Q1. How large is a child's imagination?
Q2. How shallow is the soul of the Minister for Exams?

'Fat' is an adjective Patten has recently come to favour. It crops up again in 'In Perspective', a poem placed towards the end of a brilliantly sequenced selection, seeped in sea imagery, but this time new challenges appear to lie

across the rich earth, the fat orchards, the fields I hardly knew,
Happiness came bounding towards me,
A hungry puppy, mistaking me for its master.

Armada proved to be what Patten's readership had been waiting for. As Matt Holland comments in *Poetry Review*:

Patten has lost none of his talent for using plain language, free of pondered and paraded poeticisms, yet full of language charged with meaning… His judicious use of the personal pronoun 'I' is masterful giving just the right amount of feeling to engage the reader/listener in a very intimate way while not indulging in a discharge of self-pity.

Charles Causley, whose admiration of Patten's narrative gift has been unwavering, feels 'he hasn't written his best work yet. That is still to come. He's deceptively simple at times, which is why he's so revealing.'

Armada reveals a poet who has, in Auden's words, followed 'to the bottom of the night', but tempers any storm-sheltered hints of 'mistaking paradise for that home across the road' with the resounding finality of 'The Brackets':

de la Mare (1873-1956)
Farjeon (1881-1965)
Graves (1895-1985)

Patten scans the contents list commenting on the the unfairness of his boyhood hero, the short-lived Wilfred Owen (1893-1918) on the earlier list:

The names of friends crop up.
Some are gone –
Tumour-ridden, the brackets close in.
They drop against the ends of names,
Not orderly, but any old how.
Henri, Mitchell, McGough – watch it mates,
The brackets, any day now.

1997 began with Roger McGough being awarded the O.B.E. in tandem with Paul McCartney's knighthood. Genuinely honoured and describing himself as a poet to the Queen, (who replied 'very good'), he did disclose to at least one interviewer that he fully accepted that 'one man's poetry can mean simply another man's waste of time'.

A year which saw the deaths of the two remaining founding fathers of the Beat Generation, Allen Ginsberg and the seemingly indestructible William Burroughs, also saw in May the return by a landslide of the first Labour government in eighteen years, led by Tony Blair. The optimism of the sixties, kindled by new bands such as Oasis's unbridled admiration for The Beatles, seemed to be back.

Thirty years on from *The Mersey Sound* – such a watershed in British Poetry – meant anniversary radio programmes and a full-scale commemorative tour. This ran throughout the early months of the year playing to packed houses, including an anecdotal re-enactment sketch of how it all began at Streate's. Looking back to those days, Henri admitted that at one time he felt 'maybe it could be just a fad', and that at some stage he would have to go back to the real world and get a job:

> I never really thought it would last. Actually I didn't mind if the poetry didn't, I never had this Keatsian idea of looking at eternity; I was much more interested in the Andy Warhol idea of here and now. And yet oddly enough it has lasted. I'm still writing; there is still an interest in people buying the books and coming to listen to the readings. And it's something I hadn't anticipated. But if it all went away, if all those dire things that were said thirty years ago came true, I'd still be doing it anyway. I'd still write for me – and hope I could still persuade some musicians to put music to my words. I don't think I could stop doing it now.

Patten, once so wary of live readings, fully endorses this:

> We've never stopped reading together or performing together. And we've never stopped being friends for the last thirty-five years. Over the years my readings have got better because I've done so many. So I think technically the performances have improved.

McGough's technical skills, noticed so long ago in John Willett's reviews of the early Happenings, have been continually met by his ability to realise poem after poem out of thin air and send them straight back into the public domain. Mid 1997 he rang his young daughter from Edinburgh, asking 'What are you doing at the moment love?' 'Talking to someone on the phone.' 'Hard to argue with that one.'

Dealing with both temporal and pressing concerns, children's logic and adult fears, 'The Way Things Are', is the perfect antidote to 'Let Me Die A Youngman's Death', and is as apt an exemplification of Charles Causley's maxim that 'a good poem is always about something else other than what it's about':

> No, old people do not walk slowly
> because they have plenty of time.
> Gardening books when buried will not flower.
> Though lightly worn, a crown may leave a scar.
> I am your father and this is the way things are.

The publication of *Bad Bad Cats* brought his tally of children's books up to twenty since *Mr Noselighter* came out in 1977. He chose two poems from *Bad Bad Cats* to read on the second of two *Poetry Please* programmes commemorating his sixtieth birthday in November of 1997. The book became the unanimous choice for The Signal Poetry Award for 1998. Starting with 'The Cats Protection League':

> Midnight. A knock at the door.
> Open it? Better had.
> Three heavy cats, mean and bad.

we are then taken into a world of wordplay, parody, prosody, playground humour and street game anarchy. McGough's felines, in the underworld of protection rackets, join the exalted company of Christopher Smart's 'Jeoffrey' and Eliot's 'Macavity' as poetic cats with other secret agendas.

Discussing his early attempts at writing, he told Ian McMillan, how it enclosed him rather than freed him in any way. The work of e.e. cummings, he felt, the first truly liberating factor; giving him that freedom to do exactly what he wanted with language. McGough selected favourite poems by such diverse writers as cummings, Norman MacCaig, Theodore Roethke, Charles Causley and Elizabeth Bishop.

During the same year, Brian Patten ran an Arvon course with Sophie Hannah, one of British Poetry's brightest young talents. 'To me', Patten told one interviewer, 'writers like Sophie, Jackie Kay and Linton are the fresh voices. Too many of these New Generation writers sound like tomorrow's academics.' Unlike Charles Causley, who to Patten still sounds fresh. 'Charlie's a special man, part of that Walter de la Mare tradition. Very special.'

Patten appeared as the only solo poet at the prestigious Hay-on-Wye Festival that year, brazenly edited the *Puffin Book of Utterly Brilliant Poetry*, before reading with Lawrence Ferlinghetti in Prague. During an increasingly busy period, he wrote and presented a film for Channel 4 concerning the callous way the elderly are treated in Britain. Despite some unhelpful and unsympathetic direction, it was yet another personal triumph, featuring two outstanding performances from the poets Hugo Williams and Mimi Khalvati.

Other pairings of the Mersey Poets with bright contemporaries on tour have included Patten with Linton Kwesi Johnson, after a powerful appearance together at the Galway Festival (Patten being mistaken by one fan as Kwesi Johnson's bodyguard). McGough worked that summer with John Hegley, and Henri with Jackie Kay.

In September, at a Soho restaurant, McGough, backed by Andy Roberts, pulled out all the stops in front of an audience that included Paul McCartney, Tim Rice and Peter Blake, to celebrate the work of Buddy Holly. ('You've got to be good if Paul's there.')

'Roger's always been talented in a rather magical way', his sister Brenda Charles feels. 'As kids he was the quiet, serious one who was always good at English. Yet he never came across as ambitious in any way. He has this way with words which is totally special. Where it comes from I couldn't say.'

Her brother had recently been reading Confucius, discovering an appropriate alter ego in Book 5, in the persona of Chi Wen Tzu, an indecisive, yet invective and brilliant poet who 'always thought three times before taking action. Twice would have been quite enough'. From the character came *The Spotted Unicorn* (Viking), a poetic diary ending with three courses of action, none of which is the obvious choice:

Consider carefully what to do:

Kill wife?
Kill Lin Fang?
Design dinner service?

Another *Words on the Run* tour was planned for November and December. Questioned about his gift for language and seeming immunity from writers' block, McGough, editing *The Kingfisher Book of Poems about Love*, answered one interviewer:

I haven't had the time to be blocked. Too busy writing books. Too many probably! Looking back to my days at Hull though, I knew there was no point in me trying to get published in the university magazine because I wouldn't fit into what their idea of poetry was. I notice I've been sidelined from that Hull dynasty; which is annoying because I was actually encouraged by Larkin. He wrote to me once congratulating me on the 'used condition' of my books. Despite everything, I always felt there was an audience out there to be fed. And that audience is still frozen out by certain people who won't acknowledge it exists. Adrian felt the same, and there it was on the doorstep. And he incorporated it into his life. He has a great life Adrian. Always has had. He travels, spends time in Paris with Catherine, then New York, back to Liverpool. Paints. Writes. I often think what a great life Adrian has.

John Willett, who has always maintained that Henri laughing is one of the most infectious sights he knows, supports this but adds that 'he is complex and by no means always easy to fathom'. Heather Holden is even more emphatic:

Not Fade Away gave me such a high. He's always had that childlike quality. What he has to say is sophisticated in one sense but is also very simple and beautiful. It's that thrill about being alive and it's very unique and special. It's quite right that Adrian goes out for nice meals and tells us about them. It's quite right that he should paint. It's quite right that he should write poetry, and read aloud, travel and report back. He's got such a relish for enjoying life that is so infectious. And that's what's so brilliant about Adrian.

Adrian Henri never met his nomadic paternal grandfather, who in so many ways begins his story. Louis Ernest, the man responsible for Henri's unusual name, appearance and love of travel – particularly all things French – left the family home in Birkenhead to found a seaman's mission, never to be heard of again. No doubt he would have been proud of the achievements of a grandson so like him in 'so many different lengths of time'.

Acknowledging that Henri has always been a good tourist, Andy Roberts takes a more pragmatic view:

Never forget Adrian has a great work ethic that is often overlooked. He's never stopped producing. He's not impressed by people waiting to be discovered, or by slow developers. To him you have to produce and show what you do at all times. If you write, then you have to write and write and write. And if you paint, then you paint and paint and paint. It's for others to make of it what they will. Quantity is important to Adrian. He's a hard worker. They all are. Considering how much Roger, Adrian and Brian are in the public eye, people often forget just how many hours they sit at a desk simply writing. With the Mersey Poets, you have three people who graft at it.

None more than Henri, who recently has seen *The World is Your Lobster*, his selected children's poems published by Bloomsbury, in the process of completing a new adult collection, *The Day Of The Dead, Hope Street*, whilst finally enjoying long overdue acclaim for his continued work as a painter.

Writing in the catalogue of *The Art of Adrian Henri 1955-1985*, organised by South Hill Park, Edward Lucie-Smith echoed George Melly's earlier comments, pointing out that:

> The success which Adrian achieved as a poet had one unfortunate consequence – it distracted attention from his painting. His first literary appearance had been as a painter who also wrote poetry as an extension of the things which pre-occupied him in the studio. He became thought of as a poet who painted. Public appearances, both throughout Britain and abroad, created a persona which overshadowed his practice as an artist.

Yet Henri, like Blake, has managed successfully to be both. Since *The Entry of Christ into Liverpool* (now at the Paul Sacher collection in Basle), he has had a strong vein of urban fantasy running throughout his work. Seeing his most self-defining work exhibited again after so many years, combined with images from the darkly celebratory Mexican Day of the Dead at the Basle Carnival has recently led to *Thanksgivings and Calaveras.*

His most sustained achievement yet as a painter, the show quickly transferred from Liverpool University to the prestigious Thomas Zander Gallery in Cologne, and is the most compelling argument yet of Adrian Henri's pluralistic genius:

> calaveras calaveras calaveras
> prance castanets click
> quicken the rhythm of the dance

For Brian Patten, since being lured down to Streate's by the garlic-chewing Pete the Beat's advertisement, the irrelevant songs over the years have at times jarred, but also at times have chimed like birdsong. Although hardly hurrying to share his wonder any longer, he does it in measured steps still acknowledging what is 'bright' or 'special' in the world, quietly affirming that the last thirty-something years have been:

> Great fun. I always find it really good working with Roger and Adrian because you don't feel the onus is on you to perform or entertain. It's very much a shared thing. As for the poetry, in a sense my poems have been a poetic diary, but I suppose as my life's not unique it becomes a diary of many lives. I hope my latest poems are my best poems, but time

will be the judge of that rather than me. It all comes out in the wash in the end. Time whittles it down to maybe just one poem that might survive.

Postscript

'...all in time to the music...'

The Liverpool Playhouse has been a repertory theatre for over eighty years, before that a music-hall. The word is out that it is going bankrupt. Shrouded in late nineties' November gloom, *Big Issue* sellers lining Williamson Street, the current production is Daphne Du Maurier's *Rebecca*. Inside, there is some evidence that *Words on the Run* is playing tonight, but hardly 'the boys are back in town'. Five or six smallish posters discreetly placed.

There are places I'll remember, though some have changed:

Eddie Mooney's Streate's, once the Beat centre of the North-West, and the Basement Club in Mount Pleasant (where Yankel wanted a shilling) are long gone. The incongruous Sampson & Barlow's around the corner in London Road where Robert Creeley once read, gone too.

Some for ever, not for better:

Near Adrian Henri's place in Mount Street, O'Connor's Tavern (where Yoko received her plastic chrysanthemum, and where the gangsters could not stop the show), has been shut down, re-opened, re-named and closed once again. Parry's Bookshop where Allen Ginsberg captivated that small but appeciative gathering is now one in a string of eateries. And the Everyman Bistro – once Hope Hall – is in *The Good Food Guide*, the former mould-breaking theatre having been bailed out by the bistro. And somewhere between (Heaven and) Rushworth's and The Bluecoat Chambers, the ghosts of poets and folk singers still mix and argue amidst the dust and rubble beneath the Green Moose.

These places have their moments for lovers and friends.
Some are dead and some are living:

Words on the Run plays to a full but strangely subdued audience. The set for *Rebecca* consists of Gothic flights of steps and balustrades. It looks surreal, but wasn't that always the point? A voice (Willy Russell's) announces over the loudspeaker:

flash photography is not allowed on these premises.
But tasteful snap-shots are entirely permissable.
And remember – in case of fire, break glass.

And strolling on stage to the strumming of Russell's and Roberts's guitars –
musicians, stage left, poets, right; all in dark suits – and straight into Russell's
'Tupperware Girls', McGough, Henri and Patten (hands thrust deep into his
pockets) the back-up vocals for Russell's seventies' Rock-star chic; Roberts,
their subtle, inscrutable amenuensis. McGough, drolly dignified, wearing what
look suspiciously like winklepickers, Patten still in the same suit he has had on
for weeks, and Henri a cross between an apothecary and the Godfather.
Collectively they perform McGough's exquisite rondeau 'In Case Of Fire',
concluding:

In case of TRUTH spread word

In case of WORD keep mum

In case of MUM open arms

In case of ARMS lay down gun

In case of GUN, fire

In case of FIRE break glass.

The well-rehearsed show – dwarfed by the set's Hammer Horror gloom – plays
without a hitch. There are many high spots. Nobody misses a cue. And if they
did – well wasn't that the point? The closing chorus revolves around 'all in time,
all in time, all in time to the music', interspersed with McGough's valedictory
'from me, Brian, Willy and Ade' (Andy in time to the music), 'thanks for
coming, cue lights and fade' (all in time to the music). All in time, all in time,
all in time to the music. Then back for two calls – 'Underneath the Arches'-style
– before all five are changed (except Patten), and front-of-house by the
merchandising table which overflows with piles of brightly coloured books,
CDs, T-shirts and tapes.

Though I know I'll never lose affection for people and things:

The book-signings, the bar, the fans – 'Remember me? I'm Josie' – the agent and crew. The old friends – hangers-on in every town – the restaurant afterwards, the wine, the gossip, the top hotel. This poetry lads, where did it all go wrong?

Whether Roger McGough, Adrian Henri and Brian Patten singly or collectively, go down in the annals of history 'when it all comes out in the wash', or amount to little more than an anecdotal footnote in the myriad lists of reputations that constitute twentieth century literature, Time will be the judge. If anything is certain, then surely poetry will survive. Written by poets who have not forgotten the people. Despite the information super-highway we all seem to be travelling on, hopefully it will stick around and always remain 'a mouth'.

Whatever changes that do occur, whether ethical, demographical, or technological, poets are likely still to be on hand to remind us of that day, paraphrasing Auden further, 'as one thinks of a day when one did something slightly unusual'. Perhaps in time some future writers will stop and think about them, gratefully acknowledging the 'controversial tap-dancing poets' who were always for some 'not quite good enough', but made their mark, talked straight and shot clean from the hip. The poets admittedly who played to the gallery, but at least had one to play to.

Bibliography

Booth, Martin, *British Poetry 1964-84: Driving Through the Barricades* (Routledge & Kegan Paul, 1985).

Coleman, Ray, *John Winston Lennon, 1940-1966* (Sidgwick & Jackson 1984)

Cookson, Linda, *Brian Patten* (Northcote House, in association with The British Council 1997).

Cope, Wendy, *Making Cocoa for Kingsley Amis* (Faber 1986)

Davies, Mike, (ed.) *Conversations* (Flat Earth Press 1975)

Gowar, Mick, *Living Writers* (Thomas Nelson & Sons 1992)

Green, Jonathon, *Days in the Life* (Heinemann Minerva 1988)

Lucie-Smith, Edward, (ed.) *The Liverpool Scene* (Donald Carroll Ltd. 1967)

McGear, Mike, *Thank U Very Much* (London Barker 1981)

Melly, George, *Revolt into Style* (Penguin 1970)

Motion, Andrew, *A Writer's Life* (Faber 1994)

Norman, Philip, *Shout – The True Story of the Beatles* (Elm Tree Books 1970)

Willett, John, *Art in a City* (London 1967)

Special thanks to

Dave Bateman, Vivienne Brown, Paul Butler, Charles Causley, Brenda Charles, Maurice Cockrill, Mike Evans, Yankel Feather, Fred Grubb, Avril Henri, Bob Hewitt, Heather Holden, Jerry Jones, George Melly, Andy Roberts, Annette Robinson, Juan Vitti, John Willett and Ben Wright.

Extra special thanks to

Adrian Henri, Roger McGough and Brian Patten for their co-operation, time and help during the course of this book.

Index

NEED FOR THE BIKE

PAUL FOURNEL is a French writer, poet, publisher, and cultural ambassador. He was awarded the Prix Goncourt for short fiction for *Les Athlètes dans leur tête*. His *Anquetil, Alone* was published in English by Pursuit.

ALSO BY PAUL FOURNEL

Anquetil, Alone

NEED FOR THE BIKE

PAUL FOURNEL

Translated by Allan Stoekl and
Claire Read

First published in Great Britain in 2019 by
PURSUIT BOOKS
An imprint of Profile Books Ltd
3 Holford Yard
Bevin Way
London
WC1X 9HD
www.profilebooks.com

First published in France in 2001 by Editions du Seuil, entitled *Besoin de vélo*

1 3 5 7 9 10 8 6 4 2

Translation copyright 2003 by the Board of Regents of the University of Nebraska

Revised translation, subsequently published by Rouleur
Limited as *Vélo*, copyright Claire Read, 2012

Additional material from Paul Fournel's columns in *Rouleur*
magazine is used here with their kind permission

Illustrations by Will Webb

Typeset in Granjon by MacGuru Ltd
Printed and bound in Great Britain by
CPI Group (UK) Ltd, Croydon CR0 4YY

A CIP catalogue record for this book is available from the British Library.

ISBN 978 1 78816 269 2
eISBN 978 1 78816 270 8

'There is a faster man.'
Maurice Leblanc, *Voici des ailes*

For my friend Louis, riding in the blue.

For the Baron, Chacha and Mado, Rémy, Sébastien,
Rino, Jean-Noël, Plaine, Jacques, Jean-Loup, Jean,
Titch, Furnon, Madel, Philippe, for Jean-Louis, for
Daniel, for Marc, for Denis, for Ernest, for Harry,
for Claire, for Jean-Emmanuel, for Christian …

And for all those who set out before
and whom I've forgotten.

Contents

Introduction

This is remarkable.

My experience of cycling has been captured within the pages of a book written by a man born a generation before me, in another country, whom I have never met. As I said, remarkable.

It's as if he knows me. With a poet's precision and compassion, he has got to the heart of the same compulsion I have shared to jump on a bike, and just go cycling off; a need that has been expressed differently throughout my life as I have grown older. With a philosopher's reasoning, he has unpicked and articulated my unspoken thoughts. Now he's telling me what I was thinking all along.

Paul Fournel's evocative writing impresses itself upon the reader, just as gradually, and just as completely, as the bicycle captures the soul of its rider. Anyone for whom the act of pedalling continues to fascinate and infuriate will hear his elegiac words accompanying their rides long after this book has been consumed, letter for letter, kilometre for kilometre.

Through these pages, which flow like the mysteriously forming and reforming thoughts of a ride in the Loire Valley, Fournel invites the reader to join him through a lifetime of dedication to the pursuit of an obsession for two wheels. From that miraculous moment, when, at the age of five, he 'no longer heard the noise of running behind' nor the sound of 'rhythmic breathing' on his back, Fournel's love affair with the bicycle began. It has continued unabated well into the twenty-first century. A spell of work in Cairo (where he was posted as the French cultural attaché until 2003) left him temporarily unable to cycle, and almost asphyxiated as a result. But he has recovered. He rides still.

Born in 1947 into the furnace of French cycling, Saint-Étienne, just before the golden age of the national sport bathed France in its mythical aura, Fournel grew up steeped in the classic cycling culture that many a modern reader yearns for. Such readers will wistfully inhale from these pages. His is a world of handmade steel, neither too rigid, nor too flexible, leather saddles imported from England and mispronounced, and, of course Campagnolo gears. What a time to be alive! This is first-hand testimony, forged from the same steel that made his home city of Saint-Étienne famous throughout the cycling world: elegant, durable, something to covet.

He remembers, at the age of ten, embarking on a long ride over the famous cols that surround Saint-Étienne and have seen so many battles in the Tour de France. That day his father, at the end of his reserves of strength, could ride no longer and waved his young son forward. So, alone, the young Paul angled that narrow wheel towards a future that had already been defined by the love of riding fast. A lonely baptism, a difficult rite of passage, perhaps. But one which cements a bond. Fournel also recalls sitting in the stands in the velodrome, watching the greats of French racing ripping through the still, hot air; men like Saint-Étienne's most ill-fated cycling son Roger Rivière. Some education, that.

A lifetime of publications of poetry and philosophy have always been accompanied by Fournel's strong attraction to the sport of cycling; in his blood from the very start, if that observation is not too risqué (and yes, there's a forthright chapter on doping, which may shock today's sensibilities, but speaks from the heart of a certain generation, and will still find favour with many).

On these pages Fournel inhabits, through a fusion of experience and imagination, the animus of every conceivable form of road cyclist, pushing through the levels, gaining in ambition and scope before eventually, startlingly, inhabiting the mind of the professional rider. He becomes, in words, the sprinter, the baroudeur, the rouleur, the climber. He takes up residence in the thoughts and feelings of the legendary Abdel-Kader Zaaf, who famously fell asleep under a tree when in the lead of a Tour de France stage. Through sheer force of his writer's will, Fournel calls into existence the myths and legends of a sport steeped in folklore and mystery. At one point, he even transposes himself into the body of an automaton, Jacques Anquetil, and lets the great Frenchman speak to us across acres of time. Maitre Jacques, talking to us, the generation of carbon fibre, sweat-wicking lycra and Strava.

But it is the everyday experiences of cycling that Fournel calls to life on the printed page that speak every bit as clearly and as lyrically to the reader as his writing about the races he has witnessed. Whether it's inhaling great lungfuls of summery air, breathing in deeply the 'moss and mushroom' smell of wooded glades, judging or misjudging a wet descent, or battling a limitless wind battering the west coast of Ireland, these are the shared wonders and impositions of anyone who has flown away from the rest of the world on a bicycle. Fournel finds a way of taking a complex set of impressions and contradictory impulses, and reducing them down to one very clear, perfectly formed idea.

There is talk of the quotidian violence of the bike, the pratfalls, the face-plants, the car-doorings. There is talk of familiar hunger knocks, or collapses in morale, of clicking knees and fading lights; the everyday horrors whose very survivability provides the tension and release, that tugging at the heart that a lifetime of riding a bike draws out. Whether he's battling rush hour on a Parisian hire bike or finding himself forced off the road by a Californian SUV, there is never a sense that the time will come when the bike will no longer be central to Fournel's understanding of the world and his cohabitation with the very act of being human. Get knocked down, get up again.

Yet, amid the talk of gear ratios, of tubeless tyres, of boundless hunger and great thirst, there is an acknowledgement that time cannot stay still. Your position in the grand order shifts as you accelerate over a lifetime to take your place at the front, at the peak of your powers and at the sharp point of your form. Then you drop back, gradually, almost unnoticed, holding onto those previous, dwindling reserves, but wiser and more mellow for the experience. You'd expect such good sense from an eminent philosopher. That is exactly what you get when Fournel tries to justify, or at least explain, the absurdity of the cyclist.

Why, he asks, would you want to ride like an elastic-shorted Sisyphus up Mont Ventoux, only to ride down it again and do it all again? On the face of it, this is a bit of a sucker punch. Until, that is, Fournel equates the silliness of the question with asking why you'd ever want to peel vegetables, given that you'll have to peel some more, eventually, and some more after that, just to fill your belly and fill your days.

Why, for that matter, breathe? Why live?

Ned Boulting
February 2019

Foreword

If I am to believe my computer, I have hired more than 400 Vélibs in recent months. Four hundred of Paris' public bicycles left there on the streets just for me! Never in my life would I have imagined having so many bikes; all similar, all inconvenient, all of them 20 kilos' worth of weight, all poorly designed yet all different in their ways of falling apart: bent pedal, jammed derailleur, unadjustable saddle, flat tyres, twisted wheels, nonchalant brakes, misaligned handlebars …

It is a feast for the sampler of bikes that I am – my ear always alert to the slightest grinding, my muscles attentive to the slightest suspect movement of an axle or of a bearing. I am all the more attentive and all the more entertained because I know that the liaison with this machine will be brief and that I won't have to get out my spanners and my tyre levers. At most, if the bike's condition is serious, I take care to turn the saddle around to signify to my fellow users and to the workers of the house of Vélib' that the machine is no longer of use.

As well as exquisitely moving me through the streets of Paris – which I never cease to reread at low speed – the Vélib' has the enormous advantage of making me love and rediscover, each week and each holiday, my beautiful Sunday bike. On it everything once again becomes light, silent, properly inflated and gentle; everything becomes titanium, aluminium, leather and carbon; everything becomes sharp and quick (at least until the first hill). What happiness.

For as long as I can remember, I have always ridden. My first memories are cycling memories. I entered the field of consciousness while riding and I have never stopped doing it. To ride is, for me, an enchantment – in the true sense of the term. I ride to rest and to tire myself out; I ride to dream; I ride to do myself good and to do myself harm. I ride to be alone and to share the road with friends; most often I ride for the sake of riding.

This book tries to account for this delightful and humble passion.

Violent Bike

Longchamp

I remember the dog very well. It was a golden dog of the boxer breed. I well remember that I was the last to see him alive because I was the one who hit him.

At the same moment, I felt my front wheel fold and my handlebars lever my left arm up. I felt the breeze from the peloton, which split up while yelling around me, and then I woke up, sitting on the Longchamp pavement, trying to write my phone number in the sand in case I passed out again.

There was the first hospital, where they found my arm too messed up for them; there was the ambulance with poor suspension that made me groan; there was Boucicaut hospital and the specialist emergency services for hands.

It was already 3pm, and my Sunday morning ride was taking a big bite out of the afternoon.

My arm was now calm in its cast.

The surgeon had told me: 'You've lost some bone; we're going to have to screw plates on and take some bone from your hip to do a graft,' and he went for lunch. Before going down to the operating theatre, I finished digesting the cereal bar swallowed during my race.

At exactly this point there were five of them riding at the front, and I had the sense that the great Demeyer was hiding. On the cobbles he showed himself to be cautious; he was riding strongly, as was his habit, but at the back. Moser and De Vlaeminck weren't at their best. Hinault, for his part, was pulling the train with the clenched teeth of bad days. Paris–Roubaix isn't a race where you joke around; his world champion's jersey was filthy, the kind of filth you frame under glass. The close-ups on TV showed him uncommunicative, concentrated. He wasn't trying to break away, and nothing was more exasperating than watching him carrying everybody in his panniers towards Roubaix.

They were ten Ks from the finish when the surgeon came back:

'Let's go – the theatre's ready.'

'Five minutes … I want to see the end of the race.'

'We'll tell you about it later.'

'I'll have trouble sleeping if I don't know.'

'With what we're going to give you that would surprise me!'

He made the mistake of turning his face towards the TV, and had to sit down on the edge of my bed. The race was so tense that he didn't say another word.

Kuiper entered the velodrome first, with De Vlaeminck, pallid, on his wheel. Four hundred metres from the line, the Badger took the lead and put the pressure on. Demeyer tried to inch past but could only remain level with him. Nobody else had the strength to try.

The Badger picked up his bouquet and publicly

restated that this race was bullshit. He now knew exactly what he was talking about.

Then there was the first injection, the trolley, the green gown, the second injection. Lying on the operating table, in a contented haze, I took an inventory of the gleaming tools at my bedside: nails, screws, casts, pliers, a saw …

Among them there was a Black & Decker drill, and I went under sorry that it wasn't a Peugeot … Great team, Peugeot.

Saint-Julien

I wasn't new to this game. Every cyclist, even a beginner, knows that at one time or another he will have an encounter with a car door. It could open in front of him at any time – from the right, the left, at the moment when he least expects it, at a bend in the street, at a junction, right in the middle of a straight and clear road.

As an urban cyclist, I have a complete collection to present: right door, left door, the high door of a lorry, the low door of a convertible, all accompanied by a range of reactions, from the extremely rare 'I'm sorry' to 'You should have been more careful' and the colourful 'You've scratched my paint'. At a reasonable speed this encounter ends in a broken finger, an injured shoulder, a persistent headache, a wide and dangerous swerve onto a busy pavement.

I had the honour of being initiated into this discipline at a very early age, and was awarded my first car door right at the start of my career. I was coming back from a little outing with my cousins and was riding carefully on the right, as I had been taught to do. We were coming back at a good clip because it was almost dinner time.

The door opened in front of me without the slightest scruple. My bike stayed on one side of the door, and I went flying over it, in one big lump – I wasn't yet using toe-clips at the time. I landed heavily on the other side, head first into the gravel. Half my face was pitted with dirty little pebbles. I could feel my lips and my brow swelling. I was one-eyed and mute. Would my own mother be able to recognise me?

The lady who had given me this surprise was highly embarrassed, given my tender years. She took me in her arms and carried me to her garden, while trying to come up with every imaginable way of erasing this ugly moment from our two lives. First and foremost she wanted to make sure that I hadn't broken anything and seemed to want to count my bones one by one. 'I didn't do it on purpose,' she assured me, of which I was perfectly convinced because I already knew a thousand other more efficient methods to kill your young neighbour. I thought she was a bit crazy and started to wait for my mum with some impatience.

That's when the lady had the brilliant idea of bringing me a big glass of Martini to bring me around. I downed it in one and, immediately after I got my first door, I got plastered for the first time. The lady leaned over my swollen head and, as her cheeks were fat, I felt like slapping her. I was perfectly drunk, perfectly messed up, perfectly raging, and my sole desire was to get back on my bike.

The Back Road

With the end of the Tour de France, summer had reached its sad point: long, infernally hot afternoons with nothing glorious to get your teeth into any more.

Fortunately there was still the prospect of our village's next cycling Grand Prix, when we would pass spare wheels to the riders and give them bidons in front of our house.

I was ten, I had a green bike, and I prepared for the event as if I were riding it myself. My physical training consisted of a series of frenzied sprints on the road that went from our house to the village. In those days the road was deserted, and I could sweep from left to right without any risk to André Darrigade, my major sprinting rival, with whom I jostled for first place in the last 300 metres while the courageous and powerful Roger Hassenforder, with tongue out, chased us ten lengths behind. As a general rule I crossed the line – which was right in front of our door – with my arms up, the victor. Sometimes, when the battle was too hard, I had to rock the bike back and forth right up until the final centimetre to win by a tyre length; other times I lost by a hair's breadth and pounded the top of my bars with my fists, demanding a rematch.

That afternoon the confrontation was terrible. It was intolerably hot, and we were sprinting hard in the dust of the sun. My throat was burning and my muscles tight. I have to admit that, since I was rather chubby, my quadriceps found themselves sorely tested. So I had to do this final sprint in a blind rush, back bent, head down between my shoulders, in an all-out effort.

When, with a final grunt, I raised my head to make sure I had really won, I saw the enormous lady right in front of me, a few centimetres away. It was too late to try anything, too late even to brake, and we crashed into each other in an explosion of fruits and vegetables.

My front wheel had managed to ram right into hers, tyre against tyre, and we bounced off each other. The crates that she was transporting, the bread and wine she was lugging in the shopping bag hanging from her handlebars – all of it was scattered on the road. She was planted there on her bum, her black dress hitched up around her thighs, bun drooping over her ear. I blew very hard on my burning knee; I blew very hard on my raw elbow. She simply asked me what I was doing on this side of the road, which was her side. Head lowered, I insisted on picking up absolutely every aubergine and courgette, on reattaching every luggage strap, before limping back home to cry, finally.

Longchamp

That summer I had punctured 23 times. Thanks to inflating and reinflating my tyres on the slopes and in the ditches beside the roads, my arms were bigger than my thighs. My tubular budget had blown up beyond all reason, and the absolutely last one whose purchase I had permitted was tightly secured under my saddle. It was too new, bought in haste, and cheap. In theory you never take a new tubular on a ride: it hasn't been stretched, it doesn't have the precious residue of glue, and it's difficult to ride.

When after 20k my front tyre – put on the day before – went flat thanks to an honest enough drawing pin, I quickly jumped off and regretfully put on my youngest. I put it on without fresh glue, on a badly prepared rim: it was the big mistake you make because the 24th puncture is one puncture too many; because, when you're going fast, suddenly stopping is just not acceptable; because, when the gang gets away and you have to catch up, every second is paid for by your thighs; because puncturing is not the intention of a cyclist.

Stretching the new tubular – still too small – putting

it on by tightening the wheel against my stomach, inflating it and putting the wheel back on cost me six kilometres of chasing, my nose on the handlebars, my eyes filled with sweat, and a cramp in my right shoulder. The tyre, badly mounted, suffered from a little problem near the valve, and gave a 'tock' with each turn of the wheel. I felt it in my hands and shoulders. Luckily there were some flat sections on the road, and I had the peloton in my sights.

Of course, in the fear of being left stranded, I came back to the group too quickly, as one often does when anxious to get back in the shelter of the line. I arrived seriously winded at the exact moment they decided to pick up the pace.

Having to lift my arse at the precise moment I really needed to recuperate was torture – you could give up for less. I stood up on the pedals anyway, resigned to making my thighs burn. What was going on at the front seemed to be getting serious, and the more exhausted guys started to fall back. Fighting fire with fire, I decided to bet the bank and got down in the drops, determined to close the gap. Using an old sprinter's technique, I started to rock the bike from side to side and to come down hard on the pedals. A quick glance was enough to measure the three bike lengths I had to bridge and I put my head back down for a better aero effect.

So it was in extreme close-up that I was able to see my wheel tilt, the tyre shoot off the rim and squash onto the road. Then I saw it twist up and jam behind the fork crown, inflicting on me the most brutal deceleration I've

ever experienced. The knot it made at that precise location and which I could still sketch today ... I couldn't
take my eyes off it and was able to see it from every angle
since I somersaulted over the handlebars and came to
collapse flat on my back, the bike landing on top of me
with its pitiful 24th tubular.

The road took my breath away. That was the first
time that I drowned in the tar.

San Francisco

So I was living in California, and I had carefully brought two racing bikes along with me. Once settled in San Francisco I got hold of a used mountain bike – a local product with 24 gears – that was supposed to get me up the steep streets I climbed every day on the way to work.

Californians are gentle and courteous drivers. At every junction they have four stop signs, and they respect them, very kindly giving the right of way to the first one there (who isn't just anybody). As soon as they see a pedestrian they slam on the brakes and, with a smile, let him cross. But, simply put, they hate cyclists. You'd swear they were aiming at them. It's true that nothing in the California Highway Code tells them they shouldn't run them down. And it's also true that the tough guys and girls who survive on the slopes of San Francisco are willing virtuosos. Be that as it may, my very first week there I found myself on the ground twice, once thanks to a driver who almost didn't see me, and another time thanks to a bus driver who had seen me quite well.

So I decided to take the much talked about bus to

go to work; to save my bike for weekends and for the exploration of the (magnificent) California countryside.

The next Saturday, on the climb from Stinson Beach – the one you do with the Pacific Ocean at your back and the eucalyptus-covered ridge in your nostrils – I made the acquaintance of the rustic ditch of California, pushed there in a not-so-gentle way by a driver who was determined to pass me and an oncoming car at the same time. So I lay in the ditch, hugging my bike with my thighs and flattening myself as if I were under machine-gun fire so as not to miss anything of the amazing spectacle of a Ford Explorer passing an oncoming Chevrolet Yukon.

I had just turned 50 and it seemed to me wise to save my cycling strength for Golden Gate Park on Sunday morning, when they close it to cars.

On weekdays, I therefore decided – in the defence of my thighs and calves – to go to the gym.

California gyms are open 24 hours a day. You can work on your biceps at 3am and buy your creatine at the counter. It's a place to live, and every time I went there the same guy with a red headband was staring in the same mirror at the same pointlessly flexing muscles. You also saw some really good-looking types there. 'Low Impact' and 'Tae Bo' were starting to lose their appeal, and the fashion for spinning had been launched.

The idea is to have a peloton on wheelless bikes, en route to nowhere. The yellow jersey, who you ordinarily only see the back of, stands opposite you and urges you to increase your cadence. With him you climb imaginary hills, descend shady ravines, and devour endless straight lines. The ride lasts an hour, which leaves you worn out, thighs swollen and eyes empty. The only pleasure in the whole business is this huge fan, which blows a headwind that only does you good.

For a landscape freak like me, such a ride singularly failed to have any attraction. But I decided to do it anyway, just to stay in shape.

California wants to be in the vanguard of everything, and it succeeds. So it's also in the vanguard of do-it-yourself. I was sitting on my saddle, ten minutes before setting off, pedalling gently forward and back to warm up (stationary bikes make possible tricks that even trackies can't do), when my makeshift saddle repair gave way. I fell on my back with all my (considerable) weight, my head plowing into the bike behind me. Coccyx, spinal column, skull – everyone got their money's worth.

I was so far out of it that the quickly summoned doctor made me repeat my name and count my fingers. He fixed up my wounds and hurried me to a howling ambulance that hurried me to a hospital.

From that point on my financial worries started and my health concerns became secondary ...

And yet I ride.

Not one of these accidents turned me off riding or made me regret it. As soon as I find myself on the ground I do an inventory of the damage to figure out how long it'll be before I can get back on the bike. It's also the first question I ask the doctor. Then I bargain with myself. I've ridden with stitches, with bandages, with scabs. I've ridden in limbo, in vagueness, until the luminous clarity of being in shape returns.

My desire has never been lacking.

The road between the childish desire to own a bike and the need to ride it is sunny and twisting.

Up to now every time the question has arisen in me, I've just jumped back on my lovely bike and gone for a spin.

L'Ance

After some debate, we decided to bring the girls along. We were going to have a picnic on the river bank, and their presence seemed indispensable to the older among us.

The ladies were perched on squeaky and greaseless bikes set up for shopping and for going to the beach. One swayed on her big sister's machine, and the other lifted her knees up to her shoulders as she tried to ride her little brother's boneshaker. Our team resembled anything but a peloton. It was fun for a while, but then time started to drag. At this pace, our picnic was going to turn into an afternoon snack, into dinner, into a night under the stars and big bother with our parents.

So we tried to pick up the pace by taking turns to push the ladies, enabling them to climb the hills with a little more ardour.

I ended up with the thick one. Full of goodwill, but thick. She understood perfectly well that this whole set-up was intended to help her and, grateful, she tried to help in return. At the exact moment I was to take my turn and give her a vigorous push on the bottom, she had the idea of generously saving my strength by getting out of the saddle to give it more effort. My hand encountered nothing but an emptiness which I plunged right into, my own momentum leading me into it.

By an alchemy well known to cyclists, the tiny useful objects that you see on the best bikes are easily turned into formidable weapons when the situation complicates itself. This time, it was the harmless shift lever that turned itself into a blade and came to plant itself in my right thigh.

My buddies carried out a delicate rotation of my bike in the air and removed the blade from the wound. Blood spurted, little balls of fat appeared. It all seemed to call for a few stitches.

The doctor greeted me with an air of exasperation: 'Again!' he gravely observed. 'You're pissing me off with all your messing about on your bike. I see you with your friends in town. For the inconvenience, I'm going to stitch you up – no moving for three weeks! – but I'm going to do the stitches without anaesthetic. That'll teach you.'

And he did it. He was an authentic country doc.

Desire for the Bike

Stroke of Genius

The bike is a stroke of genius. On that day in the nineteenth century when Michaux gave it a chain and pedals, it had practically attained its final form. We refine the materials, we work away at the details, but the basics of the machine are the same.

If I compare my yellow bike of 1960 to my metallic beige bike of the year 2000, their differences are minimal. The latter is lighter by three kilos and more rigid (without going too far), its gear shifters are in the brake levers, its saddle is made of plastic covered with leather (which may not be progress), the fork crown is no longer chromed. Real progress: clipless pedals, which spare me the hard work of adjusting the cleats under the shoes but which give a cyclist on foot a duck-walk that's barely compatible with the dignity of a pedestrian.

In 40 years of riding, I've seen steel replaced by aluminium, which screamed when you stood on the pedals, aluminium replaced by carbon, carbon by titanium, and titanium by steel, and so on and so on and so on ...

The fork straightened up to the point of becoming completely vertical, only to bend again. The wheelbase shortened and then it lengthened a bit. We went from ten gears to 24.

Distinguishing real progress from fashions is easy.

These are details. Costly details, certainly (one gram less ends up costing a fair amount), but they're basically unimportant.

The bike is a brilliant machine that allows a seated person to, by the power of just his or her own muscles, go twice as far and twice as fast as a person on foot.

Thanks to the bike, there is a faster man.

The bike is in itself a form of doping, which complicates things. It is the tool of natural speed; it's the shortest route towards the doubling of yourself. Twice as fast, two times less tired, twice as much wind in your face.

We can justifiably always want more.

Light Weight

To be seated on the saddle, to not carry the weight of your own body, gives bike riding something of swimming, something of flying. The saddle carries you, like water, like air. The saddle, but also the frame, and the tyres, and the compressed air in the tyres all give you wings.

The difference, however, between cycling and swimming is that the cyclist – eyes open and hair windswept – goes faster than a mere man, while the swimmer drags himself along, eyelids closed, ears plugged.

The difference between cycling and flight is that the cycling is possible and flight still isn't.

Miracle

Cycling always starts with a miracle. For days you trem-
ble, you hesitate, you tell yourself that you'll never be
free of that hand guiding you, under the saddle.

My mother and father took it in turns to hold on
to me and no doubt one or other of my cousins, the one
from whom I had inherited the little bike, the one who
was responsible for my miracle.

They'd taken the stabilisers off my back wheel,
and I followed the meadow in front of our house, in the
direction of the gentle slope, to build up momentum. I
was seeking the magical point at which a carriage that
should normally be lying down stands up, and I fell flat
on my face (yes, already) and got back on again.

And then, one morning, I no longer heard the noise
of running behind me, no more rhythmic breathing on
my back. The miracle had taken place. I was riding. I
never wanted to put my feet back down for fear that the
miracle wouldn't happen again. I was jubilant.

I did the circuit of the house, thereby proving to
myself that I was capable of taking four right turns (for
a few weeks I preferred turning right). I was no longer

afraid of anything. I zoomed past the clump of stinging nettles that usually made me so scared; I rode panic-free down the long lonely road behind the house to come out in front again, triumphant but still unable to raise my arm in a victory salute.

I've never got over this miracle.

Learning to swim didn't move me like this, and it was really only learning to read that equalled the intensity of learning to ride. Within a few months, then, I learned riding and reading, in that order. At the Christmas of my fifth year, I was a complete man: I knew my work and my pastime.

Dragon Green

He was a strange uncle, a little on the bulky side, a little cockeyed. One of those guys who wears baggy suits and big dark glasses and of whom it's said, with an air of mystery, that he ran nightclubs. They are a widely talked about part of the family history, driving through it in huge cars that purr like cats.

He was an uncle who kept children at a distance, so we sometimes worried that he was nasty. Never having known him when I was an adult, I have bad memories of him.

It was to him, however, that my father gave the role of good guy on the day I turned nine. At the time he ran a factory and in that factory they made bikes.

So it was him who brazed my first frame and built my first bike.

I chose the colour green for it, like Anquetil's (who at the time was racing on a transparent green Helyett), and equipped it with three gears – low, medium and high, which is the starter course in the school of gearing.

When it was ready I went down to the factory, which my memory renders as enormous and black, streaked with sparks, populated by masked men whose fingers spat fire, resonating with the clear din of a series of tubes on workbenches and the rainy pitter-patter of the sanding station.

It was right at the back, luminous against the dark wall, 'dragon green', out of its lair, and it was my bike.

I already knew, from having 'finished off ' a few of my older cousins' bikes, that cycling is a sport that makes your legs hurt, that demands prolonged effort and patience. But I was unaware of four essential things that my green dragon was about to start teaching me:

1. To get on your first bike is to enter into a language that you will dedicate your life to learning; it's to transform every gesture and every happening into a secret for the pedestrian.

   With my hands on the hoods, my nose was a bit too close to the handlebars. They adjusted the handlebar stem and, by turning the bike over, came up with the right height for the saddle tube, and I found myself ready to pedal, ready to take off like a shot, ready to set off strong, ready to go off to meet *la Sorcière aux dents vertes* (The Witch With the Green Teeth – bonk), confront the Man with the Hammer, all set to jostle, to follow wheels in the pack, to go flat out, to blow up, to abandon, to go to the front, to suck wheels, to slip into *bordures*, ready to swallow kilometre after kilometre, to join the Edenic clan of silky-smooth pedal strokers ...

2. To get on a bike is to enter into a history and a legend that you'll discover in thousands upon thousands of copies of *L'Équipe*.

It's to forge your own fork in Sainte-Marie-de-Campan; it's to jump into an air-taxi after having won the Dauphiné to catch the night-time start of Bordeaux–Paris; it's to win the Tour de France five times; it's to drop Merckx on the climb to Pra-Loup; it's to keep Poulidor at bay on the Puy de Dôme; it's to enter the velodrome at Roubaix alone and for the second time; it's to win the Tour of Italy in the snowstorm of the Gavia; it's, whether you like it or not, to fall and refall into the chasm of the Perjuret and to die a little every time you climb the Ventoux on the Bedoin side ...

The divine solitude of the cyclist is peopled with shadows that the sun lengthens on the grain of roads.

Sat on my first saddle, I learned to feel the breath of the great cycling peloton of all times and places.

3. To get on a bike is not to get on a machine to forget it; it's, on the contrary, to initiate a permanent debate with it.

The moment I blow on a climb, I glance nervously at the crankset of the bastard who passes me: I knew it, he has oval chainrings and 175mm cranks!

What ecstasy does an eighth sprocket on the freewheel promise? How, on the bike, can I compensate for the 500 grams I put on my belly over winter?

While the oldies still compare the relative merits of Reynolds 531s and of aluminium, the newbies question the stiffness of carbon-ceramic or the wind impact of carbon wheels.

To change a part, to repaint your frame, to screw on clipless pedals, it's to reproduce, forever, the happiness of the green dragon glowing deep in its lair.

4.　To get on a bike is to take possession of the landscape.

First that of my front wheel, then that of my father's legs (which are the legs I know best in the world), finally the immense landscape – when balance and form are there.

The next morning, I rode my first classic. Twenty-five kilometres of the Haute-Loire, which secured my definitive love for the climbs, 25 kilometres of happiness which motorways and holiday homes have today devoured.

The following year, my first stage race and my first grand cols. That's how I started my patient Tom Thumb-like work, dropping sweat on the roads of France and of the world. Mountains, plains, bushes, trees, streams, ditches, and endless snow were hidden in my green bike – to learn, all you had to do was pedal.

Haute Couture

When I lean my bike against a wall I see the eyes of passers-bys light up. Even those who you couldn't suspect of being cyclists pause for a moment and lean over the bike, taking off their hat. They're ten years old, they are 100, they're in a hurry, they have time – they always stop for a second.

The desire to have a beautiful bike is a commonly shared one. That desire, which comes with childhood; some cultivate it, others bury it, but it smoulders.

If you set aside racers, who fight over hundredths, no one needs a really nice bike. No Sunday rider has his weight down to within a kilo. But a beautiful bike has a special virtue, a secret love potion: it gives you the desire to do more. Going out on an attractive bike is a pleasure in itself. Just look at the fine gentlemen of Longchamp, who have a good old natter at the top of the hill, their bums placed on their lovely frames.

I've had nothing but beautiful bikes, cyclist haute couture, tailor-made. I've loved them all, even the aluminium one Jacques Balutin lent me that screamed each time I stood on the pedals. Even my blue carbon fibre one, the fork of which was so stiff that it froze up my back.

I prefer steel – flexible and rigid at the same time, not that heavy after all, and which you can play at having sanded down and repainted every two or three years.

I have to say that I'm lucky to be from Saint-Étienne, where, even up until a few years ago, beautiful bikes were cooked up. I paced all across the town (it's shaped like that) to go to see 'my' shop windows. I kept up with the latest stuff, peeked into the workshops, plagued the shopkeepers with questions and in this way prepared myself for my Sunday outings.

Two or three times a year my father took me along to Louis Nouvet's. He was sort of a giant (a red-headed one) who seemed to have come straight from *Of Mice and Men*; who spoke in a reedy voice further softened by a slight lisp. He brazed frames for the cycling elite: Anquetil and Poulidor, of course, but also for the whole of the touring aristocracy, the princes of challenges and the lords of 'Flèches', the barons of the 24-hour race the Vélocio. He was a direct competitor of Alex Singer or Jo Routens.

His 'factories', as my father called them, were set up in a box-like building deep in an underprivileged working-class neighbourhood. You could make him out from afar, behind the loose planks, his black goggles on his forehead, blowtorch in hand.

He started by taking your measurements, and troubled himself with everything. How many kilometres a year? Mudguards, no mudguards? Racing, no racing? Clinchers or tubulars? Fixed gear in winter?

32

While you responded, he measured the length of your legs, your waist, the length of your forearms, the size of your feet ... You would have thought he was preparing to make you a suit.

Afterwards, you had to choose the tube set (generally Reynolds 531 or Vitus 171), to choose the lugs (cut or filed), to decide on the length of the stem and the width of the handlebars. The saddle would be a retrimmed Brooks (I can still hear him utter the name in his battered English).

Then it was time to occupy yourself with the inessentials, which is to say the components.

My entire youth was marked by the magical name of Campagnolo. Nothing was better for cycling than the Italian equipment of the house of Campagnolo. Campagnolo derailleurs, brakes, pedals, cranks, chainrings were to the art of cycling what Leica is to photography, what Porsche is to cars, what Laguiole is to knives. Well made, long-lasting, expensive, inevitable. Simplex and Mavic fought in vain. The 'all Campy' bike was the *nec plus ultra*, the ultimate. Nouvet recognised that Campagnolo parts were expensive but that, with the belief of the expert, they were the 'sharpest around'. They still are, despite the Shimano vogue.

Finally you came back, for a moment, to the essential: to choose the colour. Nouvet liked metallic grey. As for me, after green, I was inclined to red for quite a while, but I also had blue flecked with black, dark grey, mauve and yellow.

Nouvet has since died and with him the secret of

his brazing, but the ritual has stayed the same with Guy Seyve, La Sablière, Ferappy.

Fashion changes, but the haute couture of Saint-Étienne remains.

Machine

During all my childhood holidays, I was lucky enough to have my bike in my room and so to was able to look at it.

I wish it were still there.

You buy a bike because it is beautiful; you choose it carefully, and then you sit on it and you don't see it any more.

I get more out of my friends' bikes than I do out of my own.

One of my pleasures is knowing that my friend Rémy rides a bike I used to own. So when I ride with him I see my old bike, and I find it pretty.

I'd like my bike to be in my room, like a sculpture, like a potentially mobile Calder. Not really hanging, but leaning there, against the white wall, in the sunlight from the window. It's red, it's top quality, it shines. I've just changed the bar tape, and it looks new. I polished the crankset this morning and put a drop of paint on the little scratch a bit of gravel drew on the frame enamel. You can't see it any more.

The great Brambilla was a courageous racer who didn't spare himself. When he felt that he hadn't been up to the job, he lay his bike in his bed and slept on the floor. That no doubt didn't improve his physical fitness, but his mental health came out of it restored.

At that time, racers took their bikes up to their rooms mainly so they wouldn't be stolen. Doing the Tour de France on a bike is very hard, but following the peloton on foot is even worse.

I've had four bikes stolen from me. Four city bikes, in Paris. They were taken from me over a span of two years. After that, Dutch-style bikes fell out of fashion, and only mountain bikes were stolen. I was saved.

I went to the flea market to try to find them, but there were so many there that looked alike that I was a bit discouraged.

It's not the same with racing bikes. Starting from a finite number of combinable elements, every rider creates his own machine, which he can recognise at first glance.

With my eyes closed I could immediately say on which of my bikes I find myself. I could describe it piece by piece. I know exactly how each differs from the one before.

I've been assured that pro racers don't have pretty bikes, and that they don't care. In reality they have very nice bikes, very refined and very reliable, but often they hide them and you have to know how to spot them. For reasons that are easily understood, racers ride on brand-name bikes with the obligatory team paint job. A cursory glance can leave you thinking that these are bikes like those you see in shop windows or in supermarkets.

That is not so: one bike can hide another. Technicians have told me a thousand little things about the tastes and obsessions of one or other rider (but when it comes to the colours, no choice). Pedro Delgado, for example, liked only the aluminium frames made by the direct competitor of his sponsor, who only made steel frames. So he used aluminium hidden under a steel paint job.

It is true, though, that certain racers couldn't care less about their machine so long as it goes – they readily said that of Anquetil. They don't even know which gears they set out with in the morning. They delegate the love of their bike to their mechanics – who are knowledgeable in that love.

Perhaps I could become a mechanic?

Class

I've always been very attentive to my position on the
bike. A good position allows you to go faster, further and
longer. So it's worth lingering over.

I take measurements; I try things; I evolve my position over time, depending on the bike I'm using and the
profile of the roads I'm following. I add measurements
to my made-to-measure bikes.

In spite of this level of care, I still look like a cow on
a bike. It's disgraceful, but that's how it is.

There's one cyclist mystery that fascinates me: some
individuals are made to go on a bike. We say they have
'class'.

Put them on any old bike and they seem at home,
beautiful, and finally complete.

This has nothing to do with their athletic ability –
you see these types among the champions but they are
also among cyclotourists. They are not spared fatigue
or the usual agonies; simply they are beautiful to see.
They're so beautiful that they're even kind of a living
lie.

Anquetil is the model of this. Even when he was

scraping bottom he seemed on parade; complicit with the wind, catlike and unreadable.

Because that right there is the lie of class: you can't read anything there other than harmony; effort leaves no trace. The racer who has class doesn't bob his head or rock his body, doesn't pedal squares. He shows none of the signs of fatigue, and he collapses, magnificent and exhausted, when you have long since given up bugging him, he seemed so at ease.

Louis Nucera was that kind of guy.

A car erased him from the cycling world, but his perfect image lives on. I see him climbing the Pilat, hands on the tops, magnificent. I see him in the valley of the Petit Morin, vying in elegance with Jean-Louis Ezine. He had the grace of those water spiders that dance on the surface without wetting their toes.

Gearing

Gearing is an obsession: 'What did you put on?' 'What do you have?' We express it by two numbers, which are the number of teeth on the front chainring and the number on the rear cog. To make it simple, let's say that the higher the first number and the lower the second, the higher the gear: 52 × 14 (you don't say the '×') is a gear for descents, 42 × 22 is a gear for mountains. For the Sunday rider – for me – gearing indicates two crucial things: the gradient of the road and the condition of the rider.

Cyclists in general are fascinated by big gears, to such an extent that you see some pedalling in slow motion on climbs for the sole pleasure of 'turning a big gear'. It's the fascination for the strong man. Outrageous stories circulate everywhere of gears as huge as plesiosaurs, Loch Ness monsters. In the mind of more than one person, to 'get into the big ring' is already to go fast.

One morning when we were riding in a group in a forest beyond Versailles, one of our buddies put in an acceleration. The group reacted immediately, getting down into the drops and with a chorus of derailleurs put into the big ring. I was keeping a careful eye on Dédé Le Dissez, who was riding with us – former pro, Poulidor's team-mate, Tour stage winner, now in the book business. He was happy with turning his legs more quickly in his little ring. I drew level with him:

'You economising on your gears, Dédé?'

'I'll shift up when it gets really fast.'

In 1996 when my friends learned that I was going to follow the Tour de France, they almost all asked me to take a close look at the gears. It was the universal demand, the central concern: 'What are they running?'

Pros have the reputation of using monster gears, which *L'Équipe* details obligingly: 54 × 11, they say, for the sprints; 44 × 19 on the climbs. All this contributes to the magical aura of the riders.

So one morning before a mountain stage I went up to one of them to ask what gearing he was using for the climbs. He gently made fun of me: 'Special gearing for the mountains is fine for you.' (He spotted me as a cyclist from my stripy tan.) 'I use race gearing. If the race is in a big gear, so am I. If it's in a small one, I'm in one too. Ask the race what gear it'll be in on the climbs today, and I'll be in it.'

Mountain Bike

The desire to have a nice made-to-measure bike that evolves with time and innovations, the desire to feel good on it, the desire to shape it to your taste, are all desires which mean that it quickly becomes, like a fountain pen, an object you can't loan out. You can't even lend it to yourself. You make it specialised, you set it aside for what it does best. You wouldn't lend it to yourself to go out and get crazy in the woods.

That's when the desire for another bike is born.

I had one just for crossing streams, an old contraption with coaster brakes, fat tyres, and moustache handlebars and which I had stripped of all its trappings. It was my bike for trails and woods, my mountain bike before their time. It was used for everything: paths, warrens, thickets, streams, the Loire.

We crossed it where it's low, where you can cross it with the water only reaching halfway up the wheels. Around there the current's fast and the bottom is carpeted with round stones covered with slippery seaweed. The winner was whoever went furthest without putting his foot down. The idea was to do a sort of flooded Paris–Roubaix: the cobbles slimy, hidden and unpredictable.

We took our run-up coming down the slope, and we hit the water bringing up spray on both sides. Then it was agreed you had to keep your balance while leaning to one side to thwart the current and to negotiate the rocks as best you could, with flexible arms and your bum out of the saddle.

As a general rule we managed to cover a few metres before toppling into the water, but sometimes a miracle took place and we held on for 15, 20 metres ... As far as I remember, nobody reached the goal of the other side, and our attempts ended with a half-flesh, half-fish peloton, which pushed its bikes laughing through the flowing Loire.

The bikes we used for these expeditions were old clunkers conceived for shopping (at the market) and squeaking returns home. They didn't always pull off the youthful rejuvenation we gave them, at a time when they should have been in retirement. Wheels buckled, frames warped, brake levers dangled.

Mine was especially hungry for headsets. The inventors of the mountain bike had the wisdom to put suspension on their forks. For me, that was still out of the question and so I often found myself once again plunged into red grease and little ball bearings, trying to give some rigour to my handlebars.

That clunker died a hero's death, its front wheel having disassociated itself from the frame. It was sacrificed so that my road bike could remain the gem that it was, knowing only the sleek, gentle tar.

Paris

In Paris – for I'm also a Parisian cyclist – I use a bike that's a real regression. It possesses everything that history has bit by bit removed from my road bike: mudguards, protections against the rain, a rack, a chain guard ... Despite being born a Peugeot, it has the dark dignity of a Dutch bike, and their weight too.

I get around town about as fast as a city bus, and in this way I cover about 1,500 kilometres a year. Hazards exist, but they can be lessened as soon as you abstain from following bike lanes (aside from those separated by low walls). It helps to have eyes all over your head, and new brakes.

This price paid, Paris is a festival of cycling. Montparnasse is a real mountain, the Champ-de-Mars is a real flat, and the Champs-Élysées is a real false flat. My friends, Claire Paulhan, Jacques Réda, Harry Mathews, all know this well because they happen to ride with me in town.

What I like above all is to go round the shops. The speed of a cyclist forces you to select what you see, to reconstruct what you sense. In this way you get to the

44

essential. It's the title of a book or a cover that your gaze brushes against, it's a newspaper which catches your eye, a potential gift in a shop window, a new bread at the baker's. That speed is the right one for my gaze. It's a writer's speed, a speed that filters and does a preliminary selection.

My city bike earns me special attention. When I take part in official functions, I park it among the limousines; the chauffeurs watching me, wide-eyed, as I pedal in suit and tie. I even had the use of a very dignified official bicycle when I was running the Ramsay publishing house.

One morning when I was having breakfast at Fouquet's (something I'm not used to) with Bernard Pivot to show him my book list, he insisted on accompanying me to the pavement to see me get on my bike and lose myself in the stream of the Champs-Élysées. On my way to the Place de la Concorde, I asked myself what car I would have to have had in order to make the same impression.

Pedalling like this around Paris is my way of making sure I get an hour and a half of light, daily exercise. Of course, you have to know how to outsmart the rain, to know to occasionally give up and to jump on a bus to stay presentable. Of course, sometimes you have to hold your nose and take care to absorb the minimum amount of oxygen necessary for the effort. Of course, sometimes you need some courage to go and visit friends who live at the summit of the mound of Montmartre. But the reward is huge when you cross a bridge over the Seine at the time the sun is setting, or when you calmly thread your way through an endless traffic jam, smiling at the drivers who drum their fingers on their steering wheel or pick their nose.

When my daughter was very small I took her to nursery on my bike. I set up a little seat on my rack and I tied her in it, with the help of her big pink scarf. She was absolutely delighted with her morning excursion and smiled throughout. The seat spent the day with her, and we were reunited in the evening to hurtle down the rue de la Convention.

Night-time in Paris is kind. The traffic is light; the side streets are deserted and silent. You can roll along in the hum of the dynamo. When our Oulipo meeting at Jacques Jouet's is finished, I like to ride across the city with Harry: the rue du Renard, the rue de Rivoli, the river banks, the rue Bonaparte ... I 'drop him off ' along the way, on the rue de Grenelle, and spin on towards the 15th arrondissement.

Sunday morning is also kind. You can follow the main roads without menace or danger. The streets of Paris are deserted since all the cyclists – including me – are in the country ...

Maniac

A little while back I noticed that, for 30 years, I had been happily mounting my bike by lifting my right leg and by passing it over the saddle.

Since then I take one turn with my right leg, and the next turn I go with my left.

Suit

You have to know how to make yourself look good for riding. You have to impress your adversary with your elegance. To look good is to already go fast.

First you think of getting the jersey of the champion of the time, hoping that it will contain a little of his strength and that it will inspire respect from others. Later you can be very particular about your image, give yourself a 'look': a cyclotourist with shorts over your cycling shorts; a monochrome look that matches the frame; settle on a grunge look; on a collective look to affirm teamwork ...

Bib shorts are made of a synthetic material, elastic all around, skin-tight. They go down low on the thigh and include shoulder straps that hold them in place. Inside, the bottom is lined with a foam pad covered with a synthetic chamois skin that protects against irritation and other kinks.

It's the piece of kit that has most evolved during my years of riding. My first shorts were wool. After a few hours – weighed down with sweat – they stretched out, didn't stay in place any more, and ended up hurting.

Every time I stood on the pedals they slid down a few centimetres, threatening to hamper my knees and to offend public decency – how true it is that, to be effective, shorts have to be straight on the skin.

Nowadays shorts stay in their place and, if you take care to slather the insides with cream, you almost forget you have buttocks.

As for the rest, things have evolved less. There's a little foam cushion in the palm of gloves. The shoes are rigid and shaped to promote pedalling, which is good; they're made of plastic, which is bad. Just about everybody now wears a helmet. Jerseys are also synthetic, which isn't so brilliant. I wear them in bright colours, not to show off but to be seen by drivers. I have them in various colours, except yellow, which is sacred. You have to be an avowed dreamer to wear the yellow jersey. Only one of them exists, that which is at the top of the pyramid, the one that you will go and look for on your bike. Any cyclist will tell you.

However, I am the happy owner of a yellow jersey that I only wear in my bedroom. It's the one my Oulipo friends gave me after I won the Goncourt Prize for short stories at Saint-Quentin. That day I gained a bike that I can't use because it's not my size and a jersey I don't want to use because it's yellow. Both of them are untouched treasures.

I own an old-style jersey, pure wool, purple with green borders, the colours of the 'Ace of Clubs' group of Saint-Étienne – the oldest bike-touring club in France. It's an honorary jersey that I was given and which I cherish. I cherish it so much that I don't wear it for fear of wearing it out, which isn't very clever.

They were faithful, those wool jerseys. They soaked up the sweat and dried on your back, and you felt like an old warrior when you came back from a ride, haloed with salt.

Shorts

One morning while I was riding in the Haute-Loire, I passed a cyclist going the other way. I gave him a little wave, as is customary among 'proper' riders ('proper' riders are those who know to whom to give a wave, the others are dicks just standing there), and it was while I was doing this that I read on his black and red shorts the phrase: 'FOURNEL, Packaging'. I turned around, caught up with him, and announced to him that I wanted his shorts because my name was written on them.

He was visibly amazed, point-blank refused to give them up, but agreed to give me the name of his club and coach, who agreed to give me the name of the club's president, with whom I could get in touch. Monsieur Fournel, manufacturer of packaging materials in the plain of Forez, sold me two pairs of shorts bearing my name, no problem at all. When you know that in cycling lingo 'to wrap it up' means to sprint, you can imagine my pride.

So I wear shorts displaying my name and my ability – implied or flaunted – as a sprinter. Since I've never had the opportunity to sprint, nobody can check.

Cyclist's Tan

The ultimate cyclist's outfit, the suit he still wears when he's given up everything, his tattoo, is his tan.

'Getting a tan' worries me. The thought of stretching myself out in the sun for ten minutes to fry myself utterly horrifies me.

It so happens that cycling is an open-air sport, often practised out in the sun. So you get a tan, even if your body forbids it. The 'cyclist's tan' starts at the middle of the arm and goes down as far as the glove. On the left side, it spares the watch. It starts halfway down the thigh and stops at the sock. It touches the cyclist from the head to the neck. If the same cyclist wants to wears a cap, you will see his white forehead which was until now the mark of the peasant from Auvergne ... None of this would suit those who are fans of going topless and wearing a thong.

One summer Rémy and I hurtled through the Alps from north to south – we went from Geneva to Saint-Tropez via all the great climbs: the Izoard, the Vars, and the Allos on the penultimate day with the Verdon as dessert. A ride that left us overdosed on sun; burnt and reburnt.

Arriving in Saint-Tropez in late afternoon, the first thing we wanted to do was swim in the Mediterranean. We caused a sensation. In this land where tanning is a cult, these two boys with their pale torsos and swarthy limbs gave subject matter for gossip and nudging. A real target for the babes.

I bear the marks of my biker's tan all winter. It's my second skin. I derive neither shame nor glory from it. I accept it and, with the first ray of sun, I put on another layer.

One day when I was at the pool a kid yelled at me: 'Hey grandad, you forgot your bike!'

It's hard to pass unnoticed.

Legs

When I ride with someone for the first time I immediately cast a glance at his legs to know at which speed we're going to go and to know what my lot will be.

You can read a cyclist by his legs.

To see – early in the morning, before the start of the stage – the tanned and oiled forest of the peloton's legs … It's a real spectacle.

Cycling lengthens muscles at the same time as making them bigger. The better the cyclist, the more defined the muscle. Freed of its fat, freed of its coating, it is like an anatomy lesson.

To add to the spectacle, racers shave, and their legs seem like pure bronze.

If you come across somebody who's a shaver, beware: generally they go fast and they're in shape (the out-of-shape rider willingly lets his leg hair grow back). The slightly chubby leg, vaguely weighed down and with indistinct contours means, on the other hand, that there remains work to do and that a gentle ride will be just that.

The slender leg, with an ever-so-small calf, is the leg

of a climber (no unnecessary weight). The voluminous thigh – that's a sprinter. The long and harmonious leg – that's a rouleur. A short femur? He'll be swift. Rounded bum? He'll set off strongly. Slender ankles and knees, he will have class.

Contrary to what's usually asserted, fat calves are of little use: the essentials of cycling power are concentrated in the back, the buttocks, and the thighs.

At the height of the season, it's difficult to forget your legs. They are the site of curious physiological phenomena. The most surprising is 'big thighs'. Having accumulated I don't know what kind of fatigue, the thighs swell up and get firmer. They don't fit into your shorts any more, or your trousers, and you find yourself burdened with two ham-like thighs whose cycling worth is relative, at least for a few days.

When you're in shape, standing still can be difficult. One of my friends was getting married, and I had to go to Mass – something I'm not used to doing. I showed myself to be unable to stand still, as the faithful do. I had the painful feeling that my legs wanted to move up into my trunk.

In that situation, only the bike can soothe the pain. After a few kilometres, it goes away – or it changes into cramps, for good.

I dream about massage. Just seeing the greediness with which racers 'go for a massage', or their bad mood when their turn doesn't come, makes me think it must be a panacea. Masseurs occupy a special place: they are confidants, friends. Just by touching the muscles they know if it's been a hard day, if their racer is 'going well' or is 'tight'. For a long time they played vague roles and carried mysterious cases – like Coppi's blind masseur, who was reputed to have supplied him with all manner of explosive items.

I dream of a masseur who would supply me with supple muscles, unknotted cramps, and kind words. That would give me two beautiful legs.

Double Bass

Throughout my childhood my extended family – cousins of both sexes – shared a wood and fibreboard house deep in a meadow in the Haute-Loire. It had been hastily constructed after the war, for refugees. The refugees had left, and we rented it by the year. Everyone in the village knew it as 'The Shack', which agreed with it perfectly.

Each family unit had at its disposal two identical rooms separated by thin wood sheeting; one of these rooms served as the kitchen-dining room, the other as the bedroom. Come the evening, the two were transformed into garages: since we dreaded robbers, rain and the sneaky effect of dew on frames, we brought the bikes in. When all the bikes were inside, getting out became impossible. The last one to go to bed brought in the last bike, the first one up took them all out.

In life's orchestra, the bike is the double bass. Hard to forget it.

Transport

When he sets foot on land, the cyclist looks like an ugly duck and immediately finds himself encumbered by his beautiful bike. A veil of nostalgia clouds his gaze – he was so close to flying, and here he is, a clumsy oaf.

I've tried everything when it comes to the matter of bike transport: boxes, bags, roof racks, baggage racks. My father even had a roof rack built to his own design. It was so huge that passers-by on the street believed it to be a television antenna.

I've known every sort of mishap. I lost a bike rack stuffed with four bikes on the Autoroute du Sud. I lost my beautiful blue bike on the Autoroute de l'Ouest – a sharp dip in the road made it shoot off the rear-mounted bike carrier, and I dragged it along for 100 metres. I held my mauve bike tight to me on an aeroplane lest they throw it in the hold like a common suitcase (I should mention that that one was made of super-thin, super-light steel – it broke not long afterwards).

No method is satisfactory, and everything calls on you to do the whole trip by bike. And in that case, you have to assure yourself that your lodging really does have a lockable, dry garage where your machine can sleep.

The prefect solution in this matter does exist, how-ever – I tried it once. We were on a little jaunt in the Swiss Alps and, at Saint-Moritz, we stayed in a luxury hotel. On our arrival, at the garage entrance, was the door-man. He immediately relieved me of my bike, parked it among the Ferraris and Rolls-Royces, then removed the saddlebag from it – which he took up to my room.

Need for Air

Territory

My childhood world was always bigger than my village. As soon as I knew how to ride I grasped the idea of a greater world. When I left to do a ride, everything that was within the circuit was 'home'. I plotted ever larger circles as my strength gradually increased – around Bas-en-Basset I took ownership of Le Vert, Tiranges, Saint-Hilaire, Aurec, Yssingeaux, Malataverne, Retournac, Usson-en-Forez, Saint-Bonnet-le-Château.

The Haute-Loire's mesh of roads is a blessing for the cyclist. They're narrow, serpentine, beautiful and little travelled. The choice of routes is vast. The gradients are variable and, though you always start at 425 metres and end up at 1,100, the profiles are always different: steady climbs, back-breakers, hairpin bends.

My village is lodged in the Loire Valley, in a little flat area, and to leave it you have to climb. Strangely enough, the six or seven hills that allow you to leave have very different landscapes: if the Tiranges climb is a beautiful ascent up the side of the valley that gradually opens out as you approach the summit, the Saint-Hilaire climb is shady, steady, hidden in a hollow that smells of moss and mushroom. The ascent via Thézenac is open, hot, hard at the beginning, and opens in its upper part on to the spectacle of the rounded volcanoes and plateaux of Velay.

In the distance, Mount Mézenc.

The villages and hamlets get some shut-eye and, even today, you can ride for three hours and only pass a couple of cars. The countryside is well kept, and little wonky fields alternate with peaceful pastures. Summer is boiling, winter is biting, the seasons are clearly defined – it's schooling in all roads and in all climates.

Little by little I widened my circles, faithfully stuck to the wheel of my father, who sheltered me from the wind and silently taught me the virtues of cyclists.

There's something of the peasant in the pedaller. They share a taste for nature, submission to the elements, patience, thrift, perseverance and the sense of acceleration. There's something of the sprint in the harvest and the grape picking. The eternal order of the fields joins with the eternal order of the road, and riders like Robic and Poulidor rode a bike the same way they worked the farm.

In this way, between the ages of nine and 15, I covered hundreds of kilometres behind my father, confidently. I learned to climb, I learned to descend, I learned to not be scared, to take advantage of everything, to be crazy at the right moment, to not be frightened of the Man with the Hammer. I changed bikes twice, I increased the height of the saddle and the handlebars and, at 15, I went to the front.

It was the gentlest way of carrying out some Freudian ritual, my father no doubt suffering from wounded cyclist's pride but comforted at least as much by his pride as a father and road captain. I was jubilant.

He immediately dubbed me 'the beast' because of the energy – perhaps unqualified – that I put into pedalling, and the nickname stuck.

And then it was on the same roads that I learned the virtues of battle and of shooting matches with Furnon, Madel, and the local lead-foots. Here, no longer a question of patience: mouth open and thighs on fire. Nothing other than the result counted.

Flats

The only thing my journeys through the Haute-Loire hid from me were the flats.

When, on the stroke of turning 20, I 'went up' to Paris on acceptable grounds, I discovered the flats. And I was stunned when I understood that I had to learn them.

I had thought that the flat was a sort of boring para-dise, a gift given to old-time riders. I was wrong. The flats call for a special cyclist science. My biggest surprise was the change in duration: on my little journeys I'd had to push hard, but every half hour of intensity earned me ten minutes of rest.

Changes in activity level and position were very fre-quent. On the flat, it's not the same deal. You can pass five or six hours without stopping pedalling, without chang-ing position, and new pains emerge: unprecedented weariness, shoulder complaints, tenderness in the neck.

Up to that point my use of the gear shifter was fairly drastic: from 42 × 22 I jumped to 52 × 14. On the flat, I had to learn the merits of going from tooth to tooth. Between 53 × 16 and 53 × 17 there can be a chasm and as a general rule it's the wind that carves it out.

The Haute-Loire isn't spared winds, but they're blocked by mountains, entangled in rises, forests, ridges. They surprise you in sudden ambushes and then disappear. On the flats they lead the dance, and their presence is continuous.

Bike position becomes key, shelter becomes a science. You find yourself constantly lying in wait for the direction of the breeze so as to find a bit of rest on a friendly wheel.

On the Vauhallan plateau the wind that blows from the west spreads out the Sunday riders in a fan, and trying to start out against it is a challenge pretty much equivalent to attacking a hill.

The reward of the flat – because there is one – is the fantastic group efficiency you can attain there. On favourable days, with four or five of equal strength and strong determination, you knock off considerable amounts of terrain at unconventional speeds. The musketeer style ('all for one and one for all') is the most seductive way of managing the flats.

By Heart

I know my corner of the Haute-Loire by heart.

To know is to have landmarks, to be able to find your way, to be able to grade yourself.

My standard measure is a hill of barely ten kilometres that comes out of the Ance valley to climb towards the village of Tiranges. It's a splendid road – a cliff path on the side of a mountain, shaded by pines, full of smells slightly more tart than those of Provence. A country road, two cars wide, and a rough surface. A road crossed by lizards and snakes, bordered by brambles, by ferns and by golden rocks. A road that feels like a path as it goes up. It was laid out more by the steps of people and animals than by the will of bulldozers. It has its fleeting inclines and its serious leg-breakers. It's charming.

I especially like it because, before going up, it saunters through the valley for five kilometres and leaves you time to warm up. The river gives out one last shot of freshness and – past the little bridge on the left, past the old abandoned bistro where in the old days a barrel organ played – the real business begins.

From the first 100 metres, I know if I'm a 39 × 24 or a 39 × 20 – in other words, whether I'm sort of in shape or in proper shape (these mystical numbers indicate the gears that are used; the first is significantly lower than the second). After that, I don't even have to look at my watch any more – just the pace of the landscape going by and the sequence of my sensations are enough to tell me where I am.

I recognise the two bends if I have to stand on the pedals, that short stretch if I find it long, and that hamlet if I have pain in my pins – generally when I get to the watering hole. This will be my pace regardless. If I have to accelerate, it'll be on leaving the forest because there my acceleration really makes the legs hurt (not just mine).

And then, on leaving the hamlet of Chasles, I know there will be a level stretch amid the rye. The view will be opened up. We'll all uncover the rounded crests of the Velay. The sparrowhawks will fly above our heads, the chickens will peck in the ditches at the side of the road, we will feel the slight breeze coming from Saint-Pal. It will be time to have a drink and to get ready for the last rise on the slope, which will take us through the hamlet of Les Arnauds. After that we will have a choice between the little road on the plateau that will take us to the hairpin bends of Cacharrat or the Tiranges road that plunges back towards the valley, dominated by the medieval château of Saint-André-de-Chalançon, perched on its outcrop.

All this is ticked off in internal minutes that tell you

whether it's May, whether it's July; whether you're shattered, whether you're in shape.

Cyclists all know this secret relationship with the world. They have a nice expression for it: 'To feel it'.

Ideal Holiday

My ideal holiday starts at the beginning of July. Work in Paris is slowing down. We have served the last cocktails. The summer books have been out for a number of weeks, the autumn novels are at the printer, the Tour de France is still in its first flat stages. The need for silence is vital. It's time to get on the road.

A little handlebar pannier with the bare minimum, and the path south. To return to the Haute-Loire, near Saint-Étienne – as I do every summer – I follow a streak of B roads that take me to meet up with the Loire; cross it at Orléans or Giens, along the river on its left bank, then the accompanying canal at Allier, then to reach Moulins, then Courpière, then Vichy, and things start to get serious in the Forez mountains: Job, Vertolaye, Ambert, Saint-Anthème, Usson, Saint-Hilaire-Cusson-la-Valmite and Bas-en-Basset.

Four days of perfect peace without saying words other than those that the refrain of my bike dictates to me; four days of militant silence to purge me of the torrent of words that is my everyday work; four days of physical violence to get revenge on my armchair. There's

nobody on these French back roads and the transformation of *Homo intellectus* into *Homo bicycletus* takes place
in private.

First, all muddled from Paris, I open a dialogue
with my thighs, to pick up the pieces. Depending on
the time of day, it is the old stuff that reawakens: an old
conflict with my knee, an old kink in the saddle area, a
burning shoulder. But one also rediscovers the old feeling of well-being: a lightness of the thigh, a swelling of
the calf, sudden power coming from my back. From the
need for silence, I slip into the need for rhythm.

Old secrets and new discoveries blend while my
body, hot and active, seeks an equilibrium with the outside. The weather forecast ceases to be abstract, and the
rain front that will cross the country from the west is
suddenly found squishing in my shoes. It could also be
the strong mistral wind that takes me by the shoulders
and carries me along towards the south at the speed of a
CGV (*cycliste à grande vitesse*).

I cover 150 to 200 kilometres a day and, if my pace
is consistent (at least while the road is flat), my mood
changes and definitely lightens along the way. I have no
more questions to ask myself; I'm alive and soaked.

Towards the end of the afternoon, when fatigue
further weighs down my luggage, I look for a TV in a
bistro to watch the end of the Tour stage.

The riders are on the flat, the stakes are minimal,
but the spectacle of the teams' manoeuvrings interests
me. As a general rule it makes a TV viewer yawn with
boredom but when you have a little education in your

thighs, the spectacle of a team going all out over the last 20k to put its sprinter into orbit is a treat. That's when you see the anonymous and proud pacesetters. Then it's left to the sprinter to sprint. This can be dangerous (Abdujaparov), powerful (Ludwig), or simply magnificent (Cipollini, Il Magnifico).

The bike gives a new flavour to simple things: the shower, the bath, the bed on which you finally stretch out, the smell of the cream you put on your legs – by magic, in gratitude, for the sake of intimacy.

When I pull into port, the remaining ten days of holiday play themselves out according to a fixed rhythm: bike in the morning, Tour de France in the afternoon. I can speak again; I'm a cyclist who chats, and I can ride with friends. The biking friends who I find where I left them last summer, around the fountain at 7am (Jean-Loup, Titch); friends passing through with whom I ride elsewhere (Jean-Noël, Rémy, Sébastien); new people, strangers, cyclists.

At the hottest point of the day, I like to watch the day's stage with my father. He's the guardian of the history and the legend of the Tour, the commentator on the commentaries. Then, when the stage is done, when the sun is still high in the sky of the Haute-Loire, it's time to get down to all the frivolous holiday activities.

Around 20 July, on a nice Sunday afternoon, the riders suddenly show up on the Champs-Élysées, and the Tour de France is over. My holiday finishes along with it, in a big bout of the blues, which I will purge on my bike on Monday morning, head to head with myself in the green mountains and the scent of pines. My summer is finished.

After that, I go 'back up' to Paris with my bike on the roof of the car – that's how much my cycling tropism points south when I'm not going in circles. Even if it's much easier to go from the Haute-Loire to Paris, even if the road descends at a steady rate for the first 200 kilometres, going to Paris is 'going up.' My schoolteachers and the Michelin Man also orient their maps that way, and in the same way they've oriented my destiny as a cyclist.

As a professional, I would have won Paris–Nice.

Giono

It was the middle of August and, rather than staying near the Mediterranean shore, caressed by the breeze and regaled by water, we took off to ride in the sun-bleached backcountry. On the afternoon of the second day, we crossed Canjuers, the great deserted plain where you occasionally come upon a tank; a desolate plateau under which, they say, war machines stir. We searched in vain for a tree, some shade.

During the ride – while my father was telling me about the Provençal novelist Jean Giono, about the peasants of Provence and the way they welcome people – I was seized by thirst, yet it was him who was talking, not me. My water bottle was empty, his too, and my young physiology – I couldn't have been more than 12 or 13 – threatened collapse. My face must have been of a red persuasive enough to make my father decide to take the dirt road that we saw on the left, and to go and knock on the door of the only farmhouse in the area and to ask for some water.

The farmer's wife half-opened her door, passed her olive-coloured head with black hair through the crack, and point-blank refused to give me anything to drink.

That's how I made my crashing entrance into Giono's world.

Around the Tour

We often set off to see the Tour de France. My father's idea was to gather up some cousins, some friends – both boys and girls – and to put together a gruppetto to go and pay homage to the racers at the top of the Alpine passes.

Paying homage to the racers means first climbing the passes on bikes, ahead of them. We made sure we had one or two drivers who weren't turned off by the spectacle of cycling – or by driving slowly – and then we worked out our itinerary.

It's pure pleasure to go up the passes in the morning, before the riders. The road is closed to cars, and to climb a col in those conditions is a gift.

If you like solitude, go up the side the racers will come down. One summer I did this with Rémy: we linked up the Izoard, Vars, and Allos, going in the opposite direction to the riders. And those three climbs stay fixed in my memory as a glorious time. You just have to get up early.

If you like crowds, go up the same side as the riders. That's the way to feel what that crowd brings to the race.

You also get the spectacle of the endless picnic that is the Tour de France, and it's a chance to pick up some first-hand information on the different types of fans.

There are the industrious types who write Richard Virenque's name in white paint on the road, and who tell you off if you ride over their fresh daubs. There are the picnickers, dyed crimson, who make up for having gone up on foot by attacking their first snack. There are the pushers who want to help you with a strong hand on your bum (when my wife is along she always gets more assistance than I do). And there are the shouters who rehearse their war chants on the amateurs passing through.

Occasionally you can pick up some real gems. I remember a big strong guy who ran a few metres behind my wife yelling: 'Go, Mama Merckx!'

You ride like this practically until the breakaway is announced. You then sit yourself down at the side of the road and you wait for the race, a cyclist on foot.

Flags

I've scaled unbelievable passes but been able to claim no glory from it because they hadn't been marked by a champion.

Once back from holiday, if I say to a friend: 'I climbed the Finestre pass,' he replies: 'I floated on my back in the Caribbean.' On the other hand, if I tell him: 'Hey, I climbed the Izoard,' his face lights up.

Ditto if I say Puy de Dôme, Alpe d'Huez, Tourmalet, Vars or Pra-Loup.

Whether they know it or not, whether they want it or not, the French have an excellent cycling education. They know the champions and the locations of their exploits. These great champions superimpose their own geography on official geography. They're like little flags stuck on the map, like landmarks.

You can even guess the age and allegiance of the person you're talking to. If his face lights up on hearing Pra-Loup, he's a Théveno-Merckxian; Puy de Dôme, he's an Anquetilo-Poulidorian; and if it's Alpe d'Huez, he's an Induraino-Züllian.

Maps

The day before an outing, or even the same morning, my father made me read the map. We stood side by side at the table, and I followed with my finger. That's how I learned the secret of B roads, back roads, and dangerous stretches marked with red dashes.

We left the main roads to the cars and sketched out our routes on everything else.

I particularly watched out for the little arrows ('quavers' my father, who knew music, called them). In those days, they scrupulously indicated the climbs on the maps: one quaver for modest inclines, two quavers for serious ascents, three quavers for walls.

It was still the era when cars got out of breath on the steep climbs and stopped, foam on their lips, to get their breath and some fresh water – human cars.

I also learned to count the kilometres by mentally adding all the little numbers that marked the route.

We did our ride and, on returning, we reread the map to check the detours that inspiration had led us to take, and to assure ourselves that we had indeed done *that*. That's how I learned to tell north from south. I am rarely lost.

For me, road maps are dream machines. I like to read them as one reads adventure stories. As a driver, I use them to find the shortest route, to find the long roads that join towns with towns without going through the countryside. As a cyclist I use them for everything else. If I know the area, every centimetre of the map is a landscape laid out before me. If I don't know it yet, every centimetre is an imagined landscape that I will explore. For example, I like maps of Brittany, which is cycling country where I've never ridden. It's my storeroom, my wine cellar. It's the masterpiece that you have in your library and which you still haven't read.

Wind

The bike is a schooling in the wind.

There are two kinds of biking wind: the object-ive wind and the relative wind. The first is that which is made by the mechanics of the world around us and the second is the work of the cyclist alone. His master-piece, you could say, for the faster he is, the more wind he creates.

The wind of the world is the one that hits you square on. I know no remedy against it other than friendship and solidarity. When you get a strong, persistent north wind full in the face, nothing beats a big-shouldered friend. You ride behind him, make yourself small, and you wait for it to pass. More pre-cisely, you wait until he pulls off and then you take your turn to do your bit.

The strongest wind that I can remember having faced is the wind of the extreme west of Ireland. I ped-alled along the coast, somewhere south of Galway, and I saw to it that I always set off riding against the wind to be sure that I could get back. I was alone, and it was a bitter fight. There was no forgiveness. All the things that can, elsewhere, allow you to cheat and to shelter yourself are not welcome here: no trees, no houses, no hedges, no hills. Nothing but the ocean wind – wet, powerful, inexhaustible. Flat out on my bike, I had the feeling I was going dead slow, condemned to using the gears of high mountains on a road that was flat.

On the way back along the Irish coast, when my little relative wind combined with the big outside wind, it was sheer pleasure. A pleasure superior to descending because I felt like I was bombing along in overdrive, going much faster than I should have been.

Having learned very early on, at my own expense, that the wind wears you out, I learned very early on to keep an eye on which direction it was blowing from. There's something of the sailor in the cyclist. It's thanks to this basic training that you learn to shelter yourself better, to take better advantage of the strength of others. When the wind blows from the side, or from an angle, the riders fan out over the full width of the road to make a rampart of their companions. These fans are called *bordures*, and if you're not in the right one, jumping from one to another is practically impossible.

The relative wind, which the cyclist makes, is that of his own speed. You can feel it when a rider brushes past you. You can also feel it when a cyclist who is faster than you overtakes you – they call it 'catching a cold'.

One day when I was going hard up the Pilat, I 'caught a cold' in this way from a young lady, as light-footed as a gazelle, who was climbing like an aeroplane. What a nice pedal stroke she had! It was a pleasure to see her, firmly in her rhythm, coming to dust me off with a gust of her breeze.

Lucky for me I was able to jump on her wheel. The cyclist, by creating a wind, hollows out a space behind in which it's easy to ride. If you stay locked onto the wheel, the cyclist will offer you a good 25 per cent less work. Thanks, gazelle.

Shelter and ambition are the best reasons to make cyclist friends. By doing so, you can benefit from the combined effort and grant yourself a moment of increased well-being before taking your turn at the front.

To really take advantage you have to stay close, in the bubble, with your front wheel only a few centimetres from the rear wheel ahead of you.

If you give up a few lengths, the wind closes in on you and 'getting back on' is not easy. When whoever's in front is pulling really hard, it can even become impossible.

In the 1996 Tour de France – in the long and rolling descent from Montgenèvre to Briançon – the peloton, made restless by the closeness of the finish, stretched out in a long unbroken line in which every rider seemed to be having problems in keeping his place. The fine Melchor Mauri, who was riding next to our car, was presented at this moment with a pickle with his gears, which forced him to forsake his spot and to quickly find himself stranded behind the peloton. Christian Palka, who was driving, told me: 'If we leave him there, he'll soon be ten minutes down. He won't get back in by himself at that speed.'

So we gave him the shelter of our car for 100 metres, to get him back in the line. On getting back in he gave us a kind wink. We had been driving at 80 kilometres an hour.

Don't repeat this story, please. It's strictly against the rules to help riders in this way and to impede the terrible will of the wind.

Sounds

The sound of a bike is the sound of the wind. The machine itself should be almost silent.

In the old days bikes dripped with oil and grease; today the oiling and greasing is more discreet, but is no less effective. A real bike does not squeak, does not rub, does not groan; it purrs. In flat country, you shouldn't hear it. If, perchance, you pass a wall, you can pick up the soft hum of the chain on the sprockets. By contrast, you hear other people's bikes much better and especially that little click, which warns you that someone has just changed gear and that you're going to have to change your pace.

Indexed gears now shield us from the scraping of the chain when it's stuck between cogs; a noise which was so irritating.

Tubulars have a whistling sound all their own, especially when you stand up on the pedals and accelerate. Now that clinchers are in general use, that whistling can go into the Sound Museum. There it will join the tinkling of the bell, the creaking of the leather saddle, the rubbing of the mudguard on the tyre.

Brakes have also shut up. The rubber of the brake pads does its job gently. It is more efficient and it is quiet.

The peloton, now that makes noise. From the outside it's a powerful and low-pitched breathing, a breathing that no mechanical noise could mask. If it were a locomotive it would be a high-speed TGV rather than a steam engine.

From the inside, the hubbub is the result of a hundred little noises that all add up. A hundred derailleurs, a hundred chains, a hundred gear changes at once, all of that locked in a mobile cocoon in which sounds pass primarily from front to back.

So long as you are skilful enough to keep your position, the peloton is a protective bubble that isolates you and pulls you forward.

If you listen closely, you can catch snippets of conversation, some laughter, some brief commands. At the start of a climb it's fun – but when you really start to gasp and fight for air and you hear somebody who's still cracking jokes, it's not as amusing.

For about ten years now, since toe-clips disappeared, the peloton makes a new sound. I became aware of it one morning around 7am in the centre of Saint-Étienne. There were 1,000 of us at the start of a hill climb and, at the pistol shot of the starter, we clicked into our 2,000 clipless pedals.

In the Sunday morning silence it was a good sound, one which said: 'Time to get going.'

Descending

Descending puts me back together. The descent reunites the skier and cyclist that are in me. Every descent on a bike is a sort of giant slalom, with its tight spots, its braking spots, and its indispensable sense of anticipation.

To be a good descender, you've got to have a deep knowledge of the road – a kind of complicity with the civil engineers, an instinctive and rapid grasp of the terrain. Every road is a design, and every descent is a design within the design.

Modern roads dictate their law with blows from bulldozers and dynamite, but the older ones embrace the contours of the ground and of the mountain.

When you go fast into a blind turn, it's imperative to have an intuitive idea of what comes next. Experience is therefore essential. The more you descend, the faster you descend.

You must be watchful and fit. Descending is the opposite of letting yourself go. That's why I have such admiration for the riders who, after a terrible fight on the climb, throw themselves full-tilt down the other side.

The great descenders are strange creatures who

you have to learn to be wary of. They're not necessarily mean, but their virtuosity can transform them. It is as though they want to send their adversaries to sleep. They go to the front, make you feel confident and then, suddenly, the person who was trying to follow finds himself on the ground, in a ditch, in a ravine. There are a few men who can turn where all the others go straight on. It is a good thing to know.

The pleasure of descending a mountain that you've descended a thousand times is to brake as little as possible, to delay breaking, to go into the corners as fast as possible, to come out with a good line to attack the following corners, to draw out an impeccable design and to give it the rhythm of music. You can sing while going down.

You can do that at medium speed and find great pleasure in it.

If, on the other hand, you're tired, or just feeling dull, a descent from a col can seem endless. If the cold muddles and numbs your fingers; if the rain muddles and overpowers your brakes; if the wind is blasting across the road, descending can be a punishment.

I remember a descent from the Ventoux into a strong and cold mistral wind that left me frozen stiff in Malaucène, incapable of warming myself up, incapable – which is even worse – of deriving the slightest trace of pleasure from the climb.

Smells

Cycling smells good.

In the Haute-Loire, it smells of pine and moss, alternating with cut hay. Here and there, a spot of cow.

In some hamlets, a cowshed takes over. But also the smells of open windows: beef stew, polish, washing powder, roast chicken. Thrown over a line, sheets and blankets give out a fleeting smell of night-time, quickly lost in the blue sky.

Summer has a very strong smell. You pass through pockets of sweet-smelling heat when the road cuts through a field of wheat or of rye, when you come out of a forest to enter a clearing. The heat activates the smell of the resins, and brings up out of the road this smell of tar, which is the underlying base of the scents of summer.

The greatest performance takes place just after rain, when the road surface is still steaming from the storm and when the deep odours of the world ascend from the earth. The returning sun dries your jersey and releases an aroma of wool and salt from you. The smell of water fades away bit by bit and for a quarter of an hour you feel as if you're riding inside a truffle.

For a long time these smells were for me the smells of cycling. When you ride fast and get out of breath, they merge and take over from one another in an ever-changing rainbow.

When my cycling domain enlarged, I had to add to my range: the smell of fish, sand and flowers in California; the smell of the wood fires of the chalets of Austria; the smell of lavender and that of thyme of Provence; the smell of salt of Ireland; the smell of the damp autumn and of mushrooms of the great undergrowth of Paris; the fine, fresh, pure smell of the high mountains.

Landscapes

Contrary to what happens when I'm in a car, when the landscape allows itself to be seen and not 'to be', on a bike I'm sitting inside it.

There is in the bike an animal relation to the world: the mountains you see are there to be scaled, the valleys are for hurtling down into, the shade is made for hiding in and for getting on with. To be in the landscape, in its heat, in its rain, in its wind, is to see it with different eyes; it's to impregnate oneself with it in a deep and instinctive way. The mountain that rises before me isn't a mountain, it's first an incline to climb, a test, a doubt, sometimes a worry. At the summit, it's a conquest, a lightness. I've taken it and it's in me.

In some ways the beautiful stretch in the forest of the Izoard is part of me, the road on the side of the Aubisque is part of me, the gorges of the Tarn and the Verdon is part of me, and the Rambouillet forest too. I've sweated them. They were never a performance; we played together.

When I set out in the morning I'm still in a home-body mood, still in a warm bed mood. I'm cold; my cyclist's micro-pains reawaken: the right knee that grumbles, a fleeting pain down in the saddle area, a really stiff back. The road is grey and vaguely hostile. I pedal in a sullen low gear. I feel that my legs are hard and that the universe is soft. I don't see anything.

After a few kilometres my temperature rises, I don't feel bad any more, and the world unfolds around me. I gently make my entrance into the landscape. An equilibrium establishes itself depending on whether it is hot, whether it is raining, whether it is windy. If I'm in shape this equilibrium will maintain itself even if the conditions change. The sharp coolness at the top of the hill will be a blessing, as will the blast of warmth when I redescend into the valley.

What I see of the world embellishes what I feel about it and about me. On the tiny little road that takes me from Thézenac to Cacharrat, one finds a brief stretch of 100 metres that the trees protect, which without doubt shelters a spring, and which guards a breath of cool air from the hottest of the summer. Thanks to this 'cool spot' – which I pass through in a few seconds and where I don't remember ever having actually stopped – I can ride for two or three hours just for the happiness of finding it again and of briefly feeling that old sensation on my skin, as old as my childhood, as old as the day I experienced it for the first time with a smile of well-being and relief.

When I ride far away, in new climates, I have to tame them before being able to discover, once and for all, the surrounding world.

When I arrived in California, where nature is a constant delight, I had to learn to ride in what for me was an unknown mix of burning sun and freezing wind – one which passes you from winter to summer depending on whether you are in the shade or in the sun and invites you to get dressed and undressed 20 times a day – before being able to feast on the sequoias and the golden prairies, on the grey and roiling Pacific that watches you pass with a scowl, and on the thousands of flowers that the wind plants at the edge of the roads.

I also have my bestiary. If my observations are correct, there are two main categories of animal: those who would like to ride a bike, and those who love to watch the spectacle of cyclists.

Cows, which we believed specialised in trains, like to feast their eyes on cyclists as well. Whether in Normandy, the Bourbonnais or the Forez, they follow you lazily with their gaze, with their gentle air.

In the Haute-Loire, hawks are also up for the spectacle. They fly in distant circles above your helmet.

I very much liked the climb up the Vars on its north side. It was a steady ascent, nice to climb, with its succession of small villages. Perhaps it was among my favourites. Today the road has been widened for coaches, and the mountain is marked all over with the scars of ski lifts – 'another one buggered up', Queneau would have said. One morning while I was climbing it alone and in silence I met, on arriving on the short flat stretch at the top, my most attentive and unexpected spectator: a marmot. This ordinarily secretive and shy creature was waiting for me, sitting on his bottom, his front paws placed on his chest, his eyes sharp. I stopped, lay my bike on the ground, and we stayed there facing each other, ten metres apart. When he was satisfied with his inspection, having sufficiently sniffed and observed me, he left to store my image for the winter.

Among the animals who would like to ride a bike, dogs are the most irresponsible. Jealous, they snap at your calves; playful, they leap about in front of your front wheel – when they don't do worse. Horses will offer you a bit of a trot on the path beside the road, happy to have the opportunity to let go.

On the tiny road that goes from Beauzac to Sarlanges, below the Frétisse, I had as fellow traveller a big hare, delightful and well behaved. We did 100 metres together. He stayed on my right, close to the ditch, and galloped. I was fascinated by the sight of his ears, which flopped in tempo with his feet, and by the sound of his running on the sand and asphalt. He wasn't scared – not even wary. He was going his way, which was my way, and then he went back into the scrubland, which was his scrubland.

I tried them out in Ireland, I rediscovered them in California during my treks along the Pacific coast. Seagulls. They're the worst. When boredom gets hold of them, they set their sights on you and dive. Their motives are strange; they don't intend to eat you, they don't want to steal your bike, but you would swear they are motivated by aggressive, secret and murky projects. As soon as they notice you, they aim for you and pass very close to the top of your head, in a rustle of wings and squawking. They can do that ten times. Three or four of them can gang up until you've gone through. They managed to scare me.

In France, the landscape changes quickly, and the speed of the cyclist allows you to sample all the variations. You can change 'regions' three or four times in the same day, and the succession of these landscapes has a strong charm. Our country is cyclable thanks to the dense mesh of its roads and the variety of its shapes. You can change gently, slipping from the Loire region to the soft plumpness of the Bourbonnais to the ancient heights of the Morvan. You can also make radical transitions: take the road south to Pau and advance straight into the barrier of the Pyrénées, or leave Lourdes and climb up to Hautacam as if scaling a wall.

The bike's speed carries out a selection on the surrounding landscape. Your eyes have to go right to the essential and keep alert if they want to grab hold of an anecdote, a bit of passing beauty, a fleeting charm.

Why did my eyes, in the immense landscape of the Vars, see only the marmot? How did they deduce that he was waiting for me there?

In the Year 2000

New Year 2000 was a commercial flop. The shopkeepers' idea was to turn the world on itself by sending everyone to the Antipodes with a party hat, streamers and a bottle of champagne. In San Francisco we were waiting for the great and the good of Paris. Those who hadn't gone to Auckland anyway.

The world's inhabitants instead chose to stay home and celebrate in other ways. Which leaves hope about the next millennium celebration. So San Francisco was calm on the night of 31 December, even a little gloomy, since the shopkeepers had boarded up their windows out of fear of the Parisians.

A week before I could have no idea of this. I had therefore decided to treat myself to a cycling celebration in the peace of the desert, far from the expected commotion. The idea was to cross Death Valley by bike.

After a night in Lone Pine, in the same motel where John Wayne and Gary Cooper stayed when they were making westerns; after a breakfast on the wooden porch of a ranch located at the valley's entrance – facing a sun rising on maximum nothingness – my son and I hit the road (my son isn't a cyclist, but he rides a bike very well).

The appeal of Death Valley is that it offers all the desert forms: dunes, rocks, salt lakes, colour palettes. The appeal of crossing it on 1 January is that the sun stays low on the horizon and brings out the entire range of colours, without overwhelming anything. Moreover, its heat is bearable.

I wanted to set out from the lowest point of the valley, about 300 metres below sea level, to climb to the summit of Dante's Peak, some 1,700 metres higher, and discover the panorama of the entire valley. The way up is beautiful, steady, with long straight lines and a terrible final kilometre. The gradient is comparable to that of a major Alpine pass. Traffic is nonexistent, and it's strongly advisable to bring water bottles and a hot-water bottle if you're planning on staying outside after night falls.

The scene is exceptional, grand, sublime, etc., but it's not for cycling. As with a lot of American landscapes, the rhythm of the bike doesn't suit it. Either the bike doesn't go fast enough or the landscape doesn't change quickly enough, but something resists their marriage. This sort of landscape has been made to measure for the car. Lost in those immense straight lines, I felt like a displaced animal, a Sempé cartoon character who's too small for his surroundings, a minuscule trace of life in the valley of death.

I discovered a new feeling there. The air was so dry that I had the feeling it was sucking up my sweat. As soon as a droplet formed on my forehead it evaporated, was absorbed, vanished into the clear blue sky. Sweat is a shell, it's armour, it surrounds and protects you from contact with the world. To work up a sweat is to pull on the matador's garb. There in Death Valley I was naked. I climbed with a quick rhythm because the road was good and the day was short, but in spite of everything I had the feeling of not managing to find the right carburation. I looked for it throughout the climb and I arrived at the top without having found it.

At the top I got my reward. The World was magical and beautiful, as old as itself, quiet like nowhere else, indifferent to the little leap of the millennium. I waited for day's end and the freezing cold of the night. The millions of stars.

We were in the year 2000 and my first resolution had been to redo this ride at the beginning of each century, to check my fitness.

Ventoux

There are plenty of passes higher than the Ventoux.
Every cyclist knows the sacred monsters with their holiest of holy places and their landscapes: the tunnel of the
Galibier; the lonely wasteland of the Izoard; the stifling
last two kilometres of the Restefonds; the hairpin bends
of Alpe d'Huez; the badly packed earth of the Gavia;
the terrible right turn of the Saint-Charles bridge in the
Iseran ... So many legendary places where cyclists head,
like pilgrims.

The Ventoux is alone. Sat on its plain. It has command over no valley, it leads nowhere. Its only purpose
is to be climbed.

It is its own climate and country. It has its own specific fauna of processionary caterpillars and beetles, and
its flora of downy poppies from Greenland and saxifrage from Spitzberg. It is a challenge to the wind and,
on days of heavenly grace, a viewpoint for an immense
panorama.

For the cyclist it is a riddle.

You never climb the same Ventoux twice. Every
cyclist has a memory of a glorious ascent. The one I

did with my sister one delightful morning in Provençal harmony and the northerly breeze. The one Jean-Noël Blanc did on the closed road, between two walls of snow, on a Ventoux his alone.

In the same way, everyone can remember those leaden days when suddenly, for no reason, the bike freezes, locked on the tarmac. Those days of dreadful sweats, those days when the fruit rots in your pockets; when, very quickly, a voiceless anguish enters.

On one of those ugly days I found myself halfway up the north side at the end of my water reserves. It was blazing hot, the heat of a stormy August bank holiday. I noticed a water spout on the side of the road and ran over to it to fill my water bottles. The dripping tap was unapproachable, black with a dense cluster of wasps and insects.

It was only 10am. Already the tar was melting, and my bottles stayed empty.

During these nightmare ascents, there are no longer any landmarks. Your eyes are glued to your front wheel, and it's your guts that you're looking at there, without really seeing them. The friend who was climbing so slowly down below passes you. In slow motion you cut a mule trail in the straight grain of the road. Cars honk their horns at you. You don't even think about going back down. You're not thinking about anything any more.

The Ventoux has no it-self. It's the greatest revelation of yourself. It simply returns your fatigue and fear. It has total knowledge of the shape you're in, your capacity for cycling happiness, and for happiness in general. It's yourself you're climbing. If you don't want to know, stay at the bottom.

Pedalling Inside

Velodrome

It was made completely of wood, like an old boat, and it creaked from every joint. It was full of smoke and dust, full of cigarette butts. You sat on benches among big blokes who shouted loudly over the brouhaha. I was very small, and I made myself even smaller in my terrorised jubilation at being in the velodrome.

Saint-Étienne was one of the rare cities to have one, but it was so dilapidated and so dangerous it was torn down. My adolescent years passed to the rhythm of the progressive forgetting of the promise to build another one. Now nobody even thinks about it.

I'm a fan of the 'squirrels'. They're the virtuosic froth of cycling. I see them as a little crazy, a little autistic; their eyes fixed on the wheel in front of them, focused on their effort, locked into their virtuosity, powerful and feline, pulled forward by their fixed gear (they can't stop pedalling), without brakes, having chosen to be what the bicycle most radically is: pure speed.

Track cycling is the essence of the bike, of cycling inwardness, of contrariness. Bikes with pure lines, stripped of everything; simple and intense rules; a changing and exhausting spectacle, a fundamental sadness among these riders deprived of the great outdoors and of countryside, deprived of it both day and night. A strange spectacle that used to be to everyone's taste, and which nobody likes any more, without one being able to know which died first – the supply or the demand.

André Pousse told me his old trackie memories – his memories of the Six Day races, his distaste for road racing, his ruses, his scheming, his sinister hunting at 2am, and the subtle tug on the neck you feel every time you come into a turn almost horizontally, and which, as the hours pass, makes your neck and shoulders heavy as stone …

When they tried to revive the old magic in Bercy, I hotfooted it over there. There was indeed a track there, there were indeed famous riders there … and not much else. The ambiance of the velodrome was missing.

In the Saint-Étienne velodrome I saw an old Coppi, I saw Anquetil, I saw Rivière battling it among themselves. I saw the mad stayers behind their motorbikes, which added a taste of petrol to the cloud of tobacco smoke – at the end of the meet, you would have said they had pedalled around inside a pipe. I saw the relay racers set off by the seat of their pants; the Madison specialists, so numerous on the track that you ended up seeing only the blur; the pure sprinters, poised at the top of their vertiginous turns, lords of the realm.

I liked to station myself at exactly the top of a turn, at the spot where the slope is steepest, where the sprinters tread water before plunging towards the baseline and surprising their adversary.

I dreamed of exploring that feeling – me, the chubby kid sitting next to Roger Rivière's actual mother, who was looking lovingly at her son.

I've retained such a vivid memory of the few evenings spent there, with my father, that the desire to ride on the track has never left me. And I've never done it – lack of track.

I've only known a substitute version of it when, much later on, I had the chance to ride a bike on the auto circuit at Monthléry. The pitch was there – and with it the worry about going fast enough so as not to touch the ground with the outside pedal – but it was missing the wood; the low, hissing noise of silk tyres; the tight angles at the corners; the asphyxiating atmosphere. The velodrome.

Memory

The bike inscribes disconcerting things in you. A thigh memory exists that is separate from ordinary memory. The body retains the memory of moments of effort. Sometimes the most difficult, the most arduous, are erased. What's left are unexpected memories of unexpected moments – moments that at the time were not felt to be exceptional but which the muscles have chosen to remember for their own reasons.

One day we descended from Saint-Véran and were caught in a storm at the bottom of the Guil valley, a classic mountain storm that pissed down very hard and soaked generously. We had to stop at a café to wait it out. After half an hour most of the storm had passed, the heavy flow of water had drained from the road, and a fine rain had settled in. None of this was very appealing, but it was rideable. So I volunteered to go and get the car, which was parked in Guillestre.

Those 20 kilometres that I rode in the rain are inscribed in my memory forever. They regularly come back up to speak to me of the bike. Is it because of the rain? Is is because of the light that gradually came back, illuminating the road? Is it because of the gentle slope that allowed me to spin with ease on the big gears? Is it because of the little rest that I had just taken? I'll never know, because my muscles play back the rough memory in its intensity and its length, but without analysis.

The Austrian skier Franz Klammer once re-enacted, in front of a movie camera, his winning run at Kitzbühel. He did it from behind his businessman's desk, wearing a tie, his eyes closed, his hands in front of his face, tracing out the curves – and he did it in the same time, give or take a few seconds.

Through effort, something – perhaps contradictory – is written in you. At one spot between Yssingeaux and Retournac the road, descending towards the valley of the Loire, sharply goes up again for 200 or 300 metres. I hate these leg-breakers that stick me to the road, that warm me up but don't leave me the least chance to really get into it, nor to get settled into a climbing rhythm.

Yet it is that damn bump that'll come back up through my thighs at the slightest opportunity, and it doesn't come back as a painful memory but rather as an incitement to accelerate. No doubt it's the terrible 'braking effect' aspect that gives it the opposite virtue.

The Texture of Roads

Suddenly the road gets smoother, my legs turn more freely. Automatically I shift into a higher gear, realign myself on the saddle. I've just changed départements, changed texture.

Every département, sometimes every district, has its own way of tarring back roads; each has its own idea of ideal asphalt, of perfect surfacing. For the cyclist, this results in a small jump when a boundary is crossed, and a new feeling to the pedalling.

In the mountains, where the cold of winter bites into the tar and the summer heat softens it, the road is made up of big, dark grains: a beluga which moves you with tiny vibrations, which numbs your perineum, which, little by little, makes your hands tingle through the gloves. On the descent the texture climbs up on both sides of your spine, as far as your shoulders, where it vibrates in tune with your arms, your palms.

On the climb, on really hard days, every bit of gravel is a minuscule mountain that you climb in addition to the mountain itself – it's then that they say the road is 'paying back' badly, which clearly means that you have to give it more.

When, in spring, I get back on my familiar roads, the frost has bitten into the surface; it has cracked it. Over winter the lorries have opened potholes. The repair crews have plugged them with a black paste that they smooth over with the back of a shovel. Generous guys make a mound, stingy ones leave a hole. In both cases I bounce around and my tyres pick up a few bits of gravel. If I don't swipe them off with my glove, they bump every 2.198 metres and I risk a flat. Heat, cold, and the passage of cars in their hundreds are needed for these dark patches to establish themselves within the general asphalt, leaving a stain on the surface that the years stretch out. On these rough-textured roads, spring rains trace out streaks of red earth; storms scatter broken branches, autumn damp leaves.

It's in the ditches by the side of these roads that nettles and brambles shoot up, calf-high. If the road crew dawdles a bit, you see green grass sprout right in the middle of the road, through the broken crust.

The road I join on arriving on the flat is fine-grained. It's light in colour and follows a canal, smooth like calm water. My breaths are longer and if I accelerate, the road 'pays back' well.

By dint of riding little back roads, long-distance trips, loops around my village, I've built up saddle memory.

From the packed dirt of the old Dolomite passes to the covering of smooth cement of the autoroutes (I've been known to ride them before their official opening to cars), via those beautiful coatings that make you feel as if you're on rubber, by the cobbles, by the roads laid down in slabs that go 'plock plock' at the expansion joints, I could draw up a catalogue of all the sensations that I have hung on to.

The cyclist's nether regions are a place of historic dramas, of furious boils, of sneaky lumps that alter the face of races. For me it's the place of a specific intelligent sensitivity. Carried blindfolded, I'm sure I could recognise, just by touching it, the texture that a road long ago inscribed in me.

Friends

When we set off side by side in the early morning, we have so much to say to each other. We haven't seen one another since the day before, a week before, a year before, but we're immediately breathing together, chatting together.

To warm up there's nothing like conversation. The pedalling rhythm that allows for chatting is the ideal one for getting going. Obviously it varies from person to person – and to see riders telling stories at 40 kilometres an hour, their hands on the tops, makes the casual rider wonder – but the principle is the same. As long as you talk while pedalling, you warm up gently. We talk about everything: about books, about films, about restaurants, about work, about life in general and about cycling in particular.

I have cycling friends who I don't see other than on the bike – I don't know them in a suit and tie. I have cycling friends who I see all the time. We're a gang; a little peloton; a breakaway with variable geometry. Certain mornings there are two of us, on others 12 of us, lost in an ocean of 4,000 cyclists.

A group of buddies on bikes is almost always a group of the same level. You have to have a real physical complicity to ride well together. That's not about all being similar or all being of equal strength – you just need each person to be able to bring something to the group.

Cyclist personalities are very well defined. As in the theatre, cycling has its types: it is a strong revealer of characters and morphologies and what is obvious to the layman about the professional riders is reproduced exactly among the amateurs. Cycling has its musclemen and its skinny guys (the 'thigh guys' and the 'chicken legs', as Jean-Noël Blanc would say); it's not very concerned about its morphotypes. There is opportunity for all.

If you take climbers, for example, there are clearly two kinds: the angels – who are as big as minnows and who seem to be sucked up to the summits – and the bulls, who fight it out with gravity, with a massive supply of power and will. In the first category there's Charly Gaul and Pantani, in the second Hinault and Indurain. Each is capable of getting the better of the other so long as he stays in the realm of his own abilities: the bulls aren't advised to follow the angels in their accelerations, and the angels mustn't allow themselves to be stifled by the regular rhythm of the bulls. Know thyself.

These broad categories are found among Sunday riders, and to put together a good group you need this kind of diversity. Everyone needs to be able to put the screws on everyone else and to keep up in all circumstances, even if you have to grit your teeth. Someone who's too fast won't help anyone develop and will get fed up waiting at the tops of climbs. Someone too slow will get sick of being stuck behind the group, stranded in no man's land. The small groups of cyclists with which I've been acquainted have balanced themselves organically around their main objective, which is to have fun riding together.

The fun comes in several ways. First of all, it's the pleasure of sharing nice things about the bike – things seen, things felt, the effort, the heat. It's also the common desire to leave, to get out – alone maybe you'd stay in bed, make up things to do, hesitate when faced with the threatening sky. It's also the happiness of pulling out all the stops, like a bunch of kids. Speeding up 'just to see' is in the cyclist's nature. The bike carries within it the freedom of racing. Even by myself I'll pull out all the stops. If I feel good, I accelerate. If I still feel good, I accelerate even more, until I don't feel so good. That's how I give myself a 'bust' (that's what they call a brief moment of tiredness, the kind that catches up with you at the end of the day).

The accelerations of one another – that you can follow – are a gift to your conditioning. They make you better, even if you're annoyed to be made to dig deep – in my case, this kind of anger never lasts more than five seconds. It's a discipline. I used to ski with Rémy, and we got on well. So I set out to convert him to the bike, and he became an impeccable cyclist – how true it is that you can take up cycling at any age. Friends in your life who are cycling friends are double friends: vanilla *and* chocolate.

The Others

You can ride long and far. Very quickly – with a good cycling technique and a little training – the body gets used to the effort and asks for more. After a few hundred kilometres you can peacefully pedal all day and consider taking on serious climbs and uneven terrain. After several hundred more, you can have fun accelerating and taking turns at the front. In this way you serenely reach the wonderful place that is 'being in shape'. So you think you're in paradise.

That's when – on your usual little route, on a climb – you catch up with another rider and you decide to stay on his wheel. Just like that you lose your paradise, you lose your native tongue.

Hell is the rhythm of other people.

When the decision to speed up or slow down doesn't belong to you any more, you are a different cyclist. Through a kind of rebellious logic, it's always when your legs are tired that the rhythm speeds up, always when you're in the process of putting on your gloves that you have to go flat out … You try out, on a small scale, the difficulty of bike racing.

If you don't want to be blown off the back, it's always in your interest to know your cycling buddies well. On Sunday mornings, in the valley of the Chevreuse, I know that Rémy will accelerate on every climb. I know Rino will punish our legs on the flat at the top. I know Sébastien will never let up and that he'll always push himself beyond his limits. That's how they are made, and that's how their souls have shaped their legs. You have to live with it.

When I followed the Tour de France, I saw professional racers pale in the morning with the thought that they might not be able to follow the pace of the peloton. I saw them again in the evening, worn out but happy to have been able to hang on to their place at the back of the pack and to still be in the Tour.

We're so busy watching the front of the race that we don't take account of the dignity and honour that lies in simply being there, in the rhythm of others. The rhythm of the best, the rhythm of those who are strong for ten minutes, the rhythm of the baroudeurs.

Racers very strongly feel the need for others, in order to build themselves up. That's exactly what they mean when they admit they're 'lacking competition'.

The others, whoever they are, make you pass another boundary in your knowledge of yourself and in your conditioning. You were good and, thanks to them, now you're even better. Soon it will fall to you to impose *your* rhythm.

Going Round

Blue Jersey

Taking advantage of the fact I was wearing a blue jersey like that of the Italian team, I slipped into the Tour de l'Avenir. The strong guys had gone past some time before, and I picked out a big blond rider in a red jersey who was going up the pass at an acceptable pace. I placed myself behind him, then beside him, and we went up the Forclaz pass together, urged on by hordes of spectators.

He was Russian and since I could speak a bit of his language (badly), we were able to exchange a few panted remarks. What he wanted to know above all was if this hell was going to last much longer; if he would have to spend still more hours scaling this endless mountain, climbing beside those low white walls that line the road and that reflect the sun's heat and light back on the cyclist. He wanted water, which I gave him; he wanted the flat stages of the Peace Race and the central Asian plains from which he hailed. A little more of this and he would have sent me into a deep depression while climbing hell for leather towards Chamonix.

For my part I was happy to be in the race and to knock off a few kilometres in good company. I carefully avoided talking to him about the Galibier, which he was going to have to climb the next day. We climbed steadily, and I took my share of pulls. I was happy to be in the Tour de l'Avenir – I was the right age. So I was able to dream in Russian for ten kilometres; then a motorcyclist came up to ask where my number was, and my career as clandestine passenger on board the race was over.

I said 'Do svidaniya, tovarich,' (Goodbye, comrade) and let my team-mate go. By then he was only two kilometres from the summit.

Racer

For a long time I wondered why I wasn't a racer. Especially during the periods when I was in shape and riding fast. I don't have an exceptional physiology at my disposal, but it's good enough. I could, perhaps, have been a racer in the ranks, been in the race at least.

One thing is certain: I could have tried.

I didn't do it.

The objective reasons are numerous: I had 'better things' to do and at the age when one tries to become a racer I had set off on other adventures. In the 1960s, sport – and especially cycling – paid badly and had no prospects. Today it would be a different story. Sport is an excellent way to glide through life.

It was also the mood of the times. The favourite sport of my school friends was exemption from PE. Any excuse would do for nibbling away at those four unfortunate hours of weekly exercise and for transforming them into heavy study hours. The most cunning guys, with help from their parents, found fabulous excuses, overwhelming themselves with colds and chronic sore throats so they could give maths the time allocated to muscles and games.

So it was natural that athletes were seen as morons ... For me, who liked sports as much as I liked studying, the pressure would increase a little more each time: how many times, when I was in preparatory classes for university, did I find myself alone under the basketball hoop? How many solitary laps of the playground did I inflict on myself?

Like any self-respecting cheater, I slipped my forbidden reading matter under my desk lid: *L'Équipe*, when folded in eighths, just fit into the space between my textbooks and exercise books and shattered the silence of the class with a racket of crumpled paper. I should be clear on this: I wasn't hiding my reading from the teacher but from my classmates. The teacher suffered from the same virus I had.

This secret muscle garden I carefully cultivated every Sunday morning on my bike naturally marked me as a member of the moron clan. I had two jobs, and it's hard to be a racer by halves.

There was also, and from the beginning, a little worm in the apple. I had the confused feeling of not liking the same cycling as my friends who were doing races. It wasn't a question of ethics or aesthetics – I never got involved in the ancient battle between touring cyclists and racers. By simple instinct, I felt closer to the latter. I pedalled like they did, I fought it out like they did, I collapsed like they did, and I had no great passion for the reasonable reason and the obligatory regularity of

Audax rides. All the same I didn't quite like the same cycling. I would have had real problems saying why.

It was only in 1996 – when I had the chance to follow the Tour and meet the champions – that I understood why I never raced. It's among former racers that one meets those who most hate cycling. They can even devote themselves to a relentless hatred, holding it responsible for their failures and their doubts.

When I was able to talk about this with them, some told me simply that they were so sick of cycling at the end of their careers that they were dying to forget the bike. Still they showed up at the Tour de France ... 'for the ambiance', they said. Others told me their job had nothing to do with bikes: it consisted of winning races, and 'going for rides' had no place in their future. Once they had retired from racing, bikes were useless.

A number of them also confessed that doping had driven them to take a long break and seriously clean themselves up, and that they had lost their taste for cycling.

Former racers are often melancholy cyclists. They've lost their good sensations (both natural and artificial), and the Sunday cyclists with whom they could share a peaceful retirement annoy them by always wanting to measure themselves against them. As if the champion of one time always has to be the champion! That ruins the very act of pedalling.

I remember the aged and pathetic Louison Bobet, who demanded that we – the kids – stay behind him on the Longchamp climb.

I'm sure I need the bike more than I need victories. I'd like to grow old as a cyclist. In ten, 20 years I'd still like to go out for a spin with Jean-Noël, with Rémy, with Sébastien.

Already I go much slower than before, but since I threw my speed to the four winds and never transformed it into bouquets or cheques, it lurks in the air of the mountains, and I breathe it in like an old perfume.

Doping

Some of the guys who raced in my area had the habit of going to obscure pharmacies to improve their performance. One day I went along with two friends who were riding a time trial on the Forez plain. The race was on a circuit of about 40 kilometres, and the starting line also served as the finish line. So it was a perfect circle, and they were hoping that the best riders could loop it in less than an hour.

A fishy bloke who we knew well, and who had no goal in life other than to ride faster than his local friends, took off like a shot and crossed the line going the other way barely ten minutes later.

Everyone was addressing him with big waves of their arms, trying to get him to show some common sense, but he didn't see any problems. He came over to me, got off his machine, and told me: 'I think I did a good time.'

We had to hide him for a few hours in the back seat of an old Citroën to keep the foam coming from his lips from official eyes, and to give him a chance to calm down.

As we said then: 'He'd even swallowed the box.'

I've got nothing against doping – the problem's more complex than a simple game of for or against. I simply never had any desire to go down that road. Even if the effect of amphetamines on muscular power is non-existent, their psychological effect on those who don't take them can be considerable.

It's commonly said that racers dope because their sport is a hard one, but their sport is also hard precisely because they dope. The milieu of racers is a doper's milieu, and the serpent of doping endlessly bites its own tail. The lie is too old, and the hypocritical abyss they've allowed to open between the official line and real practices too enormous ever to be closed.

In the peloton, to refuse to dope is to refuse to 'do the job'; it's like refusing to train or to get a massage.

Athletes have doped from day one. When the world was one of magic, dope was magic; when the world was chemical, dope was chemical; now that the world is biological, dope is biological; when, in the future, the world is genetic, dope will be genetic: swimmers will have scales and cyclists will be born with saddles between their thighs.

Doping itself has become a form of high-level competitive sport. They should test the doctors.

During the last Olympic games – in the same Arab country, at the same time, and in the same papers – you could read about the disqualification of three doping weightlifters and the protest of sporting circles that were complaining that modern doping was a privilege of rich countries!

At the entry to the locker room of the Californian gym in which I used to work out, there was a permanent notice up warning the public of the dangers associated with the use of anabolic steroids ... which you can find freely for sale at the counter on the ground floor. Whole pages of the local paper sang the praises of growth hormones banned by the International Olympic Committee.

Competition produces doping, just as taxes produce fraud. What's annoying is that while the effects and injustices of doping are well known, it often takes a long time to figure out its forms.

The younger generations now use the drugs that Coppi used to win the Tour de France to go out dancing on a Saturday night, and some racers who are nostalgic for the good old days can't train without a shot of grandpa's stuff in their backside. Without that it's a sad party and a grey road.

Frame Thoughts

Every year when I'm in France, we organise – at the time of the Saint-Étienne Book Festival – a hill climb with Jacques Plaine (I know – it's not his fault that his name means flat). He's the master of the proceedings and rides a bike when he's not running marathons.

This race – which has been christened the Autumn Suns Climb and which takes place, depending on the year, in the rain, the wind, the snow, and sometimes even in the sun – has become a great get-together. On the start line there are writers, artists, former champions, kids from the local cycling clubs, and old-timers. I've seen Pierre Béarn taking the line at the age of 94, tangling with the new tools that are toe-clips.

Jacques Plaine has chosen the Pilat climb up to the Croix de Chaubouret as the route; a severe climb whose profile I'm not crazy about. The idea being to climb it cold, and at the bottom of the gear levers, it leaves little time for savouring things. Even so, it's a very uneven course and it hurts your legs.

Once the clock has stopped at the summit, the game consists of coming back down from village to village, from prize wine to mulled wine, from sausages to small tarts, finally arriving in town in a euphoria indifferent to the brisk air and the occasional snowflake.

My friend Yvette had the good (but absent-minded) idea of asking me to write a short article for *Le Progrès* on the occasion of each running of the race. For technical reasons this article has to be submitted at 1pm. If you add the time for a shower and a clean shirt to the time taken to ride the race, I am forced to write it on the climb itself.

There are a lot of walker-poets, who write their verses to the rhythm of their feet: the Rédas, the Roubauds. Cyclist-poets are less numerous, it seems, but that's inadvertent because the bike is a good place of work for the writer. First, he can sit down; then he's surrounded by windy silence, which airs out the brain and is favourable for meditation; finally, he produces with his legs a number of different rhythms, which are just as much music to verse and prose.

The difficulty, however, is that in the case of the Autumn Suns Climb I try to climb very quickly while writing all the while. My breathing is therefore very short and my prose choppy. My lucidity is lessened and my position keeps me from seeing everything. I'm a deaf, blind and out-of-breath reporter.

Days of peaceful rides are perfect days to brew up text. I leave with a sentence, an idea, and I spin it around for a few hours. I come home with a short story almost finished, an article, the end of a piece.

When I write this way, I can tell whether it's headwind prose or tailwind prose.

On a bike, I love working with paradoxical thoughts, thoughts that appear maladapted. Thinking methodically about Proust, about Queneau, for example, about Calder, about Howard Hawks; reciting Le Pélican de Jonathan by Jacques Roubaud; reconstructing What a Man by Georges Perec and Oh l'ostrogoth by Jacques Jouet. I love experimenting with the distortions that effort causes texts and reflections to undergo. What the open air brings to them. What sweat oxidises in them. What they bring to my cycling performance.

These are displaced thoughts and I can never know precisely whether their methodical exercise influences the steadiness of my pedalling, or the steadiness of my pedalling influences the methodical side of my reflection.

Often these thoughts are crazier, freer, than they would be in a living room. Less presentable too, sometimes pitted, sometimes shaken by sudden accelerations, unforeseen shortcuts, surprise breakaways. They have nothing in common with the chit-chat topics I might share with my cycling friends: these are the thoughts and exercises of a solitary cyclist. On occasion they've served as preparation for writing.

What I can't determine with precision is the instant in which my thought escapes its subject to become a thought of pure effort. At the moment when the rhythm speeds up, at the moment when the gradient becomes steeper, at the moment fatigue gets the upper hand, thought doesn't fade away before the 'animal spirits'; on the contrary, it's reinforced and diffused throughout my entire body, becoming thigh-thought, back-braininess, calf-cunning. This unconscious transformation is beyond me and I only become aware of it much later, when the lion's share of the effort is over and thought flows back, returning to what is ordinarily considered its place.

Shrink

It seems to me that if I had a psychoanalyst I'd talk to him in any event about the haunting little phrases that the rhythm imposes on you and which can follow you for the whole ride. Also about those songs that will chant all through your morning. About those obscure thoughts you ruminate on and that are turned into purée thanks to all the angry pedal strokes. I'd talk to him about it.

To the Table

I feel the need to be hungry. A real physical hunger, a simple desire to devour.

The bike hollows you out. For a gourmand it's a blessing. The quantity of energy dispensed to pedalling is such that when evening comes around, you feel a pit in your stomach that seems unfillable. That kind of hunger doesn't form part of the panoply of the sedentary person; it's a profound happiness he'll never know.

For the cyclist two different types of meals exist, two different types of appetite: during and after.

During the effort, nourishing yourself is a complex problem. One has to indulge in things that are high-calorie, light, quickly chewed, quickly swallowed, quickly digested. 'Eat before you're hungry,' Paul de Vivie advised, and he was right.

Motivated by the desire to do the right thing – and certainly guided by the memory of the contents of the old-time racers' musettes – riders often set off with a chicken drumstick, a sticky-fruited tart, a leftover bit of steak, a ham sandwich, only to realise when it comes to mealtimes that they're not hungry. Hunger exists, but effort conceals the sensation of it, and the prospect of swallowing a chicken thigh while pedalling up an inviting false flat is enough to make you heave.

There are yet deeper mysteries. I can't think of anything better than chocolate. I eat it upon getting up in the morning and every time I come across it during the day. I like it dark, dry and hard. And yet I've never been able to swallow a square of it on the bike. The bike eliminates my taste for chocolate by turning it into a sticky, nauseating goo. No doubt I should see this as a wise lesson in the non-concurrence of pleasures. One pleasure at a time.

The effect is reversed for marzipan; I don't like it, but on a bike it's a blessing.

The cyclist on his saddle is a different person.

Rebecoming a pedestrian, the cyclist rebecomes an ordinary gourmand but with a huge hole in his stomach – peloton hunger. So the custom quickly spread, among pelotons and Sunday *gruppetti*, of putting finish lines at the entrances to good inns and of giving the winners food as well as flowers.

I'm a fervent fan of this custom, which renews the reputations of the classics. So I have very pleasant memories of a Paris–Troisgros through the Morvan, of an Arles–Bras via Mount Aigoual, of a Saint-Étienne–Loiseau through Burgundy, of a Paris–Gagnaire through the hills of the Forez, of a Saint-Étienne–Tournaire through the gorges of the Loire.

The prospect of a perfect dinner can make pedalling a delight. The Troisgros salmon scallop with sorrel, waiting at Roanne, is a real carrot dangling in front of your nose. Riding along the Cévennes mountain road you can hear the gurgling boiling of Laguiole vegetables. Towards Beauzac, at the area where the road goes above the valley of the Loire, you can already smell the green lentils of Puy done in Tournaire style.

Everything is a celebration after eight hours of riding. The simplest things – the gratin Dauphinois, bolted down at the foot of the Iseran; spaghetti after climbing the Vars; Wiener schnitzel in the evening, after the Grossglockner.

A few years ago my father and I were riding in Tyrol, Austria, and when we stopped he was overcome by an insane desire for beer. Beer, which I practically never drink, is a brilliant beverage for the Sunday cyclist: it quenches your thirst, it's packed full of carbs, and it gives you a slight buzz that erases the pain from your legs and the stiffness from your neck. Ordinarily it has the tendency to turn you into a hot-air balloon, but when you're suffering from cyclist's dehydration it's like water from the spring.

My father, then, wanted some draught beer. In his broken German he ordered one, and they gave it to him in a bottle. He drank it and ordered 'another beer, a different one,' and he was cheerfully given a bottle of brown ale, which he drank unenthusiastically. Then he repeated his demand, and the dumbfounded innkeeper finally brought him his mug of draught. These beers all came in the Austrian half-litre, and that series of three, even in Austria, made an impression. No – my father wasn't a drunk; he was just a cyclist.

One morning I was going from Paris to Saint-Étienne and I'd got up very early so decided to have my little snack break around 10am. At that point I found myself in the département of Cher, in the small village of Apremont to be precise – an old village stretching along the Allier canal, watched over by the Schneider château, and kept in all its former glory. A few Ks from there René Fallet had his cycling (and other) habits.

So I stopped at the inn and ordered some fresh bread, hard-as-rock goat cheese, and a glass of Sancerre. It was nice and hot outside, and I was happy to have already knocked off 100 kilometres and to be able to stick out my pins in the sun. The regulars tipped their caps to me, looked at my bike, had a coffee, and went on their way to work, wordlessly. When, half-choked by the cheese, I asked the bar woman to refill my glass, she objected – 'Don't even think about it! You're riding a bike. If you get drunk, you're going to risk your life.'

She had the grace to not talk to me about risking others' lives – so true it is that cyclists are gentle beings who do very little harm to their neighbours. When I showed her that I was carrying only water in my bottles, she granted me my second glass – but didn't come back.

Fatigue

What I physically feel the need for is fatigue. More precisely, the range of subtly different kinds of fatigue. For just as there exist a hundred ways of feeling good on a bike, there are a hundred ways of being tired.

The fatigue I like best is that of trips in stages. When I've pedalled all day, fatigue hits me as soon as my feet touch the ground. It accompanies me throughout the evening and into the night. It's both generalised and localised: pain in the thighs, pain in the back.

In the morning I'm completely stiff, a rusty old wreck; I have trouble getting down the stairs. I mount my bike without strength, without desire, and pedal like an old robot.

Ten kilometres later, that's all wiped away. I feel good. I even feel better than the day before – repeating the effort improves your conditioning and makes you sharper.

One summer when I was going down to Saint-Étienne with Rémy, I noticed that every morning we had our 15 minutes of silence. No doubt the cyclist's tongue – a fine muscle – also has its morning stiffness.

That was the amount of time necessary and sufficient for overcoming the fatigue and turning us back into chatterboxes. That kind of fatigue is good, it's an accomplice.

On the other hand, you have to be careful about the fatigue that builds up and which, very quickly and very sneakily, finds a way of expressing itself. It chooses a shoulder, the groin, a tendon, and it locks itself in. From that point on magic creams won't work.

The only thing you can do is go back to being a pedestrian.

After a year of intense work, I left Paris a little too hastily, without preparation, heading south – just to get out of prison. I was counting on my old 'skill' to take care of my lack of fitness. The first day was peaceful and soothing. The second morning a barely perceptible click settled into my left knee. As the day progressed it became a big click, and then a big knee.

So I had to end my trip on the train, holding my pretty bike close against me for fear of it being hung from a baggage-car hook like a common side of beef, and from there I reached my bed.

I slept for three days and nights. That good old left knee acted as an alarm bell, warning me of a profound fatigue, greater than the bike could efface.

By remaining attentive to the messages your body sends, through exercise and in pleasure, you can take an elegant inner voyage on the bike. A lasting voyage, a permanent education, continuous retraining. The dialogue you establish with your thighs is a rich one that helps you set your limits, increase your endurance, to tolerate pain and to recognise the intolerable.

I find it useful every day.

I am always on the lookout for bouts of melancholy, a deep and hidden (to me) trait of my soul, and I keep an eye out for loss of desire. I know that if I succumb to depression, it will start with a breakdown in my thighs. It will start with cycling sluggishness, and the rest will follow.

Ageing

To age on the bike is to gain endurance and wisdom. It's having the ability to go further more calmly, to train better, and, in general, to get more out of it.

But ageing is also to go slower, speeding away less quickly, soon not speeding away at all, and soon not caring that somebody else has sped right past you.

There's ruin in the cyclist's ageing as well. I rode the fastest between the ages of 28 and 32. Since then, I've been on the decline – and that's not going to change.

This decline, which happens in stages, is tolerable. You can manage it in the fatalistic mode, you can manage it in friendship – ageing in the peloton. The only indispensable things are a real love of the bike and a reasonable serenity.

The big existential advantage of this ageing of the thighs is that it always precedes the overall, inevitable ageing of the cyclist himself.

Therefore I've entrusted my bike with the mission of informing me of my ageing. It's doing nicely.

Circles

The human body, which has such pretty curves, makes very few circles. You can certainly twiddle your thumbs, but that doesn't get you very far.

To ride a bike is to make circles. You have to think about that when you pedal, as a little reminder: the movement of the legs is circular, you have to grant it this and turn the cranks roundly. Cyclists have an excellent sense of this, and as soon as the cadence falls, and fatigue mounts, they say they're 'pedalling squares'.

The cyclist is his own gyroscope. He produces not only movement but equilibrium. The faster he turns his legs, the more harmonious this equilibrium becomes: he's 'spinning'.

Spinning up a hill, for example, is to be attached to a nylon cord that leads you up to the summit. A cyclist's equilibrium is a circular equilibrium.

If your wheels spin round, your legs spin round; if your legs turn, your head will too.

When something is wrong, I ride to go back up the line of good equilibrium, to get my gyroscope going again. Enjoying a fundamentally depressive nature, I build ramparts and fortresses of cheerfulness and work; the bike is my essential metaphor, my fundamental model. As long as I'm pedalling, I'm in equilibrium; as long as I'm pedalling, I'm okay.

To build the desire for something one needs is to engage in a labour of human happiness. Need is a demanding and obscure thing that defines the dependence of one person on another. To identify it and want it is to define oneself as a person. That's the secret of culture, the secret of cuisine, the secret of kindness. It's also the secret of tiny Fournel on his bike in the vast countryside, miraculously in equilibrium on his two wheels, trying to catch his own shadow.

Blow-up

Extreme cycling fatigue is very distinctive. 'To explode', 'to hit the wall', 'to blow up' are expressions where there is no mystery as to their origins. This extreme fatigue is symbolised well by that character who's famous in all the world's pelotons and known by the moniker 'The Man with the Hammer'.

The Man with the Hammer is hidden behind a turn (you don't know which one), and he's waiting for you. When you go by, with sprightly legs, he smashes his big old hammer on your neck and turns you into a wreck. Then, however much you say that you had seen his shadow stretched out on the road for some time, no-one believes you.

You can't anticipate this kind of fatigue. It appears without warning, and it is terrible. You'd sell your soul to get rid of it.

My life as a rider is a collection of blow-ups – my own and those of others.

I've seen my brother-in-law Jacques, who's a hell of a rider, lying in the ditch on the north face of the Ventoux, 300 metres from the top, absolutely refusing to finish the climb. I've seen myself zigzagging up the Béal pass, with Jean-Loup, having forgotten my name, looking for a way out. I've seen my father abandon me, when I wasn't even ten years old, on the 100 kilometre Vélocio ride, letting me ride on with a packet of Beurre LU biscuits as my only provisions.

The worst thing to do in such cases is to rest 'just a bit' before setting off again. The second you get back on your bike the fatigue immediately returns, massively, with its garland of pain.

It's too late. Anything that could do you good – drinking, eating, stretching out – nauseates you. You'd offer your bike to the first passer-by so as not to see it again. The smidgen of thought left in your brain is a profound sense of the absurd, which makes you want to vomit.

Your sweat is like ice, your skin is pallid, and you stay curled in a ball on the side of the road. It's a rebellion by your entire body.

With experience you get the feeling you can master these blow-ups. It's not true. But you get to know them. You know that you'll get out of it, you panic less, and you recover quicker.

I think that it's in the very specific character and the suddenness of this fatigue that we can look for one of the origins of doping.

Blow-ups in races are measured in lost quarter-hours and lost races. These losses are easy enough to anticipate. In a few seconds, champions age ten years, their faces hollow, their eyes become sunken. The great

Eddy Merckx, at the moment Bernard Thévenet caught up with him on the climb to Pra-Loup, was ready for a deckchair.

It all happens as if something hatched inside you without you knowing it. A big black lump that was forming in your chest while you were peacefully pedalling. There are warning signs of a blow-up, but they aren't that different from the signs of normal tiredness. Now that I think about it, metaphysical anxiety might be one hint.

Riding is absurd – climbing to descend, going in circles, behind this mountain there's another, why hurry? Riding is absurd, like peeling vegetables, skiing, thinking deeply, or living. The moment these questions come up, while you're riding, you should take note. That's when your quads are demanding more oxygen from your heart than your lungs can provide. That's when it gets foggy. If you're on a friend's wheel, he'll pull away by two bike lengths without accelerating. You come back, standing on your pedals, but immediately lose the two lengths again. You do this elastic-band trick ten or so times, and then you let him go, certain of rejoining him soon. In fact, the next time you will see him will be when he turns around and comes back, worried, to find out what happened. At that point you will look at him as a stranger or, better yet, as a potential buyer of your disgusting bike.

One day when I was riding alone, I blew up terribly around 4pm and decided to go straight to the nearest hotel. I was such a perfect grouch – wanting them to open the garage for me, demanding a room on the ground floor (ah, the idea of going up one floor!), refusing to fill out the forms – that the staff started to get irritated. Lucky for me, the owner was a cyclist. 'Leave him in peace, he's cooked,' he said. And he took charge of things, giving me a little break for two or three hours to let me come back to reality.

Every blow-up is a furious descent to the depths of yourself, into regions where things seem to tie themselves up incessantly.

Why not give up the bike after a blow-up?

Because the blow-up is a journey, and the cyclist is first and foremost a traveller. Then because, after a blow-up, your organism is altered. There's a kind of purification in falling flat, an impression of fasting. A threshold is crossed that brings you closer to being in shape – from the very next day, when the worst of the tiredness is wiped away, you feel it. To such an extent that some racers include a blow-up in their training. I remember Fignon, a few days before the World Championships, set off to do 300 kilometres alone with a cereal bar. He went out to meet The Man with the Hammer.

If Fignon needed it, just about any clown, like me, can use a blow-up too.

In Shape

The underlying truth of the need for fatigue, its end, is the need for fitness.

Non-athletes should, at least once in their lives, indulge in the luxury of being in shape. It's a physical experience that's worth the trouble.

Even after many years of activity it remains a mystery.

After the winter break (not all cyclists have the opportunity to spend winter in the sun), the first outings are laborious. They're speckled with small pains. Little chills, cramps, loss of desire. Still, there's steady improvement and you get your bearings again.

And then one morning you feel like you've been let out of prison. The air, which is identical to the day before, seems lighter; the countryside opens up and you feel at home, in the fold of the mountain. You like the hill you're climbing, and to celebrate you upshift two cogs and accelerate. You're in shape.

Nothing can get in your way, and you pedal in happiness.

Fitness is a global state applicable to all the facets

of the bike. You pedal smoothly, as if in oil, you climb well, you descend quickly. You're capable of efforts that surprise even you. You're happy.

One summer, while I was staying in Bedoin near my friend Bens, I decided to go and climb the Ventoux. I left around 6am, to avoid the intense heat. It was early morning and the birds were singing in the vineyards. No one was around and, because the air was still brisk, I developed a quick cadence on the flat part and on the false flat that comes before the steep section.

Arriving at the fateful left turn – which rises before you like a wall and which rather bluntly indicates the beginning of the serious stuff – I got into a lower gear but maintained the same cadence. I kept that cadence to the top, wary of the blow-up hiding behind every cork oak, behind every bush, and then behind every rock – and it never came.

On reaching the summit (even the long ledge at the end seemed gentler to me), I decided to take the road down to Malaucène.

At Malaucène – where it was already hot – rather than taking the road on the left, winding through the vines (Côtes de Ventoux, *Appellation d'Origine Contrôlée*) to Bedoin, I purely and simply did a U-turn and treated myself to another Ventoux.

At noon, having showered and shaved, I was back with my friend Bens, watching the truffle oaks grow in the field opposite.

Fitness is a climb. That's why riding in the high mountains is such a beautiful metaphor. The annoying thing about climbs is that they have a summit. One day your fitness stops increasing, and it starts to become inconsistent. That's when the alternation between 'with' and 'without' days starts.

Their distribution is a surprise, and the Tour de France racers themselves confessed to me that it was their first question of the day, their first worry. They rush into the first slope (well, hill) to know whether they were, yes or no, silky mounds.

I have a compelling need for 'with' days.

From Cairo

In Cairo – where I've written some of these pages – I've had, after 45 years of continuous cycling, my first experience of cycling severance. I just don't see where I could slip a bike into this city, nor do I see – between the overburdened valley of the Nile and the deserted desert tracks – any shady countryside I could explore.

The Nile on a pedalo doesn't tempt me. The white and solitary desert doesn't appeal much more – they'd find me melted in the scanty shade of some ruin. Strangely, the only cyclists I run into in the city ride with one hand. With the other they hold up a two-square metre tray, which they balance on their heads and on which they have arranged 200 loaves – these are *baladis*, round, puffy, arranged in a pyramid (an obsession) and sold for a few piasters on street corners. Each one rides like that through the streets – straight neck, weaving among the cars, rolling worried eyes, anticipating obstacles – and stops with a sort of belly dance that enables the whole edifice to stay erect. If by chance a rider loses a loaf, he leaves it to the cars or to the children, who dive under wheels for the pleasure of a snack.

Arriving at the street corner where the soup vendor has set up his pots, the cyclist stops. Helping hands relieve him of his burden, and he sets off for another one, holding his handlebars with both hands.

I have trouble seeing myself recycled as a Cairo bread-delivery man. So I'm biding my time. My bike's wrapped up in the cellar in Paris, ready to go. I stay seated and wait – heavy and immobile.

I'm watching my thighs melt and my belly get round. I write about the bike while alternately flexing my legs under the table. I plan out routes in the desert; I read maps that show straight, arid lines stretching for 300 kilometres between oases. I ask myself where on my handlebars I could attach the compass and the GPS.

Not having a two-square-metre tray squarely on my head, I'm looking for a way to create my own shade.

For the first few days, the first few weeks, I didn't really notice I wasn't riding.

In fact – and I'm struck by this truth – it's very easy to not cycle. You hang around in bed an hour longer on Sunday; you jump behind the wheel of your car without thinking; you look for a parking space close to your office; your legs are never sore; that little pain in your knee disappears. You hardly think about it. You don't see any cyclists in the streets (not 'real' ones); you don't come across any in the country; you don't see any bikes in shop windows. You forget. Your friends write that they went out on Sunday, and they seem even further away than ever.

That lasts for a few weeks.

And then one morning – the other morning – I felt blurry. I became aware that I didn't have any contours, any edges. I no longer knew exactly where my body stopped and space started. I could have become enormous, or tiny to the point of disappearing, without noticing it. I lived in this doubt all day and all night, from time to time touching myself to make sure I really was soft.

At 2am my right calf, which is a real minx, cramped up terribly. We went for a little walk in the hallway and, taking advantage of the intimacy of night-time, it let me know very clearly that the time had come to get back on the road.

Trying to cheat, I hobbled forth the next morning to hunt down a health club – which I didn't find.

So I'm now waiting for the moment when my calf – via the little secret wire from which it normally receives short orders from my cycling brain ('we're speeding up', 'we're slowing down', 'we're attacking') – will send back its brutal message and start to pull my morale down into my ankle socks. I have the feeling it'll manage to turn me into a huge captive ape, making me hate the neighbourhoods and the landscapes, making me hate the whole country; instil in me the simple idea that the time has come to return to a country of pretty roads.

That's how my cycling calves operate: independent and wilful, and I've been living with them since that July day when I was nine years old, and, on my green dragon and on the wheel of the Baron, I attacked the climb to Pont-de-Lignon.

Ride More

Baroudeur

The baroudeur – the fighter, the adventurer, the chancer, the opportunist – is a spoilsport. A spoiler of riding in peace, a spoiler of sprinting at will. He comes to start a fire. At the slightest opportunity, he puts the hammer down. It could be on a bitch of a small climb, or at a time when the peloton slackens off ever so slightly, or on a winding road where he can hide – anything will do.

Baroudeurs aren't always liked. 'Again!' the peloton says to itself when they attack. It is the baroudeurs who hand out leg ache. Deadly accelerations are their standard.

There is no set format for a baroudeur. Neither a true sprinter, nor a true climber, nor exactly a rouleur, the baroudeur is all those at once. He is capable of all of it, but in his own time. He knows that he will not beat the sprinters at the finish and so he has to set off beforehand. He knows that he will not beat the climbers in the high mountains; he makes his kingdom the medium mountains. He knows that he will not drop everyone on the first push so he puts in a second.

The baroudeur is relentless. He particularly likes

to make his escape attempt a few kilometres from the line – right under the noses of the sprinters – and then to hold off the peloton, spreading his wonderful strength all over the road.

As a beginner, the baroudeur catches his colleagues out, but very quickly his manner is known to the peloton and he wears 'the sign'. He is a marked man. If he lifts his arse out of the saddle, the pack is on the lookout. The team-mates of the sprinters are charged with hunting him down. The leaders' team-mates have an eye on him simply because the chancers know how to take a chance and, often, to chance it is to also win it.

An Object Lesson

I'd moved up to the front of the peloton for a quiet pee
when the attack took off. I felt the draught on my back,
saw the yellow jersey go past like a rocket to my left and,
without thinking, I got out of the saddle and jumped
onto his wheel. I pedalled in the dark for two or three
kilometres, my sole horizon the buttocks of the guys
in front of me – a crazy pace. Suddenly, I didn't need
a piss any more. I felt terrible but I held on. Perhaps I
was having a good day. After those hellish kilometres,
the pressure dropped a bit and we took stock. We had
opened a gap, there were five of us out front – four big
guys and me, the baby. This was the decisive break. The
yellow jersey looked us over with a sharp eye to assess
what shape we were in, weighed us up and must have
decided it was on. He went to the front without asking
any help from any of us and launched us with his huge
gear. He didn't need us to further stretch the lead he'd
just opened. I slid in to get right behind him in the line
so I could watch him better. As long as I could hold on I
wasn't going to miss an iota of the work he was putting
in. I instantly felt the weight of his cadence in my legs,

flat out on my machine, well sheltered in his draught, suffering like a dog to stay with him. How could he be going so fast, on his own into a headwind?

It was partly because of him that I was in the professional peloton, but I'd never had the chance to observe him so closely. I liked him, I admired him, I respected him. That morning at the sign-on, I couldn't take my eyes off him. He climbed the steps of the podium and his cleats gave him the tread of a lion (they made me waddle like a duck). His bronzed legs and that smile told the whole world he was the strongest and he couldn't give a damn. He turned to face the public, drank in the cheering, and signed the register with a big scrawl of his name that spilled over the margins. Then he took time out to shake hands, sign autographs, pat some kids on the head, pinch cheeks pink with pleasure, and have a coffee. As for me, I always arrived to sign on in a muddle, slipping about, crouched over, just about disappearing under the table, my jersey only half pulled down, the number clumsily pinned on. And now I was looking at him.

He led for 15 kilometres at more than 50kph without asking for a relay. The timekeeper arrived and held the slate up under our noses: a four-minute lead, all done by the force of his pedals. Reassured, he slowed imperceptibly and paid me the compliment of waving me through. When I rode up alongside, he smiled at me and winked. We were playing a cute comedy routine. I got stuck into the relay like never before, did 500 metres flat out and I was on my own. It was an elite bunch that went past me in line: Cappilori, the Italian rouleur, reigning world champion in his rainbow jersey; Van Berg, the Belgian who had won Paris–Roubaix by a street; Choustra, the Kazakh climber who had, bizarrely, made such a showing in that year's time trial; and the man himself, in yellow. Every one had a palmarès as long as a phone book, and me who hadn't picked up a single victory in the year I'd been with the pros. I got back behind him. The speed stayed very high and, as soon as the road sloped a bit, I felt on the verge of being dropped. My earpiece started to crackle and I pulled it out so I didn't have to listen. The directeur sportif was obviously going to tell me it was all fine and to hang on as best I could. I didn't need him to tell me that. I was going to stay up in the luxury seats to see the show for as long as possible.

There followed ten steady kilometres, relaying in turn, the lead growing, and there was no doubt now that the game against the peloton was won. Behind us, they must have been riding with their hands on the tops of the bars. As to what lay ahead, I was pondering how much time I could hold on for. I knew there were two hills coming and the first would kill me off. I knew that's where he'd make his effort and that I'd crack at the first acceleration. I didn't take my eyes off him. I drank when he drank, ate when he ate, got out of the saddle to honk for a while when he did the same. He seemed to be riding without nerves, watchful only to add a bit of pressure every time he took up the relay, just to let us know that he was the boss. It seemed so easy to be a champion. I was fascinated by his cool: strong as he was but saving his strength for the right moment. If I'd had his legs, I'd have buried us. He was turning without effort. No one in the break spoke, each of us focused, intense. I felt as if I was part of a great work. When my turn came for one relay, the pain in my back shot through me and I missed my turn. Cappliori took over without saying a thing. They weren't looking for any miracles from me. They knew the peloton by heart. There were four of them in for the win and they knew it would come down to the pedals but also to moral strength. I was out on both counts.

Oddly, we went up the first hill in line. The cadence increased all the way up but no one tried to pull away. These gentlemen measured out their effort on the quiet; spent themselves without showing it. I clung on behind in my small personal hell, eyes fixed to the wheel in front, my throat burning, my muscles taut, shoulders numb. I was holding on.

The lightning struck at the summit. Just at the moment when, relieved to have finished the climb, we marginally eased off to catch our breath – that's when he let loose. He was at the back of the group and set off down the right side of the road, plunging into the descent like a cannonball. There was a moment's hesitation and Van Berg set off in pursuit. He knew he risked blowing up but somebody had to go. Choustra and Cappilori jumped onto his wheel and the elastic stretched for a moment before I got back to them with almost no strength left.

I saw him, two hairpins below us – in control, compact – and I told myself he was giving us an object lesson; that I was lucky to be there for a few minutes and that my lesson in bike riding would never be wasted. I was scared. The road was narrow and we were travelling at high speed, from gully to gully. Van Berg had a great reputation as a descender and I matched my line and braking to his. I was running out of power. Coming out of each bend, I lost a bit of ground. Even out of the saddle, I couldn't get straight back up to speed. It was a sprint every time.

Before the foot of the descent, we caught another sight of his yellow jersey ahead of us. I was sure he was slowing down on purpose so that we would rejoin him at the bottom. As soon as we got back onto his wheel, he delivered another statement: no sudden spurt this time, nothing but pure force. We'd hardly changed gear and it was time for him to go, full gas. As the speed went up again, I was surprised that my legs responded. I could follow Choustra. In front of him, Van Berg had popped and slipped away from Cappilori's wheel. Choustra plugged the gap and Van Berg tucked in behind me, quickly lost two metres, came back once, came back twice, and was dropped for good. The world champion was adrift. Ahead, the rhythm didn't slacken. Cappilori took the relay. When it came to Choustra's turn, the cadence went down a click and the yellow jersey, sensing it immediately, went back into the lead to deliver the killer blow. I jumped onto Cappilori's wheel, convinced that Choustra wouldn't last long. He held on for another two kilometres and then fell away too, demoralised.

My turn would come on the last hill. I was proud. Here I was at the head of a race with the two best cyclists in the world. Cappilori attacked the climb in the lead, standing on his pedals, in the big ring. The yellow jersey moved up alongside him, passed him without effort and gave him a jarring session of half-wheeling, setting his wheel a few exasperating centimetres ahead of Cappilori's. At each acceleration, he came back to position himself in his place. First place. Cappilori joined in the game, accelerating non-stop, and it was a treat for me to see the yellow jersey moving back up imperturbably alongside and taking two centimetres off him. Cat and mouse.

On a minimal acceleration out of one bend, Cappilori suddenly yielded. I was holding his wheel and we instantly found ourselves two lengths down. It was over. Cappilori came up beside me and smiled. He grabbed the back of my jersey and slung me forward. 'Go on, plug this hole for me – I'm cooked.' Hurtling forward, I bridged the gap, got back onto the yellow jersey's wheel, but Capplilori didn't have the strength to take advantage. Sent into orbit, I found myself alone, at the front of the race, behind the greatest cyclist of all time. Behind my champion. He wound it up full-on without turning round, without seeing me. It wasn't even certain that he was aware that I was there.

It was the most beautiful day of my life. The most beautiful race of my life, the most beautiful lesson. I didn't take my eyes off him, admiring him at full stretch, me who, ordinarily, saw him only in the distance. He was splendid. He was strong and I loved the fact that I was going to beat him.

Climber

The climber does not look like much: he is the revenge of the skinny guys, of the featherweights. The steeper the slope is, the more his power-weight ratio does wonders. You would swear that a magical force pulls him towards the summit at the same moment that gravity sticks all the big guys to the road and calls them downhill rather than up.

In contrast to the baroudeur, the climber doesn't leave the others under any illusions for long. From the first accelerations on the early slopes of a col, the peloton splits and transforms itself into a contest of grimaces and every man for himself. The climber dances, plays with the slopes and the hairpins, sometimes sitting, sometimes standing. Whereas the average cyclist opens his mouth wide and looks for a steady pace as protection against deadly accelerations, the climber takes up the pace of his kind and casts stones before taking off for good. Setting off at high speed, the small motor of the climber doesn't seem to suffer from the lack of oxygen of Alpine altitudes. The climber hides a big secret in his little torso.

If a big bloke happens to follow him, it can only be a

super champion: a Merckx, a Hinault, an Indurain. The rarefewwhoarerouleurs-baroudeurs-climbers-sprinters.

It's thanks to climbers that they invented the *gruppetto*, this little interdependent peloton exclusively reserved for non-climbers. They climb the cols at their breaking point, under the firm leadership of a few rouleurs reputed for having swallowed a stopwatch and for knowing the science that will get everyone to the end of the stage inside the time limit. The sprinters and the rouleurs like to forget the mountain stages.

Anquetil, On His Own

I am wedded to the middle of the road; I ride its crown. I cut none of its bends fine, the small economies of their slight rise and fall – such a course I leave to cheap-jacks and misers.

I retrace the pure, the exact line plotted by the surveyor. The road glides beneath my stomach. I know it by heart. I learned it from the touch under my wheels. Beyond that house, of which I catch a glimpse, the road will turn to the left and begin to climb. The whole width of it belongs to me and down it I trace the finest line possible. The narrowest of tyres have been inflated to ten kilos and I fly over my pathway of air.

I love beautiful fine-grained roads, broad and beautifully designed; roads on which you can apply all your power. Sweeping flat curves, gentle undulations, hills where you can settle in and then build your effort – the Côte de Picardie, the Côte de Châteaufort – long plateaux amid fields of wheat combed by the wind. Lower the chest further, raising the eyes only enough to note where the horizon is, more than actually seeing it, cleaving the air with the beak of my nose: $52 \times 15, 52 \times 14, 52 \times 13$. The road glides beneath my stomach like an endless black ribbon. It is my true home, my kingdom. I inhabit the road. My houses, my châteaux are overnight stops.

I take part in a sport of pelotons, and my real life is played out in solitude, against the clock. Only the race against the clock tells the truth.

The wind is a hard substance in which I bury myself, my back rounded, my nose in the centre of the handlebars, arms stuck to my sides. A motionless egg with cranks. Even in the worst moments when the clenching of my whole body becomes intolerable, I concentrate on not adjusting this position by so much as an inch. My back screams.

Speaking to journalists, I repeat my secret: start flat out, finish flat out and, in between, take an instant to catch breath, a pinch of rest, a few kilometres to relax the pressure and recruit the strength before the final acceleration. Naturally, that's not what I do but I tell anyone who wants to hear it that it is. Inevitably, my rivals all end up trying it. Perhaps he's right? Maybe that's where the secret of his power lies? They ease off on the pedals briefly and every time it's as good as won for me. While they're slowing down, I am at full gas from start to finish. I cease to be human; I am a machine, a robot in flight. I mount the attack. It's not a bike any more – it's an anvil. My arms are forks, my thighs are pistons. I am free.

I'm in pain. In my neck, my shoulders, the small of my back and then the hell of my buttocks and my thighs. You have to bear up against the burning, the knots, the biting that every pedal stroke renews, support the lead that every 15 minutes of racing adds to the muscles. Keep the mind clear to ensure that movement remains integral, pushing, pulling, lifting, crushing, without ever forgetting to maintain the circle, the perfect circle. Making the true pedal stroke; raising the ankle. Driving the biggest gear you can, as fast as you can, and not letting go. Not listening to the body and the brain which together say that this has to stop right now. Persuading yourself, to the contrary, that if you feel as bad as this, the others cannot possibly hold out.

I stockpile reserves of pain. In training, behind the derny, behind Janine's Mercedes, or even in front of it, when she is pushing me at 60kph, I go faster than in a race, faster than myself. Pain fills my training. My trainers have no right to slow down, their responsibility is to draw me into places where only I go, places of suffering that I alone know. Even if I plead with them, they must not slow. Grit the teeth, hold on, no pats on the back, ever.

On the day of the race – when I am, at last, left to myself and I'm suffering like a dog – I know that in my deepest being I am acquainted with yet more terrible pain. This gives me a minuscule margin that allows me to hurt myself more than other riders. The longer the course, the more suffering I inflict on the others and that appeases my own suffering.

Behind me, on the bumpers of the Hotchkiss, my name is written so that the public can recognise me. In black lettering on a white background: ANQUETIL. My name pursues me and drives me forward. I am chasing myself. I flee from myself.

Far off, at the end of the straight line, the car ahead has moved to one side and I've caught sight of the rider who set off three minutes in front of me. I spotted his jersey. My stare is fixed in his back like a harpoon and now I have him. He is going to pull me by the elastic that has just stretched out between us. I know that I'm going to catch him. He left three minutes before me and already he's there. The road curves round here, the bend conceals him from me, the car hides him from me but I'm not letting him go again. He's going to drag me up to him. This is the moment.

In the next few minutes, I won't feel the pain in my legs any more, I won't pose myself any more questions. I am in the suction. I've already gained a good kilometre per hour. Soon, two. At the end of the next straight, my eyes will be planted on his shoulders and he'll tug me still further forward. To take full advantage of his power, my acceleration must be progressive. I must resist the desire to sprint, to kick; I want to catch him in a whisper. I allow him the right side of the road; I will pass him on the left, flat out, with not a glance at him, my eyes glued to the road, without shifting so much as a millimetre in my saddle. I'm going to overtake him at a speed that will leave him without hope. Inevitably, he'll turn his head to the left, throw me an anxious look. Already three minutes lost. Nothing in me must move but my legs. He doesn't count. Perhaps he'll admire the Caravelle, too? He'll feel no more than the waft of the wind. My wind. I will not turn my head, I must not catch his eyes. He does not exist. Only the road in front of me exists, the road I take full down the centre. My place. I pass him.

From here on he's behind me. He's pulled me on and now he has to push me. I must use his strength once again. Pretending to frighten myself ('He's hanging on … He's going to get back,' remembering how Albert Bouvet held me off briefly on the Côte de Bullion) I press a little harder still to distance him, then feel the elastic snapping and imagine him sinking into the depths of the road, alone, emptied of self. And then I concentrate solely on the man who set off six minutes ahead, my eyes already looking for him at the end of the straight line.

In this moment of intense solitude, I am stronger than all the other men. This gift that I cultivate, this work, is my hallmark, my glory, my fortune, my châteaux and my prison. When I am not battling, alone, against the clock and the wind, I pass my time thinking up means of escape. I am a man on the run. I have only to feel myself imprisoned by a wall to want to leap over it immediately. It's an ingrained reflex. Cigarettes are forbidden; I smoke. I'm not allowed out in the evenings; I go out. Flirting is off limits; I flirt. Cycling is not my sport. I didn't choose it, the bicycle chose me. I don't love the bike, the bike loves me. It will pay the price.

Eat Before You're Hungry

(The day I became a cyclist)

I was born in Saint-Étienne, at the foot of the Col de la République. It's not my fault – I didn't do it on purpose. More significant still, I was born at a time when the town was the Mecca of the bike – the most beautiful frames were brazed here, front forks chrome-plated, components manufactured that kept Campagnolo on the hop. Cyclists of all religions came there to stock up.

Every year, cyclotourists from all round the globe – these people are used to travelling – met here to pay homage to their grand master, the man to whom they owed their identity and their code of rules: the great Vélocio. Paul de Vivie, as he was baptised, laid down the regulations of cycle tourism and gave it letters that were patent of junior nobility. A smart businessman and magazine proprietor, he cycled the byways and woodland tracks, disseminating stirring maxims and astute advice everywhere he went. Every year, in homage to his guardianship, cyclists gathered in their thousands in Saint-Étienne to ride to the summit of the Col de la République and reflect a while in front of the monument erected in his honour. The Vélocio climb was rather more than a simple tradition; it was a potent sign of universal fellowship.

Certain cyclists, however – certainly the fittest – regretted that the climb, although steep, was so short. So the organisers decided to offer an alternative ride called 'The Hundred Kilometre Vélocio', which added on the nearby cols and the Grand Bois forest. The circuit was magnificent, tough with a lot of climbing and sombre landscapes wooded with pines, enhanced by a descent through the orchards of the southern flank of the Pilat and back over the Tracol and the Burdignes. Heavy.

My father, behind whom I'd started to ride quite slowly for several months, decided that this would be the occasion of my first 'big' ride. I was ten years old and the demand was probably a bit too much for me, but he'd done everything he could in advance to help me. He even arranged to get me home in case I got into difficulties – a friend was on hand in a Peugeot 403 to race up at the first hint of a smoke signal. My father's knapsack was stuffed with food and sweaters, his bidons were full of squash and everyone was sworn to patience because we were going to need a lot of time to complete the course. We were determined to pace ourselves so that we could get to the finish and make quite sure of getting the route carnets issued to us (I kept mine in my jersey pocket) stamped at the town halls in all the little villages we passed through.

So everything had been planned for, except what happened. We rode well up the Col de la République in a great crowd and I felt strong. My father, who understood perfectly how to control my pace, kept me going at a gentle speed but without stifling me. He advised me to be cautious on the long descent. On the two following hills, he advised me on what gears to use and I twirled comfortably up to the summits. He didn't even plant his hand on my back to give me a push, and I'd have refused because right then I felt so charged with the responsibility of hauling myself up to the Grand Bois under my own power. The surprise of the day came on the Côte de Burdignes. Coming out of a bend, I overtook my father who was practically stationary. As I went by, I saw that he'd gone livid red, his face bathed in cold sweat, his eyes unfocused. He was plainly in anguish. He vomited in the ditch, his face turned green and he had to sit down on the embankment. He closed his eyes for a moment, his hands crossed over his stomach. 'Go on,' he said. 'Don't get cold. The route is arrowed – you can't get lost. I'll catch you up … if I can.'

It was a strange sensation to find myself on my own on such a narrow twisting mountain road for the first time. Especially when it hadn't been what we'd planned. A hail of unexpected questions falls on you, you'd swear they'd been written in white on the road surface as if to encourage you. Am I on the right road? Am I going too fast? Am I going fast enough? Is there still a long way to go? How many hills are there left exactly? What if I puncture? What if I fall on the descent? What if my dad is really ill? And my mum, where is my mum?

Even so young, I well knew that there weren't any wolves in the forest. But you never can be sure – even a small wolf cub lost in a glade would be big enough to gobble me up. And what of the terrible Man with the Hammer, definitely lurking behind a pine tree? On a day when there are so many cyclists about, he is never far away. I fancied I could even hear the Witch With Green Teeth gnashing. Suddenly, the trees seemed much taller and darker. The hill was very long and very steep. And there was absolutely no one else at all on the road. Hasn't it all at once got colder?

The first cyclist joined me. 'Hey, Titch, you riding on your own? That's really good.' I told him what had happened. He encouraged me. 'Okay, just keep going, at your own speed and don't forget what Vélocio said: "To avoid the bonk you must eat before you're hungry." Here.' And he handed me a Petit-Beurre LU biscuit, which I ate as I watched him race off at high speed. I felt a surge of new energy.

Five hundred metres further up, a couple on a tandem came up to me. 'Hey, it's Tom Thumb,' said the man. 'He's cute,' said the woman. 'Who abandoned you?' I gasped out the story. 'Slow down a bit,' the man urged me while the woman rummaged in her knapsack. She pulled out two slices of buttered gingerbread. 'Here,' she said. 'When you're cycling, you must eat before you're hungry.' I ate the slices as I watched the double chain wheels pedalling away. I love gingerbread with salted butter – especially because I know that it's a particular favourite of the new star of world cycling, the young Jacques Anquetil – but on top of the Petit-Beurre I discovered it rather made a glutinous lump in my tummy and I got breathless. I needed to drink.

Some distance on, I was caught by a hard man. I heard him swooping down on me with a hiss of tyres, which showed just how fast he was travelling. He braked. Sharing, but without a second to lose, he held out a Thé Brun biscuit to me in silence before sprinting off towards the summit. I chomped it up. Further on, a whole group joined me. 'Keep the packet of biscuits, kid, you need to eat before the bonk hits you.' Still higher up, a lady in knickerbockers and Argyle socks was indignant. 'It's a disgrace, leaving a mere child all alone on the road like that. At least eat something before you get hungry.' And she passed me an indigestible rice cake that I had to eat as I rode with her, checking that I finished every single crumb.

The hill grew very long. Even knowing that it was the last one and after it there remained only the big descent, it seemed to me interminable. I turned round to see if my father was coming. I felt heavy, clamped to the ground, my mouth dry as wool, my stomach bloated. I crossed the col on the verge of tears. On the descent, I had the weird sensation of dropping like a lead weight and I kept the brakes on for fear of going off the road and picking up too much speed.

Once back in the town, I was pushed over to the control desk to get my last stamp. Being the youngest entrant by far, I was applauded. Someone gave me a lemon Pschitt (a fizzy drink) and I was excused for missing one control. I needed to learn that lesson.

My father came in way down, with his pal, leaning on the 403. He had got some colour back, but couldn't ride his bike. He hugged me. He told me he was sorry, but he said that he was proud of me because now I was a real cyclist. He drew up my honour board for his friend: I'd ridden my first 100km, 60 of them in the solitude of the high mountains. I'd found my rhythm on every terrain, I had conquered my fear and I hadn't smashed myself up on the descents. I'd got my stamps at the controls and, on top of everything, I had done a good time. I could be proud of myself.

I showed how very happy I was with this praise, but I have to add, in all modesty, that I had also succeeded in digesting the first of the great Vélocio's ten commandments: now I know to eat before I'm hungry.

Self-Portrait
of Abdel-Kader Zaaf at Rest

My job is to ride a bike on the roads of the world. To ride as quickly as possible. It's a man's job, firstly because when a man rides a bike he wants to ride as far and as fast as possible; also because when a bunch of men ride bikes together they all want to ride faster than one another.

A human profession.

I am a racing cyclist.

I am French amateur champion, champion of Algeria with Vélo-Club Musulman, I ride the Tour de France in the Algerian French team. Next year I will be world champion with the main French team and I will win a stage of the Tour. I am the bravest man in the peloton, the most tanned, with the strongest jaw, and my work consists of creating the new.

All the great cycling champions create something new.

To pedal faster is first to pedal differently, so as to sow surprise and doubt in the peloton. To scare it. To pedal in a mystical way, which one would swear is impossible. Until an entire generation pedals like you.

In the life of a cyclist you can only create a single exploit.

I arrived in the peloton with a reputation as an exotic eccentric and ten years later the entire bunch watches and respects me.

Now there is me: Abdel-Kader Zaaf.

Being a great cycling champion is a condition which requires complete self-sacrifice and total concentration. I pedal full time. I pedal while praying; I pedal on the deck of the boat between Algiers and Marseille. I live with a saddle between my legs. I smile at Louison so that he will be nice to me. I am a complete headache to the manager of the Volta team, who is useless, because I know that will help me to pedal faster.

Take two Frenchmen with the same bikes and the same training, put them side by side at the start line of the Grand Prix de Pontaneveaux in Brittany and it's always me who wins in the end.

I do the ascent of the Col d'Izoard a thousand times a week. The bumps of the Massif Central, those that you take on with legs of lead – I do them each night before going to bed. I know all the stages of the Tour of Algeria by heart and, at 40 kilometres an hour, I see them unfold in slow motion.

I also prepare myself to win these mysterious criteriums that the randomness of commitments imposes on us. Twisted races like the Circuit des Vins de Gironde or the Américaine de Crozon, which the calendar obliges us to ride and that could allow Ferdi Kübler-like dicks to do well if I wasn't there.

Everything counts in your career.

One day the most important thing becomes the contents of your bidon. It's the bidon that determines the victory. You have filled it with sugar, very strong black coffee, fresh water. During the race you wondered if the coffee was strong enough, and you came second in the Grand Prix Bastos in Algiers because when the sprint started you asked yourself whether the contents of your bidon were sweet enough after all.

When I sleep I work; while eating, I work. I imagine my starts, I refine my sprints. My thighs and my buttocks are uncompromising; I constantly wear the mark of my Team Wolber cap on my forehead.

When the starter sets me free on the start line, he unleashes tonnes of work. Afterwards there is one cyclist left on the road to Toulouse, this beautiful July of 1950, in blazing heat, who has just escaped from the peloton; who has succeeded in taking 16 minutes from the other riders and who is going to win his stage of the Tour de France.

And then there is the inevitable moment that arrives in a life, a moment of real rest, of complete rest. The rest of the champion cyclist. You stopped for a moment by the side of the road, overcome by the heat. Some wine growers came to refresh you with their plonk, which you never drink. And when you set off again, you make this minute error of trajectory, this stupid little mistake (which is not due to inattention because champions don't know the meaning of inattention), which makes you set off again on the route of the Tour de France in the wrong direction. And that ... that is rest, huge rest. Nothing matters any more, you pass a group of escapees, you pass the entire peloton without even thinking of stopping, you pass the broom wagon and you arrive among the cars of the journalists, who take note and announce that you smell of wine and that you are drunk. Nothing matters any more, you are no longer a cyclist, your muscles relax, your spirit sets itself free. You know that you are going to become immortal.

Descending

I was descending very fast. As soon as I could see ahead, I began to use the whole width of the road to extend my trajectory and take the bends flat out. The road was narrow but expertly designed, the embankment was regular, the gradient steep, and the wind whistled in my helmet.

I addressed the right-hander, which was masked by a clump of trees. A light touch on the brake, right knee lifted and tilted outwards, the weight of my body leaning slightly into the bend, and I plunged to where the line I'd fixed on kissed the arc of the bend. I made it, on the rim of the ditch, at full speed, ready to accelerate away, and then I discovered the bend wasn't how I'd judged it. Here, no doubt to accommodate a rise in the ground, the road folded back and the corner bent round on itself. At the speed I was travelling, I had no chance of adjusting my line. In a flash, I realised that I was in big trouble and then I saw the black car looming up out of the bend ahead of me, driving straight for me. Instinctively, I went left and hurtled towards the ditch. My wheels skidded in the muddy gravel, the car swept by, blowing its horn, brushing my right shoulder with its wing mirror. My handlebars were shaking about, the front wheel was wobbling in the loose sand, my brakes weren't responding. Before I got in any deeper or wiped out on the stone sidewall, I went for broke and hopped – me and the whole bike, feet clipped into the pedals – in an attempt to get back onto the road. Amazingly, my tyres bit on the tarmac and I immediately got out of the saddle, accelerating like a madman, winning back all the speed I'd lost and plunging flat out to the point of the next bend. I knew that if I allowed even a single second for slowing down to reflect on what had just happened, I'd never ever again be a descender. I blasted it to the bottom and had the whole ascent of the other side to get the shivers.

Contrary to the idea widely held by non-cyclists, descending on a bike isn't always part of the pleasure. You need to have a clear mind – something you rarely have after a long climb – you need to be in shape, focused and ready to expend an energy on which you thought you could economise. You also need the perception of a highway engineer, to know how to anticipate the curve of the bends and to mould yourself to the folds of the mountain. You have to enjoy pushing the big gears to maintain your cadence and to go on hurting your legs.

Even if you combine all these qualities in yourself together with willpower and desire, it's advisable to remain vigilant because some mountain roads don't respect the harmonious plans drawn up by engineers: they were picked out in the mists of time by goats, which were either drunk or having a laugh with the sneaky aim of trapping cyclists. There are some fine examples in the Cévennes. Thus did the great Roger Rivière leave his life behind on the goat-track descent of the Col du Perjuret.

In a race, the descent can kill. The peloton appears to stretch out and take it easy but this transformation isn't by way of pleasure. The application of the brakes is brutal, the lines tight, every metre lost will be hard to win back, the speed is so high. And, then, it's very tempting to take the line of the rider immediately in front and that's when you hit a hard reality: not everyone is an equally good descender. Some great descenders are perfectly capable of lulling you, of making you feel confident while drawing you by degrees into error. And, even if they make a mistake, they know how to get out of it: Louison Bobet, who was by no means any rustic toboggan, told how on one long descent, he was overtaken several times by Fiorenzo Magni, a descender of genius, after he'd fallen and set off again at breakneck speed. One also remembers Beloki sliding heavily in melted tar on a long curve and the catlike Armstrong who was right on his wheel and opted to cut across the field to avoid him, dropping into the grass, hopping a rivulet and regaining the road on the bend further down.

Some riders take their revenge on the climbers during the descent. Often short and light in weight, the climbers sometimes have a hard job going downhill. Knowing that he was going to be caught, nothing to be done, Federico Bahamontes frankly preferred to get to the summit, calmly eat an ice cream while he waited for his pursuers, and make a peaceful descent in the bunch where he felt at home. Charly Mottet was one of the very few exceptions to the rule. He ascended like a climber and dropped like a descender. Born in the mountains, he was a giant slalom champion and that, for sure, gave him an advantage over guys from the flatlands who arrived in the peloton without ever having seen a hairpin, close up.

One morning, I was riding with my friends in a group in pelting rain and we found ourselves on a short but steep descent. We were in single file, me faithfully following the wheel of the man in front, assured that wherever he went, I'd go, too. I calculated my braking on his, my accelerations, my line, my angles. The road was very wet and we were keeping a cautious lookout ahead. Water sprayed into our socks and stabbed our eyes. My man took on a left-hand bend and I leaned over in response, swung the bars gently and went straight into the ditch, unable to steer away. I wasn't alone for long. All the men behind piled up into me, their legs, arms, machines tangled up in a big heap, with not a clue what had happened to them. We had just learned the great lesson about descenders: through some mysterious alchemy of body and soul, there are men who turn in places where others are condemned to carry straight on.

Rouleur

The rouleur has long-lasting majesty. His talent consists of a statuesque position: the rouleur knows how to stay in an impeccable (and unbearable) position for hours, body bent in two, arms at right angles, face lowered, the top of his head open to the breeze. He manages the wind like a bass manages the sea. He rides gears as heavy as anvils while having the elegance to never show it.

The less he moves, the faster he will go. It is a real spectacle for those in the know. Those not in the know find him boring because there is little which is spectacular; often, in fact, it is only disorder that gives the impression of speed.

To best express this sense of power, the peloton asserts that the rouleur 'has a big motor'. It finds in him the consistency and the power of a machine. It speaks from experience, the peloton, since when someone or other takes a fancy to attacking, the rouleur puts himself on the front to take the troops back to the fugitive and each person can experience the consequences for the muscles.

The rouleur gives the best of himself in the solitude

of the time trial, but he does not mind taking himself to the front of the peloton to stretch it out into a long line and to stick his tongue out at all the good people who are breathless in his wheel.

The flat is his kingdom. If decorated with a few cobblestones, like in Paris–Roubaix, it even allows him to fly a few centimetres above the ground. He enjoys long sweeping corners where he can follow his line without breaking his sacrosanct rhythm. When he hasn't extricated himself from the peloton thanks to his strength, he is a perfect lead-out man for his sprinter: placed in front of him, he opens up the air and dictates a high cadence. In a team, the rouleur is the indispensable base of the trade of cycling.

Bunch of Colours

I live in the peloton. It's my work. It's my home. In the morning I eat pasta because you have to eat pasta to have your place in the peloton.

Then I go back to the bedroom to get dressed. Clean clothes every morning. Cream between the thighs, fish-net vest, bib shorts, jersey. Race number 128. Brush teeth. Comb hair. Ready. Quick look in the mirror. It's to be expected: mine is a public profession. Quick look at the legs to see if the shorts go right down to the tan line. A little stroke to judge if they are well shaved. My tools.

I put on my shoes and take my place on the start line. Around the tenth row.

I never see who starts the race; I'm too far away. But we set off. At first it's not a real peloton; it's a parade with the big at the front and the small at the back. We cross the town with clean jerseys. The air is still cool. Sometimes I spot the peloton in shop windows along the route. It is beautiful, colourful, it is a procession, it blows on the spectators who huddle on the pavement.

I'm at home.

One simple rule: never in front, never behind. Easy

to say, difficult to do. If everyone wants to be in the middle there is no-one on the edges and it is no longer a bunch. At the front you find the team-mates of the champions. Behind them, the big men, those on form. Right at the back, the cooked, the injured, the clumsy. In the middle: war.

You have to respect others and be respected. That's the tricky law of the peloton. Wary-confident.

In the morning it's good. We set off calmly. The peloton chats in all its languages.

The moment of truth is when we arrive at the first incline. There I will know how I am going today. Up until then it doesn't count. The peloton stays on the large chainring to attack the slope. I lift my arse out of my saddle and I judge: if I fall back I am having a bad day; if I move up I've got good legs. When you move up, your morale goes up too. You have no choice: the peloton rides at the speed of the peloton, which is the speed of no one in the peloton.

In the afternoon, when it speeds up, you have to be alert. If your legs are too sore you quickly concede a length, then two, and then you're no longer in the peloton – it leaves for good, without you. The peloton is not sentimental.

I hate to see the pack break into several parts. It's against nature. When I am trapped behind, I do long pulls to get back on. If I've stayed in front, I discreetly go easy so that the guys get back on quicker.

Then things calm down. The peloton refills its stomach. The road widens. Throw the empty bidons on the ground, to the side, or squarely over the heads of the peloton if you're in the middle. The tiniest mistake and 30 riders are on the tarmac. A profession.

We eat, the peloton reforms and we have a good time snacking. We ride at 35–36, easy. It's a picnic.

When we have finished eating the speed goes up a notch. Going over a bump I have lost ten places. I was distracted. Legs turn. A guy pushes me on the side, he wants to pass at any cost.

It is 3.30pm. We are going to enter hell. It is hot. I am alert. A kind of silence falls on the peloton. The escapees have a 12-minute lead. The finish is in 80 kilometres. Hell. I listen out for the sound of the helicopter. It's my signal. Once the chopper is heard, life in the peloton changes. It's the TV helicopter.

As soon as you hear the noise, it's a sign that the race is going to go wild. The tough guys will ride to show off their jerseys. The sprinters will send their team-mates off to prepare the sprint. All the big engines get ready. In a few seconds we will find ourselves doing 60 and will stay at that speed for an hour and a half.

The peloton quietens. It is scared. We hear nothing but the hum of bicycles and breath. Everyone is in his place and it hurts. There are no longer any options. The slightest error in trajectory and you find yourself ejected. The slightest distraction on a traffic island and you lose 50 places. The slightest glitch and we are out the back, never to return. Once the peloton is at this speed, no lone cyclist can come back to it. The lost minutes rain down.

The pain in the legs is terrible, my breath is short, I

have a stitch in my back. With each acceleration you say to yourself that you can't follow. And then you follow. It is a matter of honour to be there.

We arrive on the outskirts of the stage town. The spectators cheer. No time to dwell on them, no time to look at yourself in shop windows. At the front, they have been unleashed. You start to see those who have finished their work at the front, finished their day, coming back. They are wizened and they turn their legs to stay in the pack at any price. Hands on the brakes, you have to avoid crashes, roadworks, splits going over bridges; you need eyes everywhere.

The *flamme rouge* of the last kilometre. That's my real finish line. At the front the sprinters fight like cat and dogs. They're doing more than 70, they're attacking like madmen. When I see them on TV, I close my eyes, because I know what's going on.

For me the race is already finished. The positions in the peloton are fixed a kilometre from the line. That line is my finish line. The peloton is intact. Compact.

There is no other. The only peloton in the world is the cycling peloton. The bunch of colours. The others, in other sports, are unimportant. The cycling one is indispensable. It is the honour of the bicycle, the honour of the bike-racing profession. It is the glory of the escapees and the winners.

The peloton is my profession.

La Reprise

The bike left my father one Sunday morning ten years ago. It happened between Bas-en-Basset and Aurec in the Haute-Loire region of France, in solitude. He was climbing a small hill that I would not describe as laughable because cyclists – even those who are used to the Ventoux or Izoard – well know that you can explode on a two-kilometre hill that doesn't go up that much.

Let's just say that this incline should not have been sufficient to end his riding.

'Something' tightened in his chest, imperiously letting him know that the bike was leaving him after 70 years of companionship.

He went home without saying anything, at the pace of his pain.

For ten years the bike has been in the garage, upright, ready to go. It is oiled, its wheels are pumped up, it is mountable, perhaps there is still something to eat in the pannier on the handlebars?

No doubt for a long time my father thought he would get back out on the road. In any case, he never said anything about it, ever. Now that he is more than 85 years old, he knows he will not set off any more.

The other day when I was driving him in his car, he asked me to take a detour so we could go back over that little hill. So I left the main road to take one of those tiny little roads that sink into the countryside and which we had surveyed so many times together.

When we arrived on the incline, he said to me: 'It's here.' I slowed down. 'I tried to go up it in the 24 tooth,' he continued, 'but the pain was too strong. I turned back.'

Then, one thing leading to another, since we were there, we followed the road. It ascended winding in the forest, all speckled by the sun, narrow, grainy, with the smell of mushroom and hot earth of this end of the summer.

At the place called The Cutaway, the slope becomes more severe. My father had changed sprocket. He went with a 22. He had never liked to ride too small a gear. There, he explained to me, his childhood friend had fallen in the clump of stinging nettles below. Then he said nothing more because the slope was too tough. I felt him try a 24 but he held on. On the descent, he explained how, 60 years earlier, he had dropped his mate Madel, passing in 52 × 14. He warned me to watch out for the left turn because it loops back on itself. Then, after the little bridge, we started to climb again.

At this point, the road climbs into the meadow. It is in full sun. There is not a cloud on the horizon and we can see the bends above, which hug the curve of the

mountain. Far away, we can make out the deep valley of
the Loire. It is lined with the shade of green trees that
will soon turn yellow. That will be the time of lovely
autumn outings when you put on long sleeves in the
early hours. My father said to me: 'I remember the time
I put on golf trousers cut to the knee and big checked
woollen socks!' We climbed in silence, our breath short.
The sweat that fell down his face, gathering in drops on
the point of his chin and falling on his frame. He rusted
more than one this way.

When we reached the summit, after the long left
turn, which was already less steep, the view opened out
on the plains just down below. The red-roofed hamlets nestled on crossroads, the beige cows on their green
background. The roads narrow and empty. Occasionally a tractor. The road is gentle, one of the rare pieces
of flat in the whole of this region. A moment to savour
letting your legs turn, hands on the tops, nose in the
evening breeze. He was in 52 × 16. We went through a
village, then another with a brief slope before plunging
towards the valley. We swallowed it up, standing on the
pedals.

'One year, I punctured twice in a row on this bitch
of a road,' he said. I remember it very well because I was
riding behind him. It was no doubt the summer during
which I punctured 16 times myself.

Crossing the hamlet, he made the same silent gesture to warn me about the manhole cover that still hadn't
been replaced in its housing. The descent is technical. If
you want to go fast you have to have the design of the

bend in your head before committing yourself totally. It's essential to know your roads well.

My father descended with his hands on the top of the handlebars, at full tilt, as usual.

Then we arrived at Aurec, on the banks of the Loire. I felt a sense of disappointment. 'Everything has changed here, look, they have built everywhere. They have redone the road. It goes straight up. They know absolutely nothing about cycling. There is nothing worse than a climb in a straight line.'

We climbed it anyway.

Through the whole of our trip, we remained side by side, shoulder to shoulder. I stayed on his left, like two peaceful cyclotourists, changing gear at the same moment, taking the corners together, rolling on.

But now that we have gone back out on the road together I know that it cannot last and that, soon, he will go on ahead of me.

Sprinter

The sprinter is all thighs. Whether he is small and power-ful like Cavendish, or big and powerful like Cipollini, he is always powerful. His job comes down to the last 500 metres of the race, but it is a big job. The sprinter is respected, first and foremost, as a virtuoso.

The sprinter is the best manager of the strength of others. He nests in the peloton throughout the day, leaving his team to impose law and order at the front. He spoils himself, riding small gears and so turning his precious legs in velvet. Then, when the finish approaches, he hides behind the train of his team-mates, who are charged with taking him close to the finish line in a good position. Only a little slower than him, they link five or six sprints together in a row, preventing the opportunists from jumping away, and launching the sprinter like a rocket into orbit.

Let us be clear, though: the sprinter is not a shirker. He is not a man of the shadows. He belongs to the world of light, though primarily light in the form of camera flashes.

In the last 500 metres, he has his head down on his job.

He is putting the tools of his trade to the test. Torsion on the handlebars, squashing of the tyres and rims, torture of the bottom bracket, efforts to drop the chain, destruction of the pedals. Going off at a patently unreasonable speed, he knows that he is guilty of a folly but he has confidence. Confidence in himself and confidence in the privileged few who still fight it out with him and who barge him with their shoulder, brushing against his spokes with their pedals, zigzagging on the road in front of him. When he is finally sure of his victory and when the finish line is his, he lifts his head and then his arms in a beautiful unfurling that resembles taking flight. At that moment of glory, he smiles at his strength and the logos inscribed on his jersey are perfectly readable. He's a good salesman, the sprinter.